But we maintain, that the power of Christ's cross and of his death . . . is so great, that it will be sufficient for the healing and restoration not only of the present and future ages, but even for those of the past.

Origen

The One Purpose of God

An Answer to the Doctrine of Eternal Punishment

Jan Bonda

Translated by
Reinder Bruinsma

WILLIAM B. EERDMANS PUBLISHING COMPANY
GRAND RAPIDS, MICHIGAN / CAMBRIDGE, U.K.

Originally published as *Het ene doel van God*
© 1993 Uitgeverij Ten Have b.v., Baarn

English translation © 1998 by
Wm. B. Eerdmans Publishing Co.
255 Jefferson Ave. S.E., Grand Rapids, Michigan 49503 /
P.O. Box 163, Cambridge CB3 9PU U.K.

Printed in the United States of America

03 02 01 00 99 98   7 6 5 4 3 2 1

Library of Congress Cataloging-in-Publication Data

Bonda, J., 1918-
The one purpose of God / Jan Bonda.
p.   cm.
Includes bibliographical references.
ISBN 0-8028-4186-4 (pbk.: alk. paper)
1. Salvation outside the church. 2. Future punishment.
3. God — Will. 4. Salvation. 5. Bible. N.T. Romans — Theology.
6. Reformed Church — Doctrines. I. Title.
BT759.B63   1998
234 — dc21   97-33626
                                        CIP

Unless otherwise noted, the Scripture quotations in this publication are from the New Revised
Standard Version Bible, copyright © 1989 by the Division of Christian Education of the
National Council of Churches of Christ in the U.S.A., and used by permission.

For Israël Paulus Tabaksblat, 1902-1992

Contents

CONTENTS

Contents

CONTENTS

Contents

CONTENTS

Contents

CONTENTS

Contents

Foreword

Few subjects, if any, are more important than that of the final destiny of human beings and God's purposes in that regard. That is the subject of this book. Despite its sometimes heavy theological content, the book is really a cry from the heart. A powerful cry for the salvation, not just of the few, but of the many — hopefully of all. The answers it gives make it a very comforting book.

The writer, Jan Bonda, is a retired pastor in the Reformed Churches in the Netherlands. He is also a man with a heavy burden on his heart. For many years already. The ultimate fate, the eternal future, of the masses who do not know Christ as well as of his next-door, nonbelieving neighbors has never been far from his mind. It has always troubled him that the Christian faith, as traditionally understood and as formulated in numerous creeds, seems so ready to consign the majority of the human race to eternal damnation. Though firmly grounded in his own tradition, the Reformed faith, as formulated in the Belgic Confession, Heidelberg Catechism, and Canons of Dort, he nevertheless takes issue with that tradition on this point. In this book Bonda does what the prophet Jeremiah was called to do, break down and build up, with the emphasis clearly on the second aspect. From the Bible he shows the untenableness of the view that the bulk of the human race will ultimately be lost forever. In this study, the core of which consists of an in-depth study of Paul's epistle to the Romans, he shows that the Bible indeed holds out hope for the many.

Anyone with a smattering of knowledge of the real world knows that it is terribly messy and hurting. Billions of people barely make a living and lead a life of drudgery and hardship. There are also the victims of injustice, poverty, sickness, exploitation, persecution and torture, massacres, genocides, war, the holocaust, epidemics, accidents, infanticide, and abortion. The list seems endless. Worst of all are the atrocities which through the centuries have been committed in the name of Christ. Thousands of defenseless people have been tortured and put to death in his Name. One is reminded of Pascal's words, "Men never do evil so completely and cheerfully as when they do it from religious conviction."

There is no denial that despite the many good things in the world which are not to be overlooked, our world is hurting. Isn't it also true that in some sense most people are at once victims and victimizers? Though, of course, the ratio differs enormously. (All of us can think of individuals we would "hate" to see go to heaven. But then, who are we to tell God what to do!) All of this makes one aware that the world's only hope is divine grace.

Salvation is only by the gift of faith in Jesus Christ (Rom. 3:21). The big question is, for whom is that grace? If all victims of injustice and the like were believing Christians, their miserable life on earth would, at least according to Christian belief, be followed by a life in a much better world. Unfortunately, the majority of these folk have never been Christian. Billions of them belong(ed) to other religions or no particular faith at all. Traditional Christian belief holds out little hope for them — actually none at all. Particularly the Calvinistic faith seems to dash all hope. Sharply put, unless one belongs to the elect, one is destined for hell. So Christianity in its traditional form consigns most of the human race to an everlasting miserable hereafter.

It boggles the mind to think that all these people will be lost forever. I, for one, have never had peace with that thought. Already a couple of decades ago, I was struck by Dr. Hendrikus Berkhof's question whether we are to think of hell as throughout all eternity being an open wound in the body of the glorified creation. I found Berkhof's answer immensely reassuring. In his view, the last judgment will mean "worldwide salvation for the outcasts and the mistreated, for the crushed and the tortured" (*Well-Founded Hope*, 1969, chapters 7 and 10). In *Christian Faith* (Eerdmans, 1979, 1986) he reiterates this emphasis. Thus he writes, "For God's sake we hope that hell will be a form of purification" (chapter 58).

My own thinking initially was very much shaped by my studies of the Old Testament. What I found there gave me the uneasy feeling that the traditional Reformed and Presbyterian confessions do not measure up to the breathtaking vistas of Israel's prophets. It has long struck me that the

Old Testament nowhere speaks of unending punishment after death. Quite the contrary. See Gen. 12:3b and numerous passages in Isaiah, such as 2:2-4, 11:9, 19:23-25, 25:7-8, and 49:6. I find it difficult to reconcile these passages with certain traditional Christian beliefs. I am buoyed by the fact that in recent years the awareness has grown stronger in evangelical circles that it is quite unthinkable that the God we meet in Jesus Christ would send the majority of the human race to a bleak, Christless eternity. Berkhof already made this point when he rejected the view held by some that "hell also serves to glorify God and . . . he has decided before all time to create a multitude of people for the purpose of eternal rejection" (*Well-Founded Hope*, chapter X).

A plodding mind, Jan Bonda carries this thinking a huge step further. According to him it is not just unthinkable; it is *unbiblical*. It is not what the Bible teaches. In my mind I can still hear his firm voice in a phone conversation across the Atlantic in which he stressed this point. I had just restated my belief that it cannot be true that the masses of the world will perish forever. To which Bonda, with characteristic Dutch bluntness, responded, "That is not the real point, it does not say so in the Bible!" (Daar gaat het niet om, het staat niet in de Bijbel!).

I will always remember that answer. It gave me the measure of the man who wrote this book. Especially, it points up the strength of this book. His conviction that the majority of the human race will not perish, in fact that there is enough evidence in the Bible to entertain the expectation that God will achieve his goal of wanting to save most, perhaps even all (Bonda struggled to come up with the right formulations, scrupulously cautious neither to say more nor less than is warranted by Scripture; see pp. 258-59), is not based on wishful thinking — bleeding-heart theology, if you will. It rests on a fresh look at and a painstakingly careful exegesis of the relevant biblical passages, particularly in Paul's letter to the Romans. The God of the Bible is not a God who easily, if ever, gives up on his human creation. God's ultimate design for humanity is not dual but singular. That is the point that is driven home in this book again and again.

The title of the book, *The One Purpose of God*, succinctly captures the point Bonda tries to make on the basis of meticulous biblical exegesis. This title is based on Paul's words in 1 Timothy 2:4 that God "desires everyone to be saved and to come to the knowledge of the truth." The book's subtitle, "An Answer to the Doctrine of Eternal Punishment," follows from that text. Once we accept Paul's conviction here at face value, the doctrine of eternal punishment becomes at least problematic. For it raises such questions as,

Will God achieve his desire? Will there be an end to God's desire of salvation for certain individuals? Particularly the question, Is a person's eternal fate irrevocably sealed at his or her death?

It is commonly held, among others by Professor Berkhof (*Christian Faith,* revised edition, 535ff.), that there are two sets of statements in Scripture. One series apparently teaches that many will be lost forever; the other series gives hope for the salvation of all. In short, there is a particularistic line as well as a universalistic line. Bonda argues that this is a misreading of Scripture. He maintains that there is only one line in Scripture: God's declared purpose in Christ that all be saved and God's unwavering determination that this come to pass.

Of course, at this point Bonda runs headlong into near-sacred traditional Christian beliefs. Particularly the Westminster Confession of Faith is very outspoken, declaring that some "cannot be saved" (10,4). This point is really no less strong in the three traditional Reformed Confessions: the Belgic Confession, Heidelberg Catechism, and Canons of Dort.

With refreshing honesty Bonda confronts the weaknesses he finds in these three creeds. Referring to the insistence in the Heidelberg Catechism (Q. & A. 11; cf. Belgic Confession, Art. 16) that God is not only a merciful God but also a just God whose justice demands that sins be punished with eternal punishment of body and soul, Bonda speaks of the "terrifying image of God" in the Catechism.

Loath as I am to go against so venerable a document as the Heidelberg Catechism, it seems to me that Bonda's point is well taken. The Reformed creeds, resting on their spiritual fathers St. Augustine and John Calvin, are, it seems to me, seriously flawed. The biblical perspective, as Bonda points out, is that of a God who goes out in search of the one sheep that became lost, not that of a God who elects some to everlasting life, bypassing all others and sending them to a never-ending "death."

Bonda also contends that there is no biblical support for the notion, expressed in the same Catechism (Q. & A. 12; cf. Q. & A. 40), that God wants to have his justice satisfied and that therefore the claims of his justice must be paid in full. Again I find myself compelled to agree. Psalm 103, for example, speaks a different language than that of the Catechism. "The Lord is slow to anger; he does not deal with us according to our sins, and he does not repay us according to our iniquities" (vv. 9-10). In Christ's death on the cross God himself took away the sin of the world (John 1:29; 6:51; 1 John 2:2). Scripture is clear that Jesus' death was a "divine necessity." But that death, as Bonda points out, was not a price to be paid to God. Calling his death a "ransom," Jesus "tells us *at what cost God saved* humanity." "The cross is a mystery, beyond any human explanation" (pp. 86-87)!

In this book Bonda does far more than "breaking down" what he considers wrongheaded beliefs. None of the Reformed confessions offers any real hope for what is often loosely called "the world." Judging by the number of those who espouse the Christian faith, the majority of the human race appears doomed, and seemingly all we can do is acquiesce. Throughout the book Bonda fights this perspective. But the thrust of his book is that of "building up"; we need not — in fact, may not — acquiesce in the eternal perdition of fellow human beings. God does not acquiesce, and neither may we. Bonda pulls out all the stops, showing that the Bible offers genuine hope for all God's human creation. Christ died for all, and God wants all to be saved. In Paul's words, "God has imprisoned all in disobedience so that he may be merciful to all" (Rom. 11:32; cf. also Rom. 5:18-19; John 1:29; 1 John 2:2).

A major part of the book (Chapters III-VIII) consists of a penetrating analysis of Paul's teaching in Romans, in particular the central place of Israel, the Jews, God's Old Testament covenant nation, in God's plan to save the world. Bonda goes to great lengths to point out that Israel was — and in a significant sense remains — God's chosen vessel to save the world. Salvation is a matter of accepting Israel's Messiah, Jesus Christ, and his atoning cross, and through him being grafted into the original tree — Israel. Refusing to spiritualize Paul's words "so all Israel will be saved" (Rom. 11:26), he faults the church for by and large having lost St. Paul's conversion zeal for his own kinfolk, the Jewish people. The church and the world are not saved without but with Israel. Apart from Israel, God's blessed reign cannot come.

A book like this is apt to be misunderstood, even misapplied, on at least three counts. For one thing, the danger is far from imaginary that the writer will be accused of teaching an easy universal salvation (*apokatastasis*). A related inherent danger is that the biblical warnings about punishment might not be taken seriously. From correspondence with him I know that the writer is deeply conscious of these possible negative reactions. He wishes to affirm that he in no way minimizes the reality and seriousness of God's judgments, both in this life and in the life to come. But he also feels he must insist, on the basis of the biblical texts, that God's judgments do not find their purpose in themselves but are meant to lead to repentance and salvation. So he seeks to preserve a careful balance between the utter seriousness of divine judgment and the hope of ultimate salvation (without

xxi

— not wanting to say more than Scripture allows — altogether ruling out the possibility of a final annihilation for some).

Thirdly, Bonda fears that his views might conceivably lead to a weakening of the church's sense of calling to go and make disciples of all nations, since presumably all will eventually make it through the pearly gates anyway. This possible charge, too, bothers him. A careful reading of the entire book should make it clear that it points the church of Jesus Christ in precisely the opposite direction. God wants the bringing in of the entire harvest, refusing to acquiesce in the perdition of even one soul; therefore, the church must be of the same mind and will. However, the harvest is not brought in without workers. Christ died for all, but unless the gospel is proclaimed people are not led to Christ (Rom. 10:14; 2 Cor. 5:18-20). There would be no future salvation for the city of Sodom, as prophesied in Ezekiel 16, if Abraham had not interceded for it; the Israelites would not have been spared in the wilderness if Moses had not put his own life on the line for them (Chapter II)!

Potentially the most controversial point Bonda makes, and one of his sharpest breaks with traditional Christian views, is that death does not automatically seal a person's eternal future once and for all. Since God is the God not only of the living but also of the dead (Rom. 14:9), the punishments in the "hereafter" are also meant to lead to salvation. Allow me to urge you to think along with the author and ponder the biblical evidence he presents (Chapter III,6).

Some final pointers. No reader should be put off by the material in the footnotes, some of it quotations in Latin. These are meant for theologians who can handle them. This book can be profitably read even without consulting these footnotes. It should be noted, too, that this book is a translation (and updating) of a book that first appeared in Dutch. That accounts for the Dutch ambience of the book, especially in its early pages.

This book embodies the ripe fruits of Bonda's many years of study of the subject. I am grateful that they are now available in the English language. To me, it is an exciting book and a comforting book; but it is also a challenging book. I, for one, am deeply grateful to my friend Jan Bonda for the trail he has blazed here and for having shown the church that there is a biblical "way out" of perplexing questions. Of course, Bonda's is hardly the final word on the questions we face. Many years of ongoing theological study and reflection are going to be needed to scrutinize everything Bonda has come up with. And isn't it true that only God Almighty can speak the final word? Yet there can be no question that the author has put the church in his debt by this penetrating study. He has given the church a fresh perspective on the unchangeable gospel, a hope and outlook it can live by, and a message of both divine judgment and hope that it can preach. The vision offered in this book has the potential of reinvigorating the church and of making Christians happier people and stronger witnesses for Christ.

In closing, I wish to mention that it was Professor Hendrikus Berkhof who strongly recommended this book to me. In the personally penned letter, his handwriting clearly showing the effects of the stroke he had suffered, he calls it a "very comforting book." More in general, he writes that "this life is but the takeoff toward a higher goal. Satan will not win. God the Creator is the Victor. God all in all!" That same Scripture-based conviction underlies the book you are now holding in your hands.

Sierd Woudstra

Preface

Throughout my life the gloomy doctrine of eternal punishment, which the church has preached for many centuries, has bothered me. After my retirement from the active ministry I at last had the opportunity to make an in-depth study of what the Bible has to say about this topic. I knew that many others had written about this subject, and I took the time to read their writings. What they wrote about the hope of salvation for all again and again strengthened my convictions. I decided, however, to take a different approach — a more systematic, biblical study that would also deal with the "difficult texts" that are invariably cited against the hope of salvation for the millions. That is what I have done in this book, and in such a way that it can be read even by those without formal theological training.

I did not dare to embark on such a project without having consulted a number of persons who have distinguished themselves in the realm of theology. First of all, I contacted Professor Herman Ridderbos, with whom I had already been in touch concerning this question. This contact, in fact, was foundational for this book. More than once I doubted the viability of the whole project. When, at one time, I had become convinced that I had no other option but to abandon it, I had a totally unexpected encounter — in a very full train — with Professor Hendrikus Berkhof. He emphatically insisted that I see the project through. I received the same encouragement from my old friend, the missiologist Professor Johannes Verkuyl, and from Professor G. P. van Itterzon, the respected church historian. They were like gifts from heaven to me.

My search finally took me to the friend to whom I have dedicated this book — Israël Tabaksblat, a Messiah-confessing Jew, who became a minister in the Dutch Reformed Church, but never really felt at home in it because of its alienation from Israel. The "Journey through Romans," the longest section of this book, was the subject of many conversations. At the end of the book I will explain what these talks have meant for me.

Dr. Jan Veenhof has been a loyal ally and companion during the writing process. From the time we first met — not long after he became a professor at the Free University in Amsterdam — this subject caught his interest. From the beginning he served — in his own words — as a "co-reader" of this book. He never doubted that I should continue along the road on which I had embarked. I doubt whether I would have reached the end, were it not for his constant encouragement.

Professor R. van den Broek was willing to read what I had written about the church fathers Origen and Augustine and about 2 Esdras. This area is outside my expertise, but with his wholehearted support I have ventured to write about this part of church tradition. This effort was preceded by a "journey through Origen," in particular through chapters 9–11 of his commentary on Romans. Many mornings Dr. Gerhard Steenstra was at my side to help me with the Latin text.

My friend and colleague Pastor Jan Brederveld, and my son Jan Willem have also been of great help in preparing this book. Their advice resulted in many alterations.

My warm thanks go to Dr. Sierd Woudstra. Unbeknownst to me, for many years already his thoughts moved in the same direction as mine. Providentially, just at the time when the efforts to get the book out in English were seriously stagnating, we became acquainted with each other. Convinced that the vision offered in this book should be made available to the English-speaking world, he offered his help to get the translation and extensive editing process back on the rails. Needless to say, I accepted his offer with both hands. In addition to spending countless hours on the book itself, he has also written the Foreword.

Many others have helped me in word and deed. I wish I could mention them all, but that would be impossible. I ask that they forgive me for not mentioning them. But I have decided to mention one person who would prefer to remain anonymous — my wife Hilde. She has supported me through the years of writing and, like no other, has shared my concern for this book and its message. She also gave it a final reading. I want to thank everyone who assisted me.

Jan Bonda

CHAPTER I

A Tradition of Acquiescence

1. An Inescapable Question — What Is God Like?

"I Had a Brother . . ."

Our question has to do with hope: Does the Bible give us ground for hope that the many who died without having sought refuge in God will be saved? The tradition of our faith teaches that there is no legitimate hope for those who died without that faith.[1] The situation at the time of death is final: "The tree lies where it has fallen." Our tradition further teaches, that we have to accept this verdict since it is in accordance with God's decree. It

---

1. The Synod of the Reformed (Gereformeerde) Churches in the Netherlands of 1905 dealt with the question whether people who had never heard the gospel would be lost. It issued the following statement: "Even though the synod does not deny that God is able even without the preaching of the Word, in particular in heathen lands, to bring to the new birth whomever he chooses, it is nonetheless of the opinion that, on the basis of the Scriptures, we cannot determine whether he indeed does so. Therefore, we feel compelled to observe the rule, given to us by the revealed Word, to leave the hidden things to the Lord our God." (*Acta of the General Synod of the Reformed Churches in the Netherlands, 1905*, p. 85). H. Bavinck writes: "On the basis of Scripture, we cannot, both with regard to the salvation of the heathen and to that of children who died at a young age, come to any decision, other than that we should refrain from a definite positive or negative conclusion" (*Dogmatiek*, 4:708). These statements are a step forward, yet they affirm that the Bible provides no hope for the salvation of the many who never heard the gospel. It could be "Yes" or "No." And there is absolutely no hope for those who did hear the gospel but rejected it. This last aspect causes the most anxiety.

does not want to deviate from what the Bible says. But — and this is the question that will occupy us — does our tradition in fact not say something different? Do the Scriptures really teach us that there is no hope for those who died in that state? *Is it true that God wants us passively to accept the fact that our fellow human beings are lost?*

"I had a brother" — our conversation began with these words. I was talking with an elderly woman. It happened long ago. Her brother had died at an early age. He died without God. Something had happened. The girl he was about to marry had deserted him and had married his friend. As a result he felt resentment against God. God had deserted him. Sometime later he became ill; the illness proved to be terminal. Death was imminent. But he did not change. He did not want to hear a word about God. He wanted no Bible, no prayer, no preacher at his bedside! When his final moments came, he told his parents that he did not want anything related to God at his funeral! That was what she told me. For a few moments we sat in silence. Then she looked at me and said: "My brother is lost." She kept looking at me.

Was I to agree with her? I could not. I knew what is normally said in such cases. But of what use were those words of comfort, "God's mercies are manifold," for this woman? What would God do for her brother, who refused to have anything to do with God? — that was the big question. Then, too, there is that other line of reasoning to defuse the anxiety: "Could it be that, on the threshold of eternity, in his heart he called upon God; nobody knows what happens in the human heart!" But what good would any "maybe" do for this woman! Her brother had been too close to her for such words to comfort her. Any comfort would have to be firmly grounded — in the Bible itself. And in the Bible we find those implacable words: "Whoever disobeys the Son will not see life, but must endure God's wrath" (John 3:36). Her brother had done precisely what this text warns against. With firmness and persistence he had said "No" to God. That is how he died. There is no way around it: if the Bible is true, he was lost.

Did this mean that all she could do was accept God's judgment? Was that what I was to say? I could not bring myself to do that. "Why don't you pray for your brother," I suggested, realizing that I had deviated from the Reformed path. That she would not do! That was impossible, she said. That was Roman Catholic! Prayer for the dead — there was nothing in the Bible about that. What good would it do? Her brother's fate had been determined — once and for all. One simply had to accept that. But she was unable to do so. Others might be able to accept such things, but she could not. That was the greatness of this woman. It was her brother — and he was lost! She simply could not forget him, and she did not want to forget him!

Pray! — why had I said this? I could not submit to the despair that stared at me through her eyes. That could not be the message God wanted me to deliver in these circumstances. He might be lost, but was it God's intention that he would remain lost? Suddenly I realized: this woman's longings were after God's heart. The very fact that this woman could not accept the lostness of her brother had to be genuine faith!

I was not thinking of the kind of prayer that must move God to save her brother. But the Bible does say: "Cast all your anxiety upon him, for he cares for you" (1 Pet. 5:7). If this anxiety was God's desire, it simply could not be true that she would find a closed door in her approach to God. There had to be a way for her to come to God in her distress. There had to be hope for her brother!

The apostle Paul had written something about this "passive acceptance." "I have great sorrow and unceasing anguish in my heart. . . ." In this passage he writes about his brothers, the Jews, who had rejected the Messiah and therefore were outside God's salvation. This woman knew about such great sorrow and unceasing anguish. Paul then adds that he could wish himself to be cut off from Christ if that would help his brothers (Rom. 9:2, 3). That is quite different from simply accepting that they would be lost. We might say: The Jews of his days had not yet died, while the brother of this woman was dead. There is hope for conversion as long as there is life. But also in Paul's days, every day Jews died without having come to faith in Jesus. What did Paul think of that? Did he give up on them because they had died? No. Paul did not share the despair about the destiny of the dead that we know in our tradition. Reading on, we come upon words of boundless hope! "God has imprisoned all in disobedience so that he may be merciful to all" (Rom. 11:32). That is not the kind of hope that ends at the grave! Apparently we have lost something in our faith tradition; something of the hope by which the New Testament believers lived. It is imperative that we know more about this hope!

"He Wants It Even More Than You Do"

A few years earlier I had a somewhat similar conversation. I spoke with a man of just under sixty years of age. I had heard that he was seriously ill and decided to visit him. He was not a member of the church. Like so many, he had grown up in a Christian family, but at an early age he had turned away from the church. Now he was about to die, and he knew it. I was welcome. But our conversation was far from smooth. "Actually," he said, "I have never ceased to believe." But at the same time it was quite clear: His faith did not give him any support. Nor was he looking for that support. What was the reason?

One afternoon he opened up. He began to talk about his spouse. At that particular time she was not at home. She had always been a wonderful wife for him. Now, during his sickness, how patiently she cared for him! But she did not believe! She came from a family where religion was taboo. That was his big problem: If he were now to seek salvation from God, what would God do with his wife? "You mean," I said, "that you might then be saved and she would not?" Yes, that was it. With dismay I remembered what I was supposed to say. Jesus had said something difficult about this matter: "Whoever comes to me and does not hate father and mother . . . yes, even his own life, cannot be my disciple" (Luke 14:26; cf. Matt. 10:37). He had to decide: Should he follow Jesus or his wife? That was what I was supposed to say. But is that what Jesus intended? Suddenly our conversation took a sharp turn. Was his problem that he would be saved and his wife would be lost — that he would have to abandon her? Did he want his wife to be saved if he were to receive salvation for himself? Yes, that was what he wanted. "Then you must go to Jesus," I answered, "because he desires her salvation even more than you do."

Had I said too much? I was far from sure whether or not I had. But something struck me. It was the same thing that impressed me in my conversation with the woman I discussed earlier. This must be God's desire! Or would God want it differently? Would God want him to be unconcerned about the salvation of his wife, and concerned only about his own? Was that the kind of choice Jesus referred to? No, God is not like that! On that fact I had dared to stake my hope.

From that time on we could talk. His illness was long and painful. I prayed that God would relieve his pain, but that did not happen. Something else did, however. He found his way to God. In one of our last conversations I asked him what I should pray for. "Pray?" he asked. "I want to thank God. I am so grateful that I found the way." Then, with just the two of us in that hospital room, he began to thank God. After that I heard him pray for his wife. He committed her destiny into the hands of the Father whom he had found. Shortly afterward he died.

A Farewell Letter

I have a letter in front of me. I have known the writer from the time I was a student. He had become a neurologist and a psychiatrist. The letter is addressed to a circle of friends. It bids them farewell. He was terminally ill, and he knew his life would soon come to an end. It is a shocking letter. In it he reveals to his friends that toward the end of his life he broke with his faith. Several times he had discussed this matter with them. He wanted to talk about it once more, with his friends in his home, where he wanted to read the letter to them.

I quote a few lines from this letter. "It is difficult for me tonight, being with you, to have to say a few things that may be painful to some of you. In all honesty I cannot do otherwise. But I will do my best not to hurt any of you." He then speaks of the "venom of sin, guilt, damnation, death, and the power of the devil" (from Lord's Day 1, Heidelberg Catechism), which flows weekly, or perhaps monthly, from the pulpit to the people, and even to their children.

He finds the wording of the baptismal service particularly offensive, and quotes extensively from it:

> O almighty, eternal God, Thou who hast according to Thy severe judgment punished the unbelieving and unrepentant world with the flood, and hast according to Thy great mercy saved and protected believing Noah and his family; Thou who hast drowned the obstinate Pharaoh and all his host in the Red Sea and led Thy people Israel through the midst of the sea upon dry ground — by which baptism was signified. . . .

It is a liturgy by which the churches have lived for centuries. "Now I am disgusted with what I so long took for granted. . . . How can it be that for centuries the Calvinistic brethren, and not just some ultraconservatives, with unashamed sadism brainwashed devout believers with this ideology of hell and damnation"?

But he not only objected to this liturgy, as is clear from these examples. The Bible itself, God's written "good news," "gives a picture of God as full of jealousy and revenge, a destroyer of generations (the third and the fourth), and at one time of almost all people — except 'Noah and his family'. . . ." For two thirds of his life he had believed this message with all his heart. He had been a faithful churchgoer. "Now I say that I received stones for bread. A 'Father' who for no good reason involved me in guilt that was not mine. One who did not show his 'goodwill' toward humankind, as I had been fond of singing during the Christmas season."

Yes, he knew that some theologians speak in different terms about hell. If what they said were true, he would look differently upon the matter. But what else did they do, he said, than merely "touch up" or obscure what the Bible so clearly declared? They could not convince him that the Bible itself did not teach this doctrine of hell. He saw no other choice: Either the God of the Bible or nothing! He could not believe in a "God of theologians."

So, later in life, he had distanced himself from the Christian faith. The book of Ecclesiastes, he writes, had been an "eye opener" for him. He had nothing left! But he experienced this fact as extremely positive. "The normative, dogmatic, logical, icy belief in justification[2] has fortunately been . . . beneficially undermined and dismantled into a kind of human happiness, even now, that does not need to be gold-plated in a hereafter." He hoped he would have opportunity to discuss the matter further with his friends. "I think all the time about the meaning of life, in particular the goodness of life, and about the horror of death." So ends this letter.

These are the words of a person who felt hurt, who had lost his faith but could not stop searching, and who looked for it where he had lost it. He read Ecclesiastes. The Bible, in spite of everything! And he remained in touch with those who had kept their faith. Shortly before his death — which was soon to follow — he had felt the urge to read this letter to them and talk with them about it. And that is what happened. But they could not change his mind. "Why not?" I asked one of them after I had read the letter. They did not know what to do with the problem of their friend. It was undeniable, they feared, that that is how the Bible talked about God.

Must We Remain Silent?

This letter has meant much to me. The dogma that God wants everlasting punishment for the vast majority of humanity had always bothered me. Some of those with whom I discussed the topic also had their doubts about this traditional teaching, but preferred to remain silent. They pointed to the seriousness of the biblical warning. In times such as ours, in which people tend to let go of all norms, it would be wrong to undermine the warnings of the Bible. And that is what you did if you were to suggest that

2. The "belief in justice" is reflected in what the Heidelberg Catechism says about God: God is not only compassionate but also just (Q. 11). I once heard this statement expressed even more simply: "I do believe that God is just, but I do not believe that He is love."

the Bible offers the possibility of salvation after punishment. But there was something else. They agreed: It was impossible to believe that God would allow people to suffer endlessly; it was contrary to what Jesus said and showed about God's love. *Nevertheless, should we not face the fact that a number of biblical passages do teach everlasting punishment?* They feared that this was indeed the case, and that prevented them from speaking out on the issue.

After reading the letter from this former fellow student, I knew that it was better to speak out. I was looking at three things. He had rebelled — and remember, he was a psychiatrist — against this terrifying "image of God," a God who wills the destruction of the majority of humankind. He could no longer with a clear conscience bow before such a "god." Was that wrong? Could it be God's will that he would bow before such a god? That was the first consideration. Second, there was his unshakable conviction that the tradition simply reworded what the Bible itself taught. For him, any attempt to phrase this differently was equal to obscuring what the Bible said. Finally, a searching human being had lost his faith in God. Nothing could be done about that, because that was how he died.

The second matter continued to haunt me: Is this how Scripture really speaks about God? Does it talk like this about the divine judgment? I believed that there were good grounds to question this supposition. Was it not high time that the church dealt with this matter? That does not happen when everyone keeps silent.

Despair and Hope in Our Tradition

In the following pages we will get a glimpse of what the "church of the ages" has taught about eternal punishment. This topic may not make for pleasant reading. But we have to point to the source of the profound pessimism that we find in our tradition of faith. Thus we cannot avoid paying attention to the content and place of eternal punishment in the history of the church.

Before we begin, let me point to something that should not be lost sight of. What we are about to survey is the teaching of the church. But there is more to say about our tradition. It is not true that it is totally governed by this dogma. Many, if not most, believers have been very much aware of the difficult Bible texts about eternal punishment, but they have nonetheless clung to the words that assure us of God's love. Therefore, the hope that was built on that love has never been extinguished throughout the history of the church. But that hope was contradicted by the church itself. There was no real answer to these "threatening texts." Therefore, it was impossible to give others, who were vexed by these texts, the help they needed. We saw this in the writer of the letter referred to above: His friends had no answer. The aim of this book is to make a contribution toward finding a biblical answer that disproves the terrifying image of God found in our tradition; an answer that will lead to a biblically founded hope for the world — a hope for the living and for the dead.

2. Election

Tradition and Scripture

If the fathers of the Reformation emphasized one thing, it is our responsibility to search the Bible for ourselves, to see whether what has been transmitted to us by former generations does indeed harmonize with the Word of God. We read in the Belgic Confession of 1562 (Art. 7):

> Neither may we compare any writing of men, though ever so holy, with those divine Scriptures; nor ought we to compare custom, or the great multitude, or antiquity, or succession of times or persons, or councils, decrees, statutes, with the truth of God, for the truth is above all: *for all men are themselves liars,* and more vain than vanity itself (Ps. 62:10).[3]

The believers of that time trusted the promise of the Spirit, given to them to understand the Word of God. And on the basis of what they read in the Bible, they said "No" to things that for centuries had been taught by the church.

But they did not claim infallibility: "for all men are themselves liars, and more vain than vanity itself." Therefore, the church will always have the duty, while praying for the promise of the Spirit, to examine what has

---

3. Philip Schaff, *The Creeds of Christendom* (New York, 1931), 3:388. The Belgic Confession is in close harmony with the Gallic Confession of the French Protestant Church. In the confession of the Anglican Church, the Thirty-nine Articles of Religion of 1562, we read: "Holy Scripture containeth all things necessary to salvation: so that whatsoever is not read therein, nor may be proved thereby, is not to be required of any man, that it should be believed as an article of faith, or be thought requisite or necessary to salvation" (Art. 6).

been taught by previous generations in the light of Scripture. If the church discovers that the Bible teaches something else, it must have the courage to follow the Bible and abandon tradition. Respect for and gratitude toward earlier generations do not free us from this task. In fact, this is precisely what they have charged us to do. Only if we do this will we be able to deliver the faith of our parents and ancestors to the next generation as a living faith.

In the next chapter we will discover whether Scripture teaches us to take the lost state of our fellow human beings for granted. But first we must face the fact that we have been taught this acquiescence in the long tradition of our faith! We must therefore direct our attention to the dogma of election and reprobation as we find it in the confessional documents of the Reformed and Presbyterian churches.

The Belgic Confession says:

> We believe that all posterity of Adam, being thus fallen into perdition and ruin by the sin of our first parents, God then did manifest Himself such as He is; that is to say, *merciful and just*: merciful, since He delivers and preserves from this perdition all whom He, in his eternal and unchangeable counsel, of mere goodness has elected in Christ Jesus our Lord, without any respect to their works: *just*, in leaving others in the fall and perdition wherein they have involved themselves. (Art. 16; italics supplied)[4]

What is God like? One the one hand, God is compassionate. And, on the other hand, he is just. God shows compassion, in that he saves people who do not deserve to be saved. But, at the same time, he is just. That is clear from the fact that he does not save other people but leaves them in the lost state in which they find themselves through their own fault. Their guilt is no bigger than or different from that of those who are saved. We should not conclude that God is unable to save them. But, in their case, he does not choose to save. Why not? Because he wants to demonstrate that he is a just God, who punishes evil. That makes it necessary for some people to be lost. The elect will recognize this:

> . . . they shall see the terrible vengeance which God shall execute on the wicked . . . who shall be convicted by the testimony of their own con-

---

4. Schaff, *Creeds*, p. 401. A similar statement, more extensive and closer to the Canons of Dort, is found in the Westminster Confession of Faith, approved in 1647 by the General Assembly of the Church of Scotland, III *(Of God's Eternal Decree)*.

sciences, and, being immortal, shall be tormented in the everlasting fire which is prepared for the devil and his angels. Matthew 25:46. (Art. 37)[5]

The Heidelberg Catechism of 1563 describes why this punishment must be *without end*. Does that not conflict with God's compassion? The answer is:

> God is indeed merciful, but He is likewise just; wherefore his justice requires that sin, which is committed against the most high majesty of God, be also punished with extreme, that is, with everlasting punishment both of body and soul. (Q. 11)[6]

Once again the contrast: compassionate but also just. Thus God is the saving God for a number of people, but the punishing God for the vast majority. The question may, however, be asked: Is it just that a person be punished with eternal punishment for sins committed during a life of limited duration? "Yes," is the answer, since the sin is not against a human being but against God, the highest majesty. For that reason the punishment must also be the highest and the most severe: it must be *eternal*. Those who believe in Christ are saved from that punishment, but all others are not. When an explanation is given of the second coming of Christ, we read that it is our comfort that he

> shall condemn all his and my enemies to everlasting condemnation, but shall take me, with all his chosen ones, to Himself, into heavenly joy and glory. (Q. 52)[7]

Thus we are taught that there are elect and non-elect.

Differences of opinion arose over the doctrine of election, and therefore it was unequivocally defined in a later confessional document, the Canons of the Synod of Dort of 1619. In it we read:

> That some receive the gift of faith from God, and others do not receive it, proceeds from God's eternal decree. . . . According to which decree He graciously softens the heart of the elect, however obstinate, and inclines them to believe; while He leaves the non-elect in His just judgment to their own wickedness and obduracy. And herein is especially displayed the pro-

---

5. Schaff, *Creeds*, 3:435.
6. Schaff, *Creeds*, 3:311.
7. Schaff, *Creeds*, 3:324.

found, the merciful, and at the same time the righteous discrimination between men, equally involved in ruin; or that decree of election and reprobation, revealed in the Word of God. . . . (I, 6).

Election is the unchangeable purpose of God, whereby, before the foundation of the world, He has out of mere grace, according to the sovereign good pleasure of his own will, chosen . . . a certain number of persons to redemption in Christ. . . . (I, 7)[8]

What we said about the harsh image of God in our faith tradition is not the result of our imagination!

No Calvinistic Invention — Augustine

Usually this teaching about the dark side of God's dealings with humankind is seen as Calvin's invention: *the harsh Calvinistic image of God.* There is no question that the confessional documents cited above hark back to Calvin. But it would be a misunderstanding to think that this teaching was initiated by Calvin. It is not so well known that Luther taught the same view in a no less outspoken way in his famous book about "the bondage of the human will." He never ceased to insist that none of his other books so perfectly expressed his views.[9] It is true that the Lutheran Church subsequently softened some of this harshness, in contrast to the Reformed tradition. But that does not imply that the Lutherans in any way downplayed the doctrine of eternal punishment. The Augsburg Confession emphatically teaches the endlessness of the punishment (Art. 17).[10]

Did the teaching that God does not want to save all people originate with the Reformation? Certainly not! First of all, the two reformers referred to above were disciples of Augustine, the church father of the entire Western Church, including the Roman Catholic Church. Second, it would be incor-

8. Schaff, *Creeds,* 3:582.

9. Wilhelm Niesel, *Das Evangelium und die Kirchen. Ein Lehrbuch der Symbolik* (2nd ed.; Neukirchen, 1960), pp. 193-202.

10. "Also they teach that at the Consummation of the World Christ will appear for judgment, and will raise up all the dead; He will give to the godly and elect eternal life and everlasting joys, but ungodly men and the devils He will condemn to be tormented without end [Latin: *ut sine fine crucientur*]. They condemn the Anabaptists, who think that there will be an end to the punishments of the condemned men and devils." *The Augsburg Confession,* Art. 17 (St. Louis, n.d.).

rect to assume that the dogma of eternal damnation derives from the dogma of election. Let us first look at the origin of that teaching.

Eternal damnation was first taught by Augustine. Strangely enough, it resulted from his great discovery: the truth about God's grace. Our salvation is *free:* we are not saved because we are better than the many who are lost. This had been Augustine's own experience: He knew that God had overcome his stubbornness and that he owed his salvation solely to God's determination to save people — in spite of their own godlessness. This will is the will of his grace.

But this grace, apparently, has its limits. For most people will in the end be lost. How do we know this? From the evident fact that most people do not die as true Christians, and whoever dies in that state is lost.[11] This was Augustine's undeniable point of departure. It was what the church in his days taught, as we will see later. For the moment we need to deal with the question: Why are all people not saved? In the days of Augustine people would answer: "Because they do not want to be saved." This we read in his "Handbook" (the *Enchiridion*). But according to the church father this could not be the correct response. If God had desired their salvation, he would have done for them what he did for those who will be saved. This is indicated in the following lines:

> And, moreover, who will be so foolish and blasphemous as to say that God cannot change the evil wills of men, whichever, whenever, and wheresoever He chooses, and direct them to what is good? But when He does this, He does it of mercy; when He does it not, it is of justice that He does it not; for "He hath mercy on whom He will have mercy, and whom He wills He hardeneth" (Rom. 9:18).[12]

Thus, they will be lost because God does not want their salvation! We discern in Augustine the same distinction we saw in the confessional documents mentioned above: on the one hand God's mercy, and on the other

---

11. Augustine, *Enchiridion,* 97, in Whitney J. Oates, ed., *Basic Writings of Saint Augustine* (New York, 1948), 1:658-732. Augustine persisted in his teaching that there is no salvation outside the church, as Cyprian (ca. 200-258) had already stated. Therefore, unbaptized children would not be saved; though for them the (endless!) punishment would be the least severe (*Enchiridion,* 93); cf. *De Natura et Gratia,* 4:4; 8:9; in Bibliothèque Augustinienne, 21:251, 259, 601ff. n. 31).

12. *Enchiridion,* 97, 98.

hand his justice, that is to say: his judgment. We find this distinction between the two sides of God for the first time in Augustine.

But is there not a text with a different message, which indicates that God "desires everyone to be saved and to come to the knowledge of the truth" (1 Tim. 2:4)? How can this be true if in reality most people will be lost? Will they be lost in spite of the fact that God wants to save them? Augustine had to face that question.

> For, as a matter of fact, not all, not even a majority, are saved: so that it would seem that what God wills is not done, man's will interfering with, and hindering the will of God.

This appears to be so in Jesus' complaint over Jerusalem.

> Our Lord says plainly . . . when upbraiding the impious city: "How often would I have gathered thy children together, even as a hen gathereth her chickens under her wings, and ye would not!" (Matt. 23:37) as if the will of God had been overcome by the will of men, and when the weakest stood in the way with their want of will, the will of the strongest could not be carried out.

Impossible! How could the Omnipotent be thwarted by children in what he wants? Strangely enough, Augustine here feels that Jesus differentiates between children and adults. Jesus intended to gather the small children from Jerusalem, but not all of them. From among all the children, against the will of Jerusalem itself, Jesus gathered only those he wanted. This was, according to the church father, Jesus' intention.[13]

But is that what the text says? Not exactly, but Augustine sees no other option, for the judgment has been executed over Jerusalem; Jerusalem did not repent and has been destroyed, and therefore it must be considered lost. Thus, it cannot be true that Jesus wanted to gather all of Jerusalem, as a hen gathers her chicks — if that were the case, it would have happened! For God was perfectly capable to change the evil wills of human beings for the better!

We notice that the church father completely ignores any future salvation after the judgment, as announced by Jesus: ". . . until you say: Blessed is he who comes in the name of the Lord" (Matt. 23:39). Augustine firmly believes that there cannot be any salvation after the judgment for those upon whom the judgment has fallen. He does not attempt to prove this

---

13. Both quotations are from *Enchiridion*, 97.

13

belief from Scripture. It was self-evident; it was the church's teaching. It could not be otherwise: God is able to conquer the stubbornness of the people by his grace; but *it does not happen because he does not want it to happen.*

Nevertheless, he had to deal with a text that seemingly expressed the opposite point of view: "God desires everyone to be saved." He did not know what to do with this text:

> Accordingly, when we hear and read in Scripture that He "will have all men to be saved," although we know well that all men are not saved, we are not on that account to restrict the omnipotence of God, but are rather to understand the Scripture, "Who will have all men to be saved," as meaning that no man is saved unless God wills his salvation: not that there is no man whose salvation He does not will, but that no man is saved apart from his will. . . .

Is this indeed what the text says? No, but we know that not all people are saved. Therefore, when we read: God desires that everyone be saved, it simply cannot mean that in actual fact all people are included. Augustine understands that his answer — "that no man is saved apart from his will" — is insufficient. He adds a torrent of words, which we will quote in its entirety, since this abundance of words demonstrates how Augustine struggled with this text:

> . . . that we are to understand by "all men," the human race in all its varieties of rank and circumstances — kings, subjects; noble, plebeian, high, low, learned, and unlearned; the sound in body, the feeble, the clever, the dull, the foolish, the rich, the poor, and those of middling circum-stances; males, females, infants, boys, youth; young, middle-aged, and old men; of every tongue, of every fashion, of all arts, of all professions, with all the innumerable differences of will and conscience, and whatever else there is that makes a distinction among men. For which of all these classes is there out of which God does not will that men should be saved in all nations through his only-begotten Son, our Lord, and therefore does save them; for the Omnipotent cannot will in vain, whatsoever He may will? . . . Our Lord, too, makes use of the same mode of speech in the gospel, when He says to the Pharisees, "Ye tithe mint, and rue, and *every* herb." For the Pharisees did not tithe what belonged to others, not all the herbs of inhabitants of other lands. As, then, in this place we must understand by "every herb," every kind of herb, so in the former passage we may understand by "all men," *every sort of men.* And we may interpret it in any

14

other way we please, so long as we are not compelled to believe that the omnipotent God has willed anything to be done which was not done.[14]

With these words Augustine tries to convince his readers. Apparently, he is far from sure that he will succeed. But if these words do not convince, he will have to find some other arguments. For under no circumstance can he accept the view that the text means that God wants to save everyone.

We would not have quoted this "explanation" at such length if it were not repeated even in our own time to demonstrate that God does not want all people to be saved. But by now it should be clear how little this has to do with a careful exegesis of this Bible text.

There is no doubt: Augustine taught that God does not want everyone to be saved. This is clearly implied in his doctrine of election. For that reason many refer to the *grim image of God* of Augustine, and even more to the grimness of the Calvinistic tradition. For precisely in the doctrine of election of that tradition, we find the truest reproduction of Augustine's views. We do not deny this grimness — on the contrary. Calvin agreed that it was horrifying. The divine decree of election and damnation, he writes, "is *dreadful* [*decretum horribile*] indeed, I confess. Yet no one can deny that God foreknew what end man was to have before He created him, and consequently foreknew because He so ordained by his decree."[15]

It bothered Calvin intensely. He writes in his commentary on Isaiah (25:1): "For truly pious people naturally wish that all people would be saved."[16] But he refuses to make things rosier than the Bible teaches. If the Bible teaches the eternal damnation of humanity, it must be faced and be taught without detracting from it, even though it horrifies us. In this "without detracting from it" lies the meaning of Augustine's doctrine of election. But it would be incorrect to ascribe this frightful image of God to either Augustine or Calvin, as is often done.[17] Why? Because the doctrine

---

14. Both quotations are from *Enchiridion*, 103 (italics mine).

15. *Institutes*, 3:23.7. John T. McNeill, ed. *Institutes of the Christian Religion,* The Library of Christian Classics, vols. 20 and 21 (Philadelphia, 1975), 21:955 (italics mine: "Decretum quidem horribile, fateor").

16. Calvin, *Commentary on the Book of the Prophet Isaiah,* trans. William Pringle (repr. Grand Rapids, 1948).

17. We read, e.g., in B. Altaner and A. Stuiber, *Patrologie* (8th ed.; Freiburg, 1978), p. 442, that Augustine's doctrine of grace (and the doctrine of election that follows from it) is undergirded by a horrifying concept of God ("von einem schauererregenden Gottesbegriff getragen"), and that from the beginning it evoked protest within the

of eternal damnation was already being preached long before Augustine developed his doctrine of election!

3. A Horrifying Image of God

Eternal Punishment, the Teaching of the Church

Augustine is, as we saw, the father of the traditional doctrine of election. But he is not the father of the teaching of eternal damnation! Our tradition has accepted that as self-evident: from the beginning, we are told, the church has taught the doctrine of the eternity of hell, as did the apostles. Whether that is indeed so will become clear only after we have listened to the apostles themselves. For the moment, our goal is more limited: We want to discover whether the endlessness of divine punishment was taught in Augustine's days as a fixed doctrine. In the *Enchiridion* we read how the church father was confronted with the problem:

> It is in vain, then, that some, indeed very many, moan over the eternal punishment, and perpetual, unintermittent torments of the lost, and say they do not believe it shall so be; not, indeed, that they directly oppose themselves to Holy Scripture, but at the suggestion of their own feelings, they soften down everything that seems hard, and give a milder turn to statements which they think are rather designed to terrify than to be received as literally true. For "Hath God," they say, "forgotten to be gracious? Hath He in anger shut up his tender mercies?"[18]

We see that in those days the eternal duration of God's punishment was indeed being preached from the pulpits. For these believers objected to what they heard in church. And they appeal to the words of Scripture: Even in his wrath God will be the God of compassion and grace, and for that reason his wrath shall not be without end. Their objections were not against some invention of Augustine! His doctrine of election was a novelty, and

---

church and caused serious aberrations ("schwere Irrungen"). In referring to these serious aberrations the author clearly has Calvin's doctrine of election in mind.

18. *Enchiridion,* 112. The edition in Bibliothèque Augustienne (9:307) refers to "la grande extension de l'erreur" that was combated by Augustine. Cf. the note regarding the "Erreur des miséricordieux" (p. 388); the idea that only a minority of the believers was affected is rejected; in fact, it is argued, the "error" was widely accepted.

it surely did not carry any authority in the church of his days; there is no indication that his contemporaries were even aware of it. Notice: they did not deny the reality of the punishment, but they could not believe that God would let it continue without end, as they were taught.

That this doctrine was taught we also hear from Augustine's famous contemporary: John Chrysostom (ca. 350-407), who had nothing to do with Augustine's doctrine of election. In one of his sermons he states that one of the most important questions is, Will the fire of hell ever end? But that it is without end, he says, has been confirmed by Christ: their fire will not be extinguished and their worm will not die. People asked him: How can God be just if he allows the punishment to continue forever? But, so the church father replies, such questions should not be asked, if God's Word is clear on the matter. If his hearers do what is right they have nothing to fear, that is, for themselves! He does not elaborate on the fate of others! Chrysostom knows that hell is a harsh word. And the more he realizes how the doctrine of hell is grounded in Scripture, the more he shudders. "But we must teach it, in order that we will not end up in hell."[19]

Apparently, Augustine also had to deal with these objections from his audience. He does not strike out at them as dangerous heretics. They are good people, filled with compassion for their fellow human beings. But, he says, they rely more on their sentiments than on Scripture. The Bible only is authoritative, and we are not free to take from it what we find acceptable, while rejecting what we do not like. Augustine does mention that it was precisely the Bible to which these believers appealed in defense of that "human feeling," but, he explains, God's compassion in his wrath can — "without any problem"(!) — be explained in a different way. It can be argued that it concerns only those who are defined as "objects of mercy" (Rom. 9:23), that is, the elect. He does not ask whether this is what Scripture really intends. He has no doubt whatsoever that the punishment is eternal, and this belief must be at the basis of any exegesis of the Bible. He simply wants to correct these sensitive Christians in a gentle manner. We hear the same when he addresses them in his *City of God*. There he refers to them as "tender-hearted":

> Now must I have a gentle disputation with certain tender hearts of our
> own religion, who think that God, who has justly doomed the condemned

19. John Chrysostom, in *Texte der Kirchenväter* (Munich, 1964), 4:566, in a sermon on the first letter to the Corinthians.

into hell fire, will after a certain space, which his goodness shall think fit for the merit of each man's guilt, deliver them from that torment.[20]

How does Augustine deal with these "tender-hearted" believers? He wants to convince them, and with them all believers, of what the church teaches: God has determined that the vast majority of humankind will be eternally punished. Which arguments does he adduce?

A Defense for Endlessness

In his defense of the endlessness of divine punishment, the church father appeals to a statement of Jesus: "And these will go away into eternal punishment, but the righteous into eternal life" (Matt. 25:46). The word "eternal" in the context of "eternal punishment," must, so Augustine argues, mean "endlessness," because otherwise the word would also imply finality when used in the context of "eternal life."[21]

The church father does not stop to ask whether the word "eternal" in the Bible always implies "endlessness." He says only: If here, in this text, you do not accept this meaning, you must conclude that eternal life will also come to an end. We will later deal with this "proof."[22] We meet another argument for the endlessness of God's punishment in the words addressed to the "tender-hearted" believers, which we quoted above. Once you believe that God's compassion is so abundant that he will not keep the people in hell, you must take another step.

> And of this opinion was Origen, in far more pitiful manner, for he held that the devils themselves after a set time expired should be loosed from their torments, and become bright angels in heaven, as they were before.

This statement, Augustine added, amply justified the church in condemning Origen. The latter had indeed argued that God had a salvific

20. *The City of God,* 21.17 in Henry Bettenson, ed., *St. Augustine: The City of God* (New York, 1984) p. 995. Cf. *La Cité de Dieu,* in Bibliothèque Augustienne, 19-22:806-9, n. 45, "Les Miséricordes," which states that the error was not widely disseminated.

21. *Enchiridion,* 112. In one of his sermons Chrysostom appeals to Matthew 25:46 in the same manner (*Letter to the Romans,* hom. 25; Nicene and Post-Nicene Fathers [Grand Rapids, repr. 1974], 11:527).

22. For comments on the word "eternal" when referring to punishment, see VII, 3 below.

purpose in his impending punishment: the return of lost humanity. Augustine does not say that for this reason Origen was condemned. Origen's condemnation, he says, resulted from the fact that he had taught that eventually even the devil would be saved. But the people with whom Augustine has to deal do not want to go to that extreme. Their compassion is for their fellow human beings. But they err nonetheless when in their "tenderness of heart" they hold

> that this freedom out of hell shall only be extended unto the souls of the damned after a certain time appointed for every one, so that all at length shall come to be saints in heaven. But if this opinion be good and true, because it is merciful, why then the farther it extends, the better it is; so that it may as well include the freedom of the devils also, after a long continuance of time! Why then ends it with mankind only, and excludes them? . . . Nay, but it dares go no farther, for they dare not extend their pity unto the devil. But if any one does so, he goes beyond them in charity, and yet sins in erring more deformedly and more perversely against the express Word of God, though he appears to show the more pity herein.[23]

The church father indicates that to desire the salvation of all people is a dangerous error. For those who think that all people must be saved, must also want the devil's salvation. The "tender-hearted" recoiled from that conclusion, yet this was the inevitable consequence: As soon as you said one thing, you also had to say the other. Why? Does the Bible force us to do so? We will not go into the question what theory or system of logic led Augustine to this reasoning.[24] For us it suffices to know that the Bible does not provide any ground for this. Once again we meet — after his "exegesis" of 1 Timothy 2:4 — the curious arguments Augustine used in order to "prove" that it cannot be true that God desires all people to be saved. We simply add in passing that even today some supporters of the doctrine of eternal punishment use this argument (the salvation of the devil).

23. Both quotations are from *The City of God,* 21.17; cf. the final part of 21:18. The first condemnation of Origen must have been around 400. Denzinger (*Enchiridion Symbolorum,* no. 93, n.) mentions the condemnation of his errors, without identifying what they consisted of.
24. About this bone of contention (the salvation of Satan), see I, n. 54.

THE ONE PURPOSE OF GOD

The Image of God: The Dual Purpose of God

We now come to the arguments that have most deeply influenced our tradition, and that have led to the "image of God" transmitted to us by the church father. For he wants to explain to believers how it makes sense that many will be lost. It cannot be otherwise, he writes in his "handbook," for the larger number of the lost makes those who are saved realize that they, too, would have been among this multitude of the lost if God in his compassion had not saved them from this multitude. Those who are saved recognize:

> . . . that those who are redeemed should be redeemed in such a way as to show, by the greater number of who are unredeemed and left in their just condemnation, what the whole race deserved, and whither the deserved judgment of God would lead even the redeemed, did not his undeserved mercy interpose, so that every mouth might be stopped of those who wish to glory in their own merits, and that he that glorieth might glory in the Lord.[25]

We find the same thought in *The City of God*. All human beings are condemned as a result of Adam's transgression, and can be saved only through God's compassion and undeserved grace. Humankind is divided between "those in whom the power of merciful grace was demonstrated" and "those in whom is shown the might of just retribution." Both could not be shown in all humans.

> . . . for if all had remained condemned to the punishment entailed by just condemnation, then God's merciful grace would not have been seen at work in anyone; on the other hand, if all had been transferred from darkness to light, the truth of God's vengeance would not have been made evident. Now there are many more condemned by vengeance than are released by mercy; and the reason for this is that in this way [it may] be made plain what was the due of all mankind. . . . But the fact that so many are released from it is the ground for heart-felt thanksgiving for the free bounty of our Deliverer.[26]

Once again we are confronted with this duality of mercy and justice in God. His compassionate, undeserved grace precedes everything else. To

25. *Enchiridion*, 99.
26. *The City of God*, 21.12.

20

this the "tender-hearted" believers appealed in their resistance to the endlessness of the punishment. They could not harmonize endless punishment with what Scripture says about God as the Compassionate One. Nor could Augustine! But the endlessness of the punishment was beyond discussion. Thus, there must be some other element in God. This Augustine found in what the Bible says about God's "righteousness" (Lat. *iustitia*), which he interpreted as "revenging justice." We will simply ignore the fact that nowhere in Scripture does the word " righteousness" refer to God's act of punishing. There is no question that the Bible teaches unequivocally that God punishes evil. Our concern is the contrast Augustine discerns in God: retribution as opposed to compassion. *God wants two things.* For some people He wants to be the *Compassionate One.* But for most people he wants to be something else: the *One who is just* — the Judge, who "requires that sin, which is committed against the most high majesty of God, be also punished with extreme, that is, with everlasting punishment" (the Heidelberg Catechism, Q. 11). Since Augustine, this theory of the two contrasting divine goals has dominated the western faith tradition.

Original Sin

But prior to this theory of the necessity of eternal punishment over against eternal salvation, we hear something else. Is endless punishment just retribution for sins committed during a life of limited duration?

> Now the reason why eternal punishment appears harsh and unjust to human sensibilities, is that in this feeble condition of those sensibilities under their condition of mortality man lacks the sensibility of the highest and purest wisdom, the sense which should enable him to feel the gravity of the wickedness in the first act of disobedience. For the more intimate the first man's enjoyment of God, the greater his impiety in abandoning God. By so doing he merited eternal evil, in that he destroyed in himself a good that might have been eternal. In consequence, the whole of mankind is a "condemned lump"; for he who committed the first sin was punished, and along with him all the stock which had its roots in him.[27]

---

27. *The City of God,* 21.12.

In order to judge whether the measure of eternal punishment matches the transgression, one must understand the immensity of the treasure humankind rejected. They have repudiated an eternal prize, and it is therefore reasonable that they receive eternal punishment. We are referring to the sin committed by Adam and Eve. We do not know how immense the treasure was that God had given them and that they intentionally forfeited. Therefore, we are in no position to say that their punishment is too severe. We must leave that judgment to God.

But is it fair that we are punished for what our first parents did? We are told only: "He who committed the first sin was punished, and along with him all the stock which had its roots in him."[28] The doctrine of original sin is the cornerstone of Augustine's doctrine of election. His system collapses without the concept of original sin. Thus this concept *must* be assumed! He hardly ever deals with the fairness of the punishment. The human race had to be divided in such a way that in some the compassion of God would be demonstrated, while in others God's just retribution would be manifest. From the beginning God had this dual purpose for humanity. Can it be right that God should reach his goal in this way, by imputing the first sin to all of Adam's descendants, and subsequently saving only a few of them? This question also belongs to the things we cannot judge and must leave to God.

The Image of God: Does God Want Evil? The Contrast

In writing about the origin of the devil, Augustine states that he was created as a good angel. He did not become evil because God wanted this to happen, but of his own free choice. But then we read something shocking:

> Now God, when He created the Devil, was without doubt well aware of his future wickedness, and had foreseen the good that He Himself would bring out of that evil. That is why the psalm says, "This is the dragon which you fashioned for him to mock at" (Ps. 104:26). In the creation of the Devil, though by God's goodness he was made in a state of good, God had already, in virtue of his foreknowledge, laid plans for making good use of him even in his evil state.

28. Cf. *The City of God*, 13.3 and 14.1; *Enchiridion*, 26, 50, 98. See below (with reference to Rom. 5:12), III, 5.

Thus, God saw that this angel would choose evil. But he foreknew how much benefit he would derive from this choice. Of course, he could have decided not to create this angel that would become the devil. Then evil would not have entered the world. But! — it suited him that there would be evil, and he therefore created this particular angel and allowed him to bring about evil. When evil had come about, God allowed humanity to become evil. Augustine tries to argue that God did not want evil. That is what the Bible teaches. Then how can it be that it nevertheless exists? This the Bible does not explain. What then are we to think of this explanation by the church father? The doctrine of eternal punishment implies that God wants the evil, which now exists, to be perpetuated. For he wants to punish eternally. That would be impossible if evil no longer existed. But if it is true that God wants evil not to disappear but to continue, how can it be said that God does not want evil? Here we see where the doctrine of eternal punishment leads us!

What is the good that derives from the evil? We read:

> For God would never have created a man, let alone an angel, in the foreknowledge of his future evil state, if He had not known at the same time how He would put such creatures to good use, and thus enrich the course of world history by the kind of antithesis which gives beauty to a poem. "Antithesis" provides the most attractive figures in literary composition. . . . The opposition of such contraries gives an added beauty to speech; and in the same way there is a beauty in the composition of the world's history arising from the antithesis of contraries — a kind of eloquence in events, instead of in words.[29]

In the *Enchiridion* we find the same idea. "For He judged it better to bring good out of evil, than not to permit any evil to exist."[30] Evil

> . . . only enhances our admiration of the good; for we enjoy and value the good more when we compare it with evil. For the Almighty God, who, as even the heathen acknowledge, has supreme power over all things, being Himself supremely good, would never permit the existence of anything evil among his works if He were not so omnipotent and good that He can bring good even out of evil.[31]

29. *The City of God*, 11.17. The metaphors of these antitheses reflect linguistic convention.
30. *Enchiridion*, 27.
31. *Enchiridion*, 11.

From our earlier quotations, we learned that the lost state of the vast majority demonstrates from what punishment the few have been saved. There we saw how the contrast functions: The divergence between the doom of the majority and the salvation of the few leads those few to "heartfelt thanksgiving for the free bounty of our Deliverer." The salvation of the few thus *requires* the lostness of the many if there is to be complete and full bliss. God uses this lostness to reveal how, through his grace, he *freely* gives them his salvation.

Does this mean that salvation is bought with the lost state of the doomed; that it is enjoyed at the expense of their lostness? We cannot but get that impression. What would we think of someone who would bring happiness to others in such a way? And what would we think of people who want to be made happy in such a way? It is a question in itself where Augustine found this idea, but one thing is clear: What he writes about the origin of evil and the beautiful contrast does not come from Scripture.[32]

Do We Do Justice to Augustine?

But do we do justice to the church father in quoting him as we did? Did he not also say many other things about God? True enough. But the question here is not what this great church father has meant for western Christianity. It is rather what posterity did with his defense of eternal punishment. By transmitting this defense, century after century, his followers have given these words a weight they did not possess in Augustine's own mind — the weight of the "church of the ages." The task of posterity was to compare these words with Scripture before handing them down to the next

---

32. The origin of this dualism in Augustine's concept of God remains an open question. A. Adam (*Lehrbuch der Dogmengeschichte* [2nd ed.; Gutersloh, 1979], 1:291-96; cf. pp. 207-10), with others, looks for the source in Manicheism, which resulted from Persian influences. Manicheism was a Christian sect that was the major opponent of the church for a few centuries. J. van Oort denies this in his study of "The City of God" (*Jeruzalem en Babylon* [The Hague, 1986]). His third thesis is: "The extensive similarities between Manichean teachings and Augustine (pp. 291-96) must be explained on the basis of their shared Judeo-Christian background" (see pp. 230-300). This is outside the scope of this study. Our question is not whether there has been Judeo-Christian background for the teaching that God wants eternal separation, but whether this dualism is *biblical*. Cf. I, 5 (regarding 2 Esdras).

generations. There is ample reason to question whether posterity did what it should have done in this matter.[33]

But then there is another question we should not pass over. If eternal punishment was the goal for which God created the majority, would it not have been better for them not to have been created at all? There is one passage in *The City of God* that might especially clarify Augustine's thinking about the doom of the many who will be lost.

> Mere existence is desirable in virtue of a kind of natural property. So much so that even those who are wretched are for this very reason unwilling to die. . . . If those wretches were offered immortality, on the condition that their misery would be undying, with the alternative that if they refused to live for ever in the same misery they would cease to have any existence at all, and would perish utterly, then they would certainly be overjoyed to choose perpetual misery in preference to complete annihilation.[34]

In Augustine's philosophy it is always better to exist than not to exist, even when this existence is unhappy.[35] This kind of philosophy is meaningless to us. We cannot believe that an endless existence of torture is preferable to nonexistence. If we view suffering in this way, even hell would be something more to be grateful for than to complain about. We will leave this matter for what it is. In fact Augustine does not mention hell at this point. We get the impression that he viewed hell as less horrendous than did later tradition.

Apart from Chrysostom, his contemporary, we know of no other church father from this early period who so emphatically taught the eternal nature of punishment in hell. But after him this was, at least in the western church, the only valid doctrine.

33. According to Hans Urs von Balthasar, the generations after Augustine in almost docile obedience accepted "the darkness of his predestination doctrine." He sees it as the great merit of Karl Barth that (in *CD*, II/2, chap. 7) he broke with this doctrinal tradition "Christlicher Universalismus," in the Festschrift *Antwort, Karl Barth zum 70. Geburtstag* [Zollikon-Zürich, 1956], p. 240). This chapter of the *Church Dogmatics* fully convinced me of the unbiblical character of the doctrine of predestination as taught by the church.

34. *The City of God,* 11.27.

35. For the significance of Neoplatonism for Augustine, see John Hick, *Evil and the God of Love* (2nd ed.; London, 1977).

4. A Tradition of Acquiescence and Anxiety

Unquestioning Acceptance

In his era Augustine was the great defender of the faith of the church. He was convinced that "tender-hearted" believers should not oppose what the church taught about eternal punishment. It is terrifying, he writes, to think of a future of eternal pain for the majority of people — and especially that this is what God wants! Thus he searched for arguments that would help them to accept the lost state of the many. If God is good — and that is undoubtedly the ground for all faith in God — then endless punishment must be something good! Augustine tried to demonstrate how it makes sense that God divided humankind into two groups; how he intended that one group would be eternally saved, while a larger group would be eternally lost.

Though we want to deal mostly with the Protestant tradition, we must not forget that its terrifying image of God does not differ essentially from what we find in the Roman Catholic tradition. A few examples will suffice.

In Dante's (1265-1321) *Divina Commedia*, we find the famous words that the poet saw above the entrance to hell: "Abandon every hope, you who enter here." He does not speak of election or reprobation. But the absence of grace for those who are lost is no less prominent. At a given moment Dante is unable to hold his tears. Then the guide tells him that he would be foolish to have compassion, for here piety can exist only when there is no more compassion, and vice versa: No one can have faith if he allows himself to be compassionate.[36] Again, passive acceptance! A true believer does not trust his human feelings, for in so doing he would rebel against God's decision.

We meet the same viewpoint in Thomas Aquinas (1225-74). He, too, teaches that we must simply accept the endless doom of the many. The saved will see how the lost are punished, but they will not pity them. Thomas has to explain this. Pity is possible, he argues, only if one desires that the fate of the unfortunate ones be changed. But in the case of the doomed this change would be undesirable, for that would be contrary to divine justice. The saved will in fact rejoice at the pains of those who are condemned. Their own bliss will be all the more enjoyable in the contrast with the misfortune of the lost.[37]

36. Dante Alighieri, *Divina Commedia*, I, "Hell," song #3, line 9 and song 20, lines 25-30.

37. Thomas Aquinas, *Summa Theologica*, Suppl., Q. 94.

26

This is what the great teacher of the Roman Catholic tradition taught. It corresponds with what Augustine said! There is the same duality in God: God is compassionate but he is also just. His justice is part of his goodness. Thus, the joy of the saved will not be marred by the misery of the lost. This joy is not the result of ignorance of their pains. No, they see their suffering and rejoice in it. That is unquestioning acceptance. Thus we find in this tradition the same passive acquiescence in the eternal doom of the many!

The Wish That God Were Different

There cannot remain any doubt: The entire western church has taught God's intransigence toward the lost. The Christian tradition has become one of acquiescence. But it is also a tradition in which opposition to the kind of God it proclaims never lets up. For all Augustine's attempts to reconcile believers with this doctrine have failed! And — significantly enough — it proved subsequently impossible to find other, better arguments! The theologian who succeeds in convincing believers that the doctrine of eternal punishment does not lead to a terrifying image of God has yet to arise. Wherever the concept of eternal punishment is propagated, it inevitably leads to the "picture of God" that Augustine designed! After sixteen centuries no other conclusion is possible.

We have grown up with Augustine's arguments. Our youth were taught them in catechism. The Bible may say: "God desires everyone to be saved" (1 Tim. 2:4), but that does not mean that God wants to save all people. The text rather applies to all classes of people. It does say that God is love, but it is a different kind of love, for his love is *holy* love, a love focused on himself. Similarly, God is gracious, but his grace is sovereign. That word had an ominous sound to it, just as the word "free" did: sovereign grace was free grace. That meant: God reserved for himself the liberty to give his grace to those he selected, and this was apparent in that he did not give it to all. Furthermore, "the beauty of the contrast": Only against the darkness of eternal damnation do we discern the full radiance of God's grace for the saved!

We listened to this teaching and accepted it. It was horrifying, but nothing could be done about it. Who were we to argue with God! He was the Omnipotent. Those who disagreed with him would incur his wrath! You had no option but to accept it passively. But it kept churning in your thoughts. You could not voice it because to do so was sinful. Nonetheless, it was always there: How marvelous would it be if God were different!

For how many has this doctrine — that God wants the doom of the many, and that those who believe must simply accept this fact — been the main reason why they could stand it no longer in the church and why they lost their faith? We saw this from the letter from which we quoted at the beginning of this chapter. We also want to mention an example from the Roman Catholic tradition. Tormented by the doctrine of hell — the lost state of the many — the French author Charles Péguy (1873-1914) for a long time turned his back on the Christian religion. "A religion which has decided to acquiesce in the eternal lostness of brothers is fundamentally egoistic with regard to salvation, and this is basically 'bourgeois' and 'capitalistic'." He returned to the church in 1908, having realized that his refusal to accept the fate of the many was not in conflict with the faith of the early church. "Together . . . we must come to our loving God. Together we must face Him. What would He think of us, if we were to arrive home without the others!"[38] Here we meet someone who found his way back to God through his conviction that God wants the salvation of all people — and that he desires that we want that together with him!

Blasphemy?

In the 1960s a formal objection was lodged with the Synod of the Reformed Churches in the Netherlands against some statements in the Canons of Dort. It concerned the passages quoted above. But the emphasis was upon yet another passage that, it was argued, raised the question of possible blasphemy. That passage reads:

> What peculiarly tends to illustrate and recommend to us the eternal and unmerited grace of election is the express testimony of sacred Scripture, that not all, but some only, are elected, while others are passed by in the eternal decree; whom God, out of his sovereign, most just, irreprehensible and unchangeable good pleasure, hath decreed to leave in the common misery . . . and not to bestow upon them saving faith and the grace of conversion; but . . . for the declaration of his justice, to condemn and punish them forever. (I, 15)

38. Péguy, "La damnation est mon seul problème"; quoted in Hans Urs von Balthasar, *Herrlichkeit*, vol. 2, "Fächer der Stille" (Einsiedeln, 1962), p. 775, in his essay about Péguy (pp. 769-880). For Péguy, see also Gisbert Greshake (another Roman Catholic theologian), *Stärker als der Tod* (7th ed.; Mainz, 1976), pp, 5, 85-90. The last quotation (following Greshake) is from his work "Mystère de la Charité de Jeanne d'Arc." Both theologians support Péguy.

Immediately we recognize what Augustine said about the beauty of the *contrast:* the divine light against the dark background of the state of doom. But what do we in fact say about him when we teach that from eternity he decided to send most people to eternal damnation, in order that his grace toward others might appear more laudable. "We should never," says the author of this objection, "in what we say about God, however unintentional it may be, evoke the image of a ruthless, indifferent or arbitrary Omnipotent. And the question which kept haunting me, was whether the authors of the Canons of Dort, in spite of all their efforts to avoid this, had been guilty of blasphemy." In 1970 the synod of the Reformed churches recognized the validity of this objection against the eternal decision of God to predestine the majority of humanity to endless punishment as confessed in the Canons. But in its official pronouncement it did not address the main objection: that what the Canons said was blasphemy.[39]

A few years later — in 1983 — a conflict arose precisely over this point in the *Reformed Journal,* a periodical of Reformed comment and opinion. Thomas Talbott — a professor of philosophy — attacked the confession of his church. He called the Calvinistic doctrine of election *a form of theological blasphemy.* He argued that it ascribed satanic attributes to God: The heavenly Father, whose essence is perfect love, was being confused with the devil himself! The root of Talbott's disagreement was not in the doctrine of election as such, nor in that of the future judgment. He protested against a doctrine of election that claims that God refuses to save people he could save, that he punishes eternally without any intention to save. Those who truly believe that God is such a God, he wrote, cannot love him with all their heart and cannot love their neighbors as themselves. How can the very same God, who commands us to love our neighbors as ourselves, ask us to concur with their endless tortures? How can I love him with all my heart and at the same time keep silent when he predestines my little daughter to eternal damnation? Someone who passively accepts this view does not love

---

39. *Acta of the General Synod of the Reformed (Gereformeerde) Churches in the Netherlands,* 1969, 1970, Art. 376; *Rapporten,* pp. 455-68. The writer of the notice of objection, Dr. B. J. Brouwer, is a historian. His objection is not included with the documents, but he allowed me to read it. The reason why this accusation of blasphemy was not supported by the synod, we read in the report, is that blaspemy was not the *intention* of the original authors. The synod of the Dutch Reformed (Hervormde) Church took a similar action in 1960, in reaction to an objection from A. Duetz, a Dutch Reformed minister. See *De Uitverkiezing, richtlijnen aanvaard door de Generale Synode der Nederlandse Hervormde Kerk* (The Hague, 1962).

his child! God demands that we should love even our enemies, but would God himself not do so? Is that what the Bible teaches? Notice the example of the apostle Paul: He wished that he were himself accursed and cut off from Christ for the sake of his brothers who had rejected Christ (Rom. 9:1-3)![40]

As was to be expected, a number of theologians took it upon themselves to defend the confession of their church against this frontal attack. One of them was Dr. John Piper. He argued that it was impossible to speak about God's love in such simplistic terms. There is undoubtedly a love of God for all people, even for his enemies. Jesus referred to this love in the Sermon on the Mount: "He makes his sun shine on the evil and on the good, and sends rain on the righteous and on the unrighteous" (Matt. 5:45). But this love for his enemies does not preclude his decision to send them to eternal doom. For it is not the love of his election. That is reserved for the elect. Thus there are two sorts of divine love. All the arguments we discussed earlier were brought to bear, including the contention that "the sovereign grace of God" shines all the more brightly in contrast to the eternal darkness that is the destiny of the lost.

The writer concluded his argument with an answer to the question how one could possibly love God if he had predestined his children to eternal doom. He wrote: "I have three sons. Each evening, after they have fallen asleep . . . I open the door of their bedroom and go from bed to bed. I lay my hands on them and pray for them. . . . But I realize that possibly God has not chosen my sons to be his sons. And, although I think I would be willing to give my life for their salvation, I would not rebel against the Almighty if they would be lost. He is God. I am a mere human being. The potter has absolute authority over the clay. It is my duty to bow before his undeniably pure character, and to believe that the Judge of all the earth has the right on his side, and will always do what is just."[41]

Submit — for he is God! Accept, acknowledge, and agree that he is good even if he wants our children to be punished throughout eternity.

40. Thomas Talbott, "On Predestination, Reprobation and the Love of God," *Reformed Journal*, February 1983: "The Reformed doctrine of predestination . . . is a form of blasphemy in this sense: those who accept the doctrine inevitably attribute Satanic qualities to God: they inevitably confuse the Father in heaven, whose essence is perfect love, with the Devil himself."

41. John Piper, "How Does a Sovereign God Love?" *Reformed Journal*, April 1983. The discussion was continued in the June, July, and September issues.

That is what the tradition wants to teach us. It is forced to teach us that, as long as it accepts eternal punishment as a biblical doctrine. Augustine was the first to grasp this and to express it in words. After him no one could deny it: If there is eternal punishment, it is because that is how God wants it to be. And if God wants it, we can only submit.

Here, after Augustine, we again see the strange arguments that are used to defend the teaching of eternal punishment, as well as the horrifying images of the future that result. But where does the Bible speak in such terms about God and about the future he has in store for humankind? If this is how this doctrine is to be defended, is it defensible? One thing stands out clearly: *This is not what the Bible teaches!*

A Letter from 1630, Dirk Rafaëlsz. Camphuysen

The tension between tradition and Bible is — in a quite different way — the subject of a short treatise that was published in 1630 and entitled "Extract uyt D.C.R. Brief."[42] It is part of a letter from the poet Dirk Rafaëlsz. Camphuysen (1586-1627) and was published three years after his death. Camphuysen was well known for his "Stichtelijke Rijmen" (Pious Rhymes), which were reprinted time and again. He was a minister, but he had to leave the ministry after he refused to abide by the teachings of the Canons of Dort.

The letter is pastoral in intent. It deals with the terror the believer experiences as a result of the doctrine of hell. Camphuysen relates how he felt tormented by this doctrine to such an extent that he was almost ready to abandon the Christian faith. But through a pamphlet by the Italian reformer Socinus — regarded as a heretic because of his opposition to the

42. Camphuysen's letter was published as "Extract uyt D.R.C. Brief. Dat het gevoelen van de Vernietiging ende Eyndelijcke Straffe der Onrechtvaerdigen &c. niet soo schadelijck nochte gevaerlijck is; Ende dienvolgens wel mach ontdeckt ende ter stichtinge voorgehouden ende verbreydt worden." I consulted the 1631 edition, published as a supplement (pp. 211-28) in Thien Predicatiën by V. Smaltius and printed in Crakow, Poland, in 1631. I also referred to the 1666 edition, which was included as a tract (pp. 33-46) in *Van den Standt der Dooden,* by Ernestus Sonnerus (Ernst Soner of Sohner, 1572-1612) (Vrijstadt [Amsterdam], 1666); it is found in the library of the University of Amsterdam: no. 1513 F52. For details about Camphuysen, see L. A. Rademaker, *Didericus Camphuysen* (Gouda, 1898). Rademaker fails to mention this letter. The letter is mentioned and cited, however, in D. P. Walker, *The Decline of Hell: Seventeenth-Century Discussions of Eternal Torment* (Chicago, 1964), pp. 84-92.

doctrine of the Trinity — he had come to see light in "the thick and total darkness of the fable of hell and endless doom." He writes about his liberating experience in the following words:

> As far as I am concerned, I thank and praise therefore from my innermost soul God the Father of our Lord Jesus Christ. For the enlightenment in this treatise . . . has helped me, while I was about to reject the entire Christian religion, to love this religion, to hold it in esteem, to consider it as reasonable and to experience it through God's grace with my total being.[43]

Camphuysen knows: Many Christians somehow find it possible to escape the anxiety caused by hell. They do not follow Christ in all seriousness, for they think: "God is merciful. Thus, thinking that things are not so serious, they push the eternal pain of hell away from them, believing that it concerns others rather than themselves." But not everyone manages to take the commandments and the gospel so lightly. The argument "God is merciful," used by others to trivialize God's commandments, does not put their minds at ease. They need more ("overflowing godliness"); they see how far they fall short in this respect — and fear hell! This doctrine ("this opinion") of endless torture leads them to despair, melancholy, and even suicide.

> This opinion creates despair, or at least serious melancholy, in those who have pious hearts but little understanding. They cannot accept these wrong fundamentals, which lead to either godlessness or lukewarmness, realizing that they are expected to manifest overflowing godliness.
>
> As a result, they fear that this endless trouble will fall upon them, and this creates so much anxiety and pain in their souls, that these people despair of their lives and choose death by their own hands. Examples of this are far from few, and some I know personally. Others do not go so far, but are in great desperation and fear that they might end similarly. Consequently, they experience extreme vexations and melancholy (at times to the point that they lose their minds), which they call assaults of Satan and which, in particular in the Reformed Churches, are the subject of daily prayers.

Then he focuses on something that should not escape us: *Is it not remarkable that the Bible nowhere mentions these fears?*

---

43. *Extract uyt D.R.C. Brief,* 1666, p. 37.

For (remarkably enough) we find none of these anxieties and so-called temptations in the New Testament, nor any remedies for them. But all consolations are intended to alleviate the sadness and tortments which . . . could result from serious problems and difficulties, or even from persisting worries concerning offenses or past sins.

Scripture does not provide any help ("remedy") against this anxiety, for nowhere does it teach the eternal torments of hell. He therefore protests against the idea that one could in fact think about hell in a way that differs from tradition, *but that it is better to remain silent,* since to speak about it would lessen the power of the warning of judgment. To remain silent means that the traditional view will continue as the teaching of the Bible. The consequences are cited: extreme vexations, psychological problems, and suicide. One must exercise caution,

> but this caution must not be taken so far that . . . one hides the truth. For, if that were correct, then we should hide the whole gospel teaching, yes, even the complete Bible. All that is written in the Holy Scriptures should not be hidden from those who are allowed to read them. And all people are free to read the entire Holy Scriptures. . . .[44]

Believers must thus be told that Scripture does not teach eternal punishment. However, this does not mean that the coming judgment is not a serious matter. Camphuysen believed that the punishment mentioned in the Bible entails the annihilation of the godless.[45] On this point we do not follow him. But his arguments against the prevailing doctrine of hell and against the silence of those who have other opinions have lost nothing of their relevance.[46]

44. *Extract uyt D.R.C. Brief,* pp. 41-42.
45. On the annihilation of "heathen, Turks, unbelievers, and the ungodly" (Heydenen, Turcken, ongelovige, godtloose menschen), see Rademaker, *Camphuysen,* pp. 219-20. This is also defended in the "Brief." Camphuysen objected only against the fear of hell; he does not refer to the salvation of the many.
46. Walker's study (*The Decline of Hell*), which led me to Camphuysen, is invaluable for any attempt to understand the lively debates about the doctrine of hell in post-Reformation times. The idea that hell is not endless was regarded as dangerous: sermons on hell were required to keep crime under control. See also F. Groth, *"Die Wiederbringung aller Dinge" im Württembergischen Pietismus, theologiegeschichtliche Studien zum eschatologischen Heilsuniversalismus Württembergischer Pietisten des 18. Jahrhunderts* (Göttingen, 1984); and G. Rowell, *Hell and the Victorians: A Study of the Nineteenth-*

Our study of the Bible will focus on the divergence between tradition and Scripture.[47] But before we begin our investigation, we must take a look at the history of the church of the first centuries, the time before Augustine.

5. Was Eternal Punishment Taught from the Beginning?

A Pagan Intrusion? An Early Church Father

We saw that Augustine had no doubt whatsoever that the majority of humanity would be lost. But this was not the only view in his time. We also took up his admonition to the "tender-hearted" believers. Their view was in fact held by the majority of the church members. Were these "tender-hearted" believers a new phenomenon that appeared in his time, or can we point to Christians even earlier in the history of the church who refused to believe in eternal punishment? Yes, we can. We find this view clearly expressed by the first great church father, Origen (185-254). We read in Augustine's writings that Origen was condemned for his belief that God would extend his mercy even to the devil. But we discover also that he was condemned for another reason:

Century Theological Controversies concerning Eternal Punishment and the Future Life (Oxford, 1974). For a more recent contribution, see J. Sanders, No Other Name: An Investigation into the Destiny of the Unevangelized (Grand Rapids, 1992). This book is required reading for all who are looking for a survey of current discussions about the fate of unbelievers. It also deals with various positions that have been advocated in the history of the church. The book is well documented and includes publications and translations in English; the Württemberg fathers, however, are not mentioned. Finally, see N. M. de S. Cameron, ed., Universalism and the Doctrine of Hell — papers presented at the Fourth Edinburgh Conference in Christian Dogmatics, 1991. (Carlisle/Grand Rapids, 1992).

47. In the last-mentioned collection of essays (above, n. 11), D. J. Powys (in "The Nineteenth- and Twentieth-Century Debates about Hell and Universalism") points to the impasse in the discussion about this issue. For over a century the same points of view have been reiterated. A breakthrough, he writes, requires: "1. the elimination of all unjustified presuppositions; 2. a new openness to the biblical data; 3. a willingness to embrace and apply biblical convictions and presuppositions to the question; 4. if necessary, a willingness to move independently of traditional orthodoxy. . . . Future constructive contributions to the debate will be made by those deeply committed to fresh, radical, and unbridled examination of the biblical data" (p. 135).

. . . in particular [for] his theory of incessant alternations of misery and bliss, the endless going back and forth between those states at predetermined epochs. For in fact he lost even the appearance of compassion in that he assigned to the saints genuine misery, by which they paid their penalties, and a false bliss, in which they could not experience the joy of everlasting good in genuine security — I mean that they could not be certain of it without any apprehension.[48]

Thus, this condemnation concerns, in particular, the eternal cycle, which he supposedly propagated. This is the principal objection, which even today is mentioned against the belief that God wants to save all people: it supposedly is a pagan intrusion, which entered the church through Origen. We read, for instance, in Bavinck's *Reformed Dogmatics*: "The doctrine of the eternal return of all things in the godhead is already found in Indian and Greek philosophy; from there it found its way into Gnosticism and Neoplatonism and was first introduced into Christian theology by Origen. All spirits return to God in the same state wherein they originally existed with Him. Since the free will remains unchanged, it can just as well change from the good to the bad, as from the bad to the good. Thus, there is an eternal interchange between apostasy and the return of all things, and endless creation and destruction of the material world."[49]

The church was right in rejecting this idea of an eternal cycle from salvation to doom and vice versa. This, indeed, is a pagan way of thinking. But that does not necessarily imply that the idea that a return to God of all that is lost is imported from paganism. As if there could not be a return of all to God without an eternal falling away! That is precisely what Origen intended to say. Unfortunately, he did cause considerable confusion.

Origen was the first great theologian and exegete of Christendom. He brilliantly defended the Christian faith in an era when the church was attacked from all sides by pagan philosophers and was confused by the adherents of many complicated currents of religious thought. The concept of successive cycles of worlds or eras was very popular in his time. Origen was able to fit this theory into what he read in the Bible, except that the cycles would *not* go on forever. He believed in a number of successive eras through which God reached the goal for his creation.

He relates how he came to that insight. He read in Hebrews 9:26 that

48. *The City of God*, 21.17.
49. Bavinck, *Dogmatiek*, 4:668.

Christ once, at the end of the ages, had come to atone for sin through his sacrifice. The word for "ages" (plural of *aiōn*) here refers to eras that have preceded our time. There will be other eras or ages in the future. Ephesians 2:7 confirms this conclusion when it tells us that "in the ages to come" God will show us the "immeasurable riches of his grace." "Whence I infer," Origen writes, "that by this passage many ages are indicated." But he immediately adds that there must be more than just these "many ages," something that might happen at "the time of universal restoration" (Acts 3:21), when everything reaches its ultimate fulfillment. Then he refers to 1 Corinthians 15:28, where Paul writes that eventually God will be all in all.[50]

But what could be the reason for these successive ages? That is where the confusion begins. Origen suggested the possibility that a rational being (human or angel), once it had been saved, might not have fully learned to live by God's grace alone, and might become proud and fall again! In a subsequent era he would then have the opportunity to learn his lesson more fully.[51] But this is nowhere to be found in the Bible, and, fortunately, the church rejected this view. But it would be incorrect to say that for Origen the end was completely identical to the beginning, and that he taught an *eternal* cycle of events. For him it was, indeed, a very long journey, but nonetheless a journey that would lead to the one goal God has for his creation: that God may be all in all. The moment will come when that goal is realized *forever!*

In his large commentary he discusses this long duration at the end of chapter 11. There it says: "From him and through him and to him are all things. To him be the glory forever!" The Greek has the words *eis tous aiōnas,* that is, until the ages — in the plural (Rom. 11:36). The fullness of all things cannot be accomplished in just one era, he writes, but extends over many ages. We would hardly dare to hope that it will ever come about. But notice Paul's "Amen," on which he further comments, "which makes us understand that this bliss is guaranteed to come through Him whom the Apocalypse describes as the 'Amen' (Rev. 3:14)."[52] However long

---

50. *De Principiis,* 2.3.5, in Fred Crombie, trans., *The Writings of Origen* (Edinburgh, 1899), 1:85-86.

51. *De Principiis,* 2.3.3.

52. *Ad Romanos* (Migne, *Patrologia Graeca,* 14:1202): ". . . et tunc 'ipsi gloria in saecula saeculorum: Amen.' 'In saecula,' propter hoc quod perfectio omnium non intra unum saeculum concluditur, sed in multa protenditur, et vix aliquando adimplenda speratur. Jungit autem et 'Amen,' ut intelligamus per illum ad istam beatitudinem veniendum, de quo scriptum est in Apocalypsi: 'Haec dicit qui est Amen.' " Migne follows the Latin text of Rufinus; the original Greek text of this commentary is not extant.

it may take, that God's intention for all things will be realized is guaranteed through Jesus Christ.

More importantly, in the same commentary Origen emphatically rejected the idea that there could ever be another fall into sin, since human beings would keep their free will and be able to sin. Origen acknowledges that rational nature (that of humans and angels) retains its free will. But then we hear something absolutely marvelous:

> But we maintain that the power of Christ's cross and of his death . . . is so great, that it will be sufficient for the healing and restoration not only of the present and future ages, but even for those of the past, and not only for this human order of which we are part, but even for the order of heavenly beings (Col. 1:20).

When the point has been reached that God is all in all, then the love of Christ has been completely fulfilled, and every human being will be kept from falling by that love which exceeds everything. For if all those things mentioned by Paul in Romans 8:38 and 39 cannot separate us from the love of God, we can be even more sure that the free will (filled with love) will not be able to separate us from his love.[53]

That is quite different from a salvation that will always be followed by a new calamity! Origen says all this in his comments on Romans 6:9. Some had argued that in the future Jesus would have to die time and again for a humanity that would continue to fall into sin. But this he denies. For Paul writes that the Christ who has risen from the dead will never die again.

We do not follow Origen in his speculation about succeeding ages and successive falls into sin. But that should not blind us to the great final destiny, which Origen saw shining for all of humanity and all of creation: God — the God of love — would be all in all. How can this view be called a *pagan intrusion?*

---

53. Migne, *PG,* 14:1052-54. "Manere quidem naturae rationabili semper liberum arbitrium non negamus; sed tantam esse vim crucis Christi, et mortis hujus, quam in saeculorum fine suscepit, asserimus, quae ad sanitatem et remedium non solum praesentis et futuri, sed etiam praeteritorum saeculorum et non solum humano huic nostro ordini, sed etiam coelestibus virtutibus ordinibusque suffuciat" (1053AB). "Et ideo merito charitas quae sola omnium major est, omnem creaturam continebit a lapsu. Tunc erit Deus omnia in omnibus" (1053C); ". . . quia si haec omnia quae enumeravit Apostolus separare nos non possunt a charitate Dei . . . multo magis libertas arbitrii nos ab ejus charitate separare non poterit" (1054A).

What Did the Church Teach in the First Centuries?

Two or three hundred years after his death, Origen was branded a heretic because he had taught that God's judgment would not last forever. But that does not tell us anything about what the church taught at the time of Origen! Was he, while he was alive, considered a heretic who constantly deviated from official church teaching?

Origen did have to face one particular accusation. He allegedly taught that the *devil* would ultimately be saved. We met this notion already with Augustine. This accusation embarrassed Origen, but he defended himself against it. He had wanted to say only that the devil *could* be saved if he repented.[54] We will leave this matter for what it is. For us it is important to underline that he did not face accusations with regard to what he clearly taught: that it was God's ultimate goal to save all people, and that all punishment after this life was to serve that purpose.[55]

Origen was highly respected in his time. This we hear from Eusebius (263-340), the author of the first church history, who has written extensively on Origen's life and work.[56] Moreover, the indisputably orthodox Athanasius (295-373) spoke with great appreciation of the "indefatigable" Origen.[57] There is not a trace of criticism in this church father regarding

---

54. Joseph Wilson Trigg, *Origen* (London, 1985), pp. 89, 138-39, 206-8. Henri Crouzel, *Origène* (Paris, 1985), pp. 41-44. The matter had come up in a debate with a Gnostic teacher. The conviction that the devil was a fallen archangel led Origen, and later Gregory of Nyssa, to speculations about his salvation as part of creation. We do not follow these church fathers in this matter. Scripture does refer to fallen angels, but does not clarify the origin of evil. We do not know what exactly constitutes the power of Evil — the Evil. We are only told that God combats it, that he will conquer it and eradicate it from his creation. And he calls us to be partners in this work. But "Evil" as such is God's problem, not ours. "The controversy with nothingness [Barth's term for Evil], its conquest, removal and abolition, are primarily and properly God's own affair. . . . It is first and foremost the problem of God Himself" (Karl Barth, *Church Dogmatics*, III/3, p. 354).

55. It has also been argued that the idea that punishment in the afterlife would have "therapeutic" value is of pagan origin. See G. Anrich, *Clemens und Origenes als Begründer der Lehre vom Fegfeuer,* Theologische Abhandlungen (Tübingen and Leipzig, 1992), pp. 95-129. Anrich, who also refers to other sources, states: "Plato is the founder of this theory," in particular in the *Gorgias.*

56. Eusebius, *Ecclesiastical History,* bk. 6.

57. Athanasius, "De Decretis" (of the synod of Nicea), 6, 27. See *Nicene and Post-Nicene Fathers,* 2nd series (repr. Grand Rapids, 1980) 4:168.

Origen's view of the return of all things to God, as if that were a dubious deviation. In fact, before Origen, Clement of Alexandria had propagated the same view without ever having been accused of disloyalty to the teachings of the church.[58]

The statement from Athanasius quoted above indicates that Origen said many things, while "searching and exercising." He suggested all kinds of options. Always very reticent: could it possibly be? — but those with other opinions were encouraged to voice them. His great disciple, the church father Gregory of Nyssa (332-394), did just that. Origen's theory of succeeding eras and a repeated falling into sin, for example, had caused considerable confusion. Certain statements of the master on this topic had left posterity with the impression that he believed in an eternal cycle of all things. Such a succession of ages for the world had more in common with the Platonic doctrine of the transmigration of the soul than with the teachings of the Bible! Gregory reached clarity on that point. A repeated falling into sin, as well as an eternal cycle of things and transmigrations of souls, was unbiblical.[59]

But here we are concerned with the return to God of all who are lost, and with the future punishment as a way of healing humankind of its sins. Gregory of Nyssa was quite unequivocal in teaching this. And — it is important that we should note this — nobody in his days even thought of denouncing this return of all things as a heresy ("a pagan intrusion")! It was not until about A.D. 600, that some in their amazement began to ask how the widely respected Gregory could have supported the doctrine of the final salvation of all.[60] At that time this belief was no longer preached from the pulpits. But also afterward he was never condemned! The Second

---

58. See Anrich, *Clemens und Origenes;* Gotthold Müller, "Origenes und die Apokatastasis," *Basler Theologische Zeitschrift* 14 (1958): 174-90.

59. S. de Boer, *De Anthropologie van Gregorius van Nyssa* (Assen, 1968), pp. 49-56; 76-84; 419-45; J. Daniélou, *Origène* (Paris, 1948), pp. 280-83. See also J. Daniélou, *L'Etre et le Temps chez Grégoire de Nysse* (Leiden, 1970), pp. 203-26 ("Apocatastase"). Gregory wrote passionately about the seriousness and the purpose of punishment and why he rejected an eternal cycle in "De anima et resurrectione" (About the soul and the resurrection). For a translation, see *Nicene and Post-Nicene Fathers,* 2nd series (Grand Rapids, 1979), 5:446-57.

60. J. Daniélou, "L'Apocatastase chez Grégoire de Nysse," *Recherches de Science Religieuse* (1940):328-47. Daniélou mentions that around ca. A.D. 500 it was commonly accepted that Origen taught a cyclic worldview, in contrast to Gregory of Nyssa, who had been correct about the return of all things (the "apokatastasis").

Council of Nicea honored him with the title "Father of the fathers." As a result, the Eastern Orthodox Church maintained that the teaching of the final salvation of all people — alongside the doctrine of eternal punishment — has rights that date back to the first centuries.[61]

In contrast to Gregory, Origen was condemned for his view that the punishment would come to an end. That happened in 543, at the insistence of the emperor, by a synod in Constantinople. The Council held ten years later in the same city decided to issue a series of condemnations: it denounced doctrines taught by some followers of Origen — the "Origenists" — but interestingly it failed to condemn the doctrine that divine punishment will come to an end.[62]

Meanwhile it is certain that in the fourth century the endlessness of the punishment was preached from the pulpits. But prior to that? How do we explain that no contemporary ever accused Clement of Alexandria, Origen, or Gregory of Nyssa for their teachings regarding the eventual salvation of all, and that their beliefs were considered heretical only from the fourth century onwards? Could it be that the salvation of all humanity had been taught even earlier? For instance, by Paul? The church fathers continually appeal to him. Was that perhaps justifiable?

In the Back of the Latin Bible: 2 Esdras

Before we begin our study of Scripture itself, we want to look at a peculiar treatise in which we find the doctrine of the "lost masses" and a futile protest against it: the apocryphical book 2 Esdras. It was written by a Jewish author around the year A.D. 100, and it deals with the destruction of Jerusalem. It is found as an addendum in the back of the Latin Bible, the Vulgate.[63]

For our purpose the *third vision* is the important one. It focuses on the fate of the many who will be lost: the many Israelites who have not lived according to the law, but also the many non-Israelites who were ignorant of the law. The writer, who has assumed the name Ezra, protests against that idea. He cannot

---

61. S. Boulgakoff, *L'Orthodoxie* (Paris, 1932), pp. 253-61; F. Heiler, *Die Ostkirchen* (Munich/Basle, 1971), p. 150.

62. *De Principiis* (ed. Görgemanns and Karpp [appendix], pp. 822-31).

63. R. H. Charles, *The Apocrypha and Pseudepigrapha of the Old Testament* (Oxford, 1913 [later reprints unchanged]), 2:542-624; J. H. Charlesworth, *The Old Testament Pseudepigrapha* (London, 1983), 1:517-59. The passages in this section are quoted from G. H. Box, ed., *The Ezra-Apocalypse* (London, 1912).

bear the thought that God has destined the mass of humanity for perdition. For that is the fate that has been presented to him as God's ultimate purpose:

> The Most High shall be revealed upon the throne of judgment: and then cometh the end, and compassion shall pass away, and pity be far off, and long-suffering withdrawn ... and recompense shall follow, and the reward be made manifest. Deeds of righteousness shall awake, and deeds of iniquity shall not sleep. And then shall the pit of torment appear, and over against it the place of refreshment. The furnace of Gehenna shall be made manifest, and over against it the Paradise of delight. (7:33-36; the translator's version of 2 Esdras is used throughout this section).

Here we find the clear conviction that the coming judgment is the end of God's mercy. The author wrestles with a view of the judgment that was current in his time. He believes that God is indeed like this, but has great difficulty with it:

> And I answered and said, If I have found favor in thy sight, show me, thy servant, this also: whether in the day of judgment the righteous shall also be able to intercede for the ungodly, or to entreat the Most High on their behalf: fathers for sons, sons for parents, brothers for brothers, kinsfolk for their nearest, friends for their dearest. (7:102, 103)

But he is told that this is impossible. Therefore Ezra asks:

> How is it that we now find that first Abraham prayed for the people of Sodom, and Moses for our fathers who sinned in the wilderness; and Joshua after him in the days of Achan; and Samuel in the days of Saul ... ? (7:106)

The answer is that this is feasible in the present world, since there is still grace, but in the future that will no longer be the case. "So shall no man then be able to have mercy on him who is condemned in the Judgment" (2 Esdras 7:106-15). The majority will be lost forever. God has no problem with this teaching:

> I will rejoice over the few that shall be saved ... and I will not grieve over the multitude of them that perish. . . . (7:60, 61) For indeed I will not concern myself about the creation of those who have sinned, or their death, judgment, or perdition. . . . (8:38)

Ezra reminds God that this declaration does not square with what Scripture says about him — namely, that he is merciful, gracious, patient,

41

bountiful, abundant in compassion, kind and forgiving (7:132-39). The response once again is that these attributes apply to the present and not to the future. The future world is not created for the many, but the few. "Many have been created, but only a few shall be saved" (8:3).

But why were things created if God destroys his own creation (8:14)? Would it not have been better if God had, when he was creating, stopped with the animals? For in bestowing reason upon human beings, he made it possible for them not to sin against God:

> And I answered and said, O Earth, what hast thou brought forth, if the mind is sprung from the dust as every other created thing! It had been better if the dust itself had even been unborn, that the mind might not have come into being from it. . . . Let the human race lament, but the beasts of the field be glad! Let all the earth-born mourn, but let the cattle and flocks rejoice! For it is far better with them than with us; for they have no judgment to look for, neither do they know of any torture or of any salvation promised to them after death. For what doth it profit us that we shall be preserved alive, but yet suffer great torment? (7:62-67)

Ezra himself receives the assurance that he will not be among those who are to be tormented, for he has a treasure of good works (7:76-77). But this thought is of almost no comfort to him:

> And I answered and said, This is my first and last word; better had it been that the earth had not produced Adam, or else, having once produced him to have restrained him from sinning. For how doth it profit us all that in the present we must live in grief and after death look for punishment? O thou Adam, what hast thou done! For though it was thou that sinned, the fall was not thine alone, but also ours who are thy descendants! For how doth it profit us that the eternal age is promised to us, whereas we have done the works that bring death? And that there is foretold to us an imperishable hope, whereas we so miserably are brought to futility? (7:116-20)

He is told that he should rather contemplate his own fate, and the glory he and his brothers will inherit (8:51). But he keeps insisting that the joy of the few does not make up for the misery of the many:

> And I answered and said, I have already said, and say now, and shall say it again: There are more who perish than shall be saved, even as the flood is greater than a drop. (9:14)

Repeatedly Ezra is told to remain silent. How could he, a mere mortal, ever comprehend the ways of the Most High (4:11)? But this does not deter him. He protests: "Wherefore have I been endowed with an understanding to discern? For I meant not to ask about the ways above but of those things we daily experience" (4:22-23). But the response, which sounds like the voice of God, refuses to give in. Ezra not only must accept it, but he is even told that it will be one of the joys of the saved to view the perplexity in which souls of the godless wander and to see the punishment that awaits them (7:93). Ezra finds it impossible to be happy about that. On the contrary, he can only conclude: *if this is the final result of God's creative activity, it would have been better if he had not created the world.*

2 Esdras and Our Tradition

Of what use is this apocryphal book to us? As has already been mentioned, we find it as an addendum in the Vulgate, the Bible of our western ecclesiastical tradition. It is a Jewish treatise, to which two Christian chapters have been added, one at the beginning and one at the end. Strangely enough, the Jews have discounted it, but it has been preserved in the tradition of the church. For it rings a bell! In this Jewish pamphlet the despair that is part of our tradition is expressed in a frankness to which we are unaccustomed. *Here we stand face to face with the doctrine of the merciless God who wants the majority of his creatures to end in perdition.*

So, this horrible image of God and this view of humanity as a mass of people forever lost were current in the church long before Augustine came up with his doctrine of election. What the church father says about God's intention for humanity is explained in this treatise without any reference to a doctrine of election! Precisely because the church of his time was preaching this doctrine — in spite of much protest from the hearers, as we saw — he developed this teaching, in which he tried to demonstrate that God is good even when he allows the many to be lost forever.

Does 2 Esdras have a message for us today? His big question is: If God has predestined the majority of his creatures for destruction, would it not have been better if he had not created them at all? This question, we believe, touches the heart of the matter. If it is true that our children might end up in the never-ending torments of hell, and if that is the certain fate of the majority of those who are born, would it not be better if no people were born? Does the joy of the few really outweigh the endless misery of the many? How can these few be happy in view of this eternal ocean of pain — and with a God who wants this to remain so?

Finally, what is the connection between this writing and the Bible? Well, at least these statements are not made in the Bible. And now for the real question: What does the Bible itself teach? Does it also contain this doctrine of the merciless God and the lost masses? Does it also teach that the believer must simply accept that the many will be lost? Or can it be that Ezra, in his refusal to acquiesce, rightly appealed to Scripture; and that this merciless image of God, which left him no peace, is foreign to Scripture? Our first task is to find out what the Bible really says.

CHAPTER II

Called Not to Acquiesce

1. Abraham Prays for Sodom

Why Does God Tell Abraham?

The Bible informs us about the lost state of humanity in whose midst we live. Right from the outset of Israel's history, we are presented with this fact. It starts with the visit of three men to Abraham, which, we are told, was a theophany (Gen. 18:1, 2). There Abraham is told that the time had come for God to fulfill his promise to him: within a year Sarah would have a son. Then follows the story of Sodom.

> Then the men set out from there, and they looked toward Sodom; and Abraham went with them to set them on their way. The LORD said, "Shall I hide from Abraham what I am about to do, seeing that Abraham is about to become a great and mighty nation, and all the nations of the earth shall be blessed in him? No, for I have chosen him, that he may charge his children and his household after him to keep the way of the LORD by doing righteousness and justice; so that the LORD may bring about for Abraham what he has promised him." Then the LORD said, "How great is the outcry against Sodom and Gomorrah and how very grave their sin! I must go down and see whether they have done altogether according to the outcry that has come to me; and if not, I will know." So the men turned from there, and went toward Sodom, while Abraham remained standing before the LORD. (18:16-22)

Earlier the Bible mentioned that things were not good in Sodom. When Lot decided to live there, we hear: "Now the people of Sodom were wicked, great sinners against the LORD" (Gen. 13:13). Sodom became a type of the future judgment of the world.

But see what happens: God wants Abraham to know what he is about to do. This action is closely related to Isaac's birth. God is going to make Abraham into a great nation. It will be unique among the nations. This people will, from father to son, keep the way of the Lord by practicing justice and righteousness — the opposite of what was being practiced in Sodom. Thus, through this people of Abraham that keeps his ways, God will fulfill what he has spoken about Abraham. Abraham will not only become a great nation, but *in him all nations of the earth will be blessed.* God had said so when he called Abraham (Gen. 12:2-3), and here he repeats his promise when Isaac's birth is announced. Sodom is one of these nations! God establishes a link between the people of Abraham and the impending judgment over Sodom. What does God want Abraham to do?

Abraham Remains Standing before the Lord

"But Abraham remained standing before the Lord." This text does not mean that Abraham was in no hurry to get home. No, it means that God cannot continue to spare Sodom! Abraham obstructs his way. He remains standing in front of the Lord!

> Then Abraham came near and said, "Will you indeed sweep away the righteous with the wicked? Suppose there are fifty righteous within the city; will you then sweep away the place and not forgive it for the fifty righteous who are in it? Far be it from you to do such a thing, to slay the righteous with the wicked! Far be that from you! Shall not the Judge of all the earth do what is just?" (18:23-25)

Abraham is thinking of Lot, who lives in Sodom with his family. But he does not think only of Lot. Abraham wants to see the entire godless city saved. He begins with the possibility of fifty righteous persons. For the sake of those fifty people, he expects God to forgive the whole city. We would argue: If justice is to be done, it stands to reason that God will save those fifty from the destruction that is about to fall upon the city. God's answer, therefore, was rather self-evident: only the righteous. But we hear something quite different: In asking for the salvation not only of the righteous but of the entire city, Abraham does exactly what God

46

intends![1] "And the Lord said, 'If I find at Sodom fifty righteous in the city, I will forgive the whole place for their sake.'" Without any second thoughts, God grants Abraham's request. He emphasizes it: The *entire* city will receive forgiveness for the sake of those fifty righteous people. But Abraham continues to worry: Maybe there are five less. Would the entire city be destroyed because of those five? Again God immediately agrees: He will not destroy the city if there are forty-five. Again Abraham challenges God. Forty. And again God follows Abraham. There is no doubt: God encourages Abraham. Abraham is on the road where God wants him to be! Thirty. Twenty. Finally, ten. And God said: "For the sake of ten, I will not destroy it." Why this bottom line? Lower than ten will not do. There must be a *people* that calls upon the name of the Lord. Ten represented the smallest unit of the people of Israel (Exod. 18:21). It is the smallest possible number: A people of ten![2] For we are concerned with the *people* — the people among whom parents, from generation to generation, teach their children to walk in the ways of God. There is no such people in Sodom now. Therefore, such a people must be found in the future. For without it, the world will face a terrible end — as in the case of Sodom. That is why Abraham will have a son, and that is why he must command his house and those after him to keep going in the way of the Lord. So God will fulfill what he promised Abraham: Through him all families of the earth will be blessed.

Can God not achieve this without such a people? Not what God *can* do is important, but what he *wants to do*. He does not want to operate without such a people. He wants to save the world through *human beings* — through a people that listens to his voice. His covenant with Abraham guarantees that there will always be such a people. It may be small at times,

1. I owe this insight to Drs. Frans H. Breukelman (1916-93). In my conversations with him it became increasingly clear that Abraham's intercession for Sodom is of fundamental significance for any response to the teaching of eternal punishment. This understanding eventually resulted in the present study. Breukelman's contribution to this book can be found in my study of Genesis 2–4, *De vrouw en haar zaad* (Kampen, 1980).

2. The Jewish concept of *minjan* is further proof that ten is the minimum number for a people. There must be minjan — a minimum of ten Jewish adult males — for any corporate act of worship. "When ten righteous souls could not be found, Abraham was silent. Because the generation of the Flood could not muster ten righteous souls, they were not saved. . . ." C. G. Montefiore and H. Loewe, *A Rabbinic Anthology* (Philadelphia, 1963), pp. 97, 107.

THE ONE PURPOSE OF GOD

but God will see to it that it will always remain. When Elijah thinks that he is the only one left, and that all Israel has chosen to follow other gods, he hears that God will leave no fewer than seven thousand in Israel who have not bowed down before Baal (1 Kings 19:10, 18). There will always be some in Israel who remain loyal to him. Thus will be fulfilled what God said about Abraham: Through this people God will save the world. For that is what God wants: to save the world. Even Sodom.

In God's Heart

But Sodom was not saved! Immediately following this conversation we read about the execution of the judgment. Unconverted, the city was swept away, pulled into the abyss of death. "By turning the cities of Sodom and Gomorrah to ashes, God condemned them to extinction, and made them an example of what is coming to the ungodly" (2 Pet. 2:6); they lie there as "an example by undergoing a punishment of eternal fire" (Jude v. 7). Sodom's destruction, Scripture says, is a type of the coming judgment.

But how does this conversation make sense, if this is the end of Sodom? God knows what he was about to do. He knows that he can not find ten righteous persons. Does he simply go through the motions with Abraham, knowing that Sodom will come to nothing? No, because Sodom will not come to nothing. The story does indeed concern the coming judgment of God. But this judgment is not discussed before it has been made clear what is in God's heart. *He wants Sodom to be saved, even when he executes judgment on the city.* That is how the story of Abraham begins: He is the God who wants to bless all nations. For that reason he called Abraham. For that reason, too, he involves Abraham in what he is about to do. He wants Abraham to know about it. Abraham would not have been the man God wanted if he had respectfully listened to God's plans and had passively accepted what would happen; if he had bowed his head in awe before the righteousness of the divine judgment. Precisely because he intercedes for Sodom, he demonstrates that he is the man through whom God will lead all nations to the salvation he has prepared for them. Therefore, the judgment will not be the end of Sodom!

The Salvation of Sister Sodom (Ezek. 16)

What value would God's promises to bless all nations of the earth have if they did not include Sodom? Not only before but also after the Flood, we

48

read that every inclination of the human heart was evil continually from youth (Gen. 6:5; 8:21). That is how the nations are, all of them, without exception! In Sodom we merely see the final end — the extreme end — of the path they all tread. They all are, just like Sodom, peoples on their way to perdition. God called Abraham away from such nations, and God wants to bless those nations through him.

The prophets teach us the purpose of that blessing. In Isaiah 2 we are told that all nations shall go up to Jerusalem, to the mountain of the Lord, where God dwells with his people Israel, that they might learn his ways (Isa. 2:1-4). It is the way of the Lord that God discussed with Abraham; there we find the people that has learned how to remain in that way — not only for their own sake but because God wants to teach all people his ways through them. In Isaiah 25 we hear that on this mountain God will prepare a banquet for all peoples. Here he will do away with death forever, and here he will wipe away the tears from all faces (Isa. 25:6-9). Death will have to give up its spoils. This is salvation from death; it is the resurrection of the dead! That is what will happen to those nations who served other gods and walked in their own ways. Now they are utterly ashamed about those ways. Isaiah 45:22-24 tells us that they come in shame (see VII, 1, 2), but they come, because they have heard about the God who is willing to save them and wants to teach them his ways.

Even if we were to hear nothing further in the Bible about Sodom, the promise to Abraham and these prophecies would be ample ground to assume that judgment and death could not be the end of God's dealings with Sodom. But Scripture does not give us only this promise for the nations in general. The salvation of Sodom is singled out! Our tradition remains silent about this issue — we will see in a moment how that came about — but we read about it in Ezek. 16. In the context of God's judgment over Jerusalem, two sisters of Jerusalem are mentioned: Samaria and Sodom. We hear that Jerusalem was even worse than her sisters, worse — we are emphatically told — than Sodom.

> Your elder sister is Samaria, who lived with her daughters to the north of you; and your younger sister, who lived to the south of you, is Sodom with her daughters. You not only followed in their ways and acted in their abominations; within a very little time you were more corrupt than they all in your ways. As I live, says the Lord GOD, your sister Sodom and her daughters have not done as you and your daughters have done. (Ezek. 16:46-48)

The sins of "sister Sodom" appear insignificant when compared to those of Jerusalem. Sodom was swept away because of what she did. Likewise, God shall return the sins of Jerusalem upon her head (v. 43). But then follows the crucial point:

> I will restore their fortunes, the fortunes of Sodom and her daughters and the fortunes of Samaria and her daughters, and I will restore your own fortunes along with theirs. . . . (v. 53)

> As for your sisters, Sodom and her daughters shall return to their former state, Samaria and her daughters shall return to their former state, and you and your daughters shall return to your former state. (v. 55)

We hear that all three sisters will return to their former state, Sodom, Samaria, and Jerusalem — notice the order! This former state, of course, does not mean that they will be as godless as before. The real intention is made clear in what follows:

> I will remember my covenant with you in the days of your youth, and I will establish with you an everlasting covenant. Then you will remember your ways, and be ashamed when I take your sisters, both your elder and your younger, and give them to you as daughters . . . when I forgive you for all that you have done, says the Lord GOD. (vv. 60-63)

We read in Ezekiel 36 what this promise means. God will give Israel a new heart. He will put his Spirit in them and make sure that they follow his decrees (36:26-27). When God gives Samaria and Sodom to Jerusalem as daughters, they will share in what God gives Jerusalem: He will also put his Spirit in them, in order that they may follow his decrees. We already learned that this declaration does not apply only to Samaria and Sodom: All the nations will stream to Jerusalem to learn to walk in the paths of the Lord (Isa. 2:1-4). This is the fulfillment of the promise to Abraham. Among all these nations are also the people of Sodom.

Translators Change the Text

Here we meet a serious discrepancy with our faith tradition. We referred to it earlier: Our tradition regards the judgment as the end of God's compassion; it is certain that the majority of people are destined for doom. They live and die without responding to God's voice. And whoever dies in such a state is lost, forever. Sodom provides an example of this.

How little the words of Ezekiel agree with our faith tradition becomes remarkably clear when we read verses 53 and 55 in the Authorized Version:

> When I shall bring again their captivity, the captivity of Sodom and her daughters, and the captivity of Samaria and her daughters, then will I bring again the captivity of thy captives in the midst of them. (16:53)

> When thy sisters, Sodom and her daughters, shall return to their former estate, and Samaria and her daughters shall return to their former estate, then thou and thy daughters shall return to your former estate. (v. 55)

Here we notice a difference: the twofold *when*. The Authorized Version says: "When I shall bring" and "When thy sisters shall return." But the New Revised Standard Version correctly translates: "I will restore" and "your sisters shall return." The word *when* is not part of the Hebrew text. One may ask: Should we not be careful not to read too much into this "When I shall bring again"? Could it not simply mean: When Sodom is saved, Jerusalem will also receive salvation? Unfortunately, it is not quite as simple as that. This becomes abundantly clear when we consult the Dutch "Statenvertaling" (comparable to the AV), which, like the English translators, uses the word *when*. In the margin of this seventeenth-century Dutch translation, the translators defend their usage of this word. They explain their choice as follows:

> That is to say: never! For Sodom and Gomorrah had been utterly destroyed, without any hope of ever being restored to their former state. This likewise applies to v. 55. However, with the exception of those whom God in his grace had elected to be a holy seed and a remnant of his church. . . .

Although in the original text the word *when* is absent, the translators have inserted it in order to arrive at the explanation that is found in the margin of this translation. What prompted them to do so? We find the answer to that question in the exegesis given by Calvin. He argues in his comments on this text that the prophet uses irony in an attempt to demonstrate how unthinkable it is that God will yet show compassion on the Jewish people.[3] Sodom's

---

3. "Ironice loquitur: et . . . ostendit fieri non posse, ut unquam populi iudaici misereatur Deus." Calvin, however, did not change his translation to suit this explanation: "Et convertam captivitatum earum. . . . Et sorores tuae Sodoma et filiae eius revertentur ad pristina sua . . ." (*Ioannis Calvini Opera*, Corpus Reformatorum [Brunswick, 1889], 40:386-88). Luther (1534) remained true to the text: "Ich wil aber ir gefengnis wenden/nemlich/das gefengnis dieser Sodom und ire töchter," and "Und deine

salvation is totally impossible, and it is just as impossible for Jerusalem to be saved!

This is no minor matter. The otherwise so conscientious translators of the Authorized Version (and of the Dutch Statenvertaling) here lead their readers in a direction that differs from what Scripture actually says. In fact, the Bible is adapted to the doctrine that the mass of humanity will be eternally lost. No wonder that what is mentioned here about Sodom's salvation could not take root in our tradition. Our forefathers never had any doubt that the Bible certainly did not intend to say that Sodom was yet to be saved. Therefore, to save their readers from confusion, they made this correction. This example shows, however, *that our tradition necessitated a change in the biblical text![4]* The Authorized Version did not want to say what Scripture does: The city that was wiped out, and that, after Lot and his family had been brought out, had no more righteous people — that same city will become a daughter of the restored Jerusalem.

Most exegetes agree that this is the correct interpretation: The text does, indeed, refer to this city that was wiped out. But, significantly enough, most of them ignore the fact that our tradition excludes the possibility of that salvation.[5] An exception is the interpretation given by B. Maarsingh. We are struck by his unreserved delight. Commenting on verse 53, he writes: "YHWH himself shall intervene; He shall grant a new future to Sodom, as well as to Samaria and Jerusalem. That is an abundant promise. For Sodom had been wiped out centuries earlier. Samaria had been destroyed and conquered in 721/720 B.C. And Jerusalem is about to fall. It almost seems like a resurrection

---

schwester diese Sodom und ire töchter sollen bekeret werden/wie sie vor gewesen sind. . . ." But the margin reads: "(Dieser Sodom) Sodom bedeut hie Juda/Allegorice." Thus: Sodom must here be a metaphor for Judah. Just like Calvin, Luther could not believe what the text said. But, yes: Judah will be saved! The question confronting them was: If we are sure that Sodom will not be saved, how is this text to be explained? (See Augustine in his dealings with 1 Tim. 2:4 in I, 2).

4. Where the AV and the Dutch Authorized Version (States-General Bible) supply words, these are normally put in italics. This is not done here, however, with the word *when.* Thus no one would suspect any alteration in the meaning of the text. The AV was published in 1611, the Dutch AV in 1637. It would be of interest to discover whether anything is known about the motives of the AV translators in supplying the word *when.*

5. A. Noordtzij, *De profeet Ezechiël* (Kampen, 1932) and G. C. Aalders, *Ezechiël.* (Kampen, 1955) do refer to the salvation of Sodom, but they ignore the fact that our tradition does not accept the salvation of those who died in their ungodliness. This is also true for W. Eichrodt, *Ezekiel* (Philadelphia, 1970), and W. Zimmerli, *Ezekiel 1 and 2* (Philadelphia, 1970 and 1983).

from the dead. Nothing is impossible for YHWH." And commenting on verse 55, Maarsingh writes: "The situation has changed dramatically. All three — Sodom, Samaria, and Jerusalem — with neighboring towns and villages, will regain their former status, fully conform to God's original plan. It will be just as in the beginning when the Garden of Eden existed, and just as in the end when the New Jerusalem will descend from on high."[6] We would only add: It does not just *seem* to be a resurrection of the dead; it truly *is* a resurrection of the dead. A century earlier, K. F. Keil, a commentator who is consulted even today, wrote that this prophecy points to the future resurrection of the dead, and teaches us that the judgments of the Old Testament must not be viewed as eternal punishments; they leave the possibility of future salvation.[7]

Those who grew up in our tradition find this declaration hard to believe: Sodom will be saved! Sodom — dead people: people who died in their rebellion against God. Their death was not the end of God's purpose to save them. We note, however, that the seriousness of the judgment is in no way softened. The judgment was executed: Sodom was destroyed and Jerusalem's evils are returned upon her head (Ezek. 16:43, 58). But God's judgment on them does not signal the end of his compassion — not for Jerusalem, nor for Sodom, and not for the world.[8]

---

6. B. Maarsingh, *Ezechiël II* (Nijkerk, 1988), pp. 28, 29. YHWH refers to the name of the LORD. See n. 11 below.

7. C. F. Keil and F. Delitzsch, *Biblical Commentary on the Book of Ezekiel* (Grand Rapids, 1975). Keil points to Jesus' words about Sodom (Matt. 10:15; 11:23-24). He believed that Sodom would be saved, since it had never heard the gospel, contrary to Capernaum. But the Bible does not indicate such a restriction. Ezekiel teaches us: When the judgment has taken place, Jerusalem will be saved. This is what Jesus himself said (Matt. 23:39).

8. Origen comments that God's judgments appear to be bitter, but in reality they serve as teaching and healing. "God is a healer, God is a father, He is a master, not a hard, but a gentle master" ("Omnia Dei, quae videntur amara esse, ad eruditionem et remedia proficiunt. Medicus est Deus, pater is Deus, dominus est, et non asper, sed lenis est dominus). He points to Sodom: " 'Sodom will be restored to its former state,' and do you still wonder whether God is good, when He punishes the people of Sodom? 'It will be more bearable for the land of Sodom and Gomorrah in the judgment,' says the Lord, in his compassion over the people of Sodom. God is, therefore, kind, God shows clemency . . ." (" 'Restituetur Sodoma in antiquum,' et adhoc dubitas, an bonus sit Dominus puniens Sodomitas? 'Tolerabilius erit terrae Sodomorum et Gomorraeorum in die iudicii' dicit Dominus miserans Sodomitas. Benignus ergo est Deus, clemens est Deus . . ." "Origenis Homiliae in Ezechielem I,2," in *Origenes Werke,* ed. W. A. Baehrens (Leipzig, 1925), 8:322-23.

A People Called to "Stand before God"

The story of Abraham's prayer for Sodom explains to us why at the beginning of its history, Israel has been placed among the nations. It is called to be a people that is to intervene on behalf of the other nations; not only on behalf of the righteous among them, but for all, even if they are as wicked as the people of Sodom. By responding to that call, Israel will be the tool in God's hand by which he saves nations from death and destruction and through which he convinces them to walk in his ways (Isa. 2:1-4).

One thing in particular should not escape us. For us this is the main point in the story of Abraham's prayer. Upon their arrival in Jerusalem, the nations of the earth meet a people there that walks in the ways of the Lord; a people from whom they can learn how to walk in his ways. But there is more. When they arrive, Israel will not be astonished. They were expected. When God gives Sodom to Jerusalem as her daughter, there will be no question whether Jerusalem is pleased with that gift. She will be a daughter Jerusalem has prayed for: A daughter as an answer to prayer! This is, in fact, the answer to Abraham's prayer. In Ezekiel 16 it is still a long way off. Jerusalem is as yet far from ready to pray for such daughters! But they will learn. When God puts his Spirit in their hearts (Ezek. 36:27), Israel will wholeheartedly respond to its calling on behalf of the nations. Following Abraham's example, it will "remain standing before God" to plead for the salvation of the nations from the powers of death and perdition.

This response also points to the calling of the church of Jesus Christ: The church has been called to intervene, to "stand in the breach," together with Israel, on behalf of a world that is lost; called not to acquiesce in the lostness of the many. This solidarity between Israel and the church is a subject we will look at again.

2. Moses Prays for Israel

"Now, Leave Me Alone!"

We now come to one of the most touching passages of Scripture. Moses is on Mount Sinai, with God. God had met him in the desert while he was tending the flocks of Jethro, his father-in-law. "I am the God of your father, the God of Abraham, the God of Isaac, and the God of Jacob," he had said. And then: "So come, I will send you to Pharaoh to bring my people, the

Israelites, out of Egypt." Moses was an old man, eighty years of age, who had fled from Egypt where his people were oppressed. He had objected: "Who am I that I should go to Pharaoh, and bring the Israelites out of Egypt." But God had said: "I will be with you" (Exod. 3:12).

Moses had gone. And God had shown that he was with him. He had delivered Israel from the land of Egypt, and now they had arrived in the Sinai desert, at the mountain. There the great encounter between Israel and God was to take place. It was the mountain where God gave the Ten Commandments. "I am the LORD your God, who brought you out of the land of Egypt, out of the house of slavery; you shall have no other gods before me" (Exod. 20:2-3), he began. God spoke to Moses on the mountaintop. A tabernacle, "a tent of meeting," was constructed (Exod. 27:21; 28:43, etc.). It was the place where God met his people. He wanted to dwell in the midst of his people:

And have them make me a sanctuary, so that I may dwell among them. (Exod. 25:8)

I will dwell among the Israelites, and I will be their God. And they shall know that I am the LORD their God, who brought them out of the land of Egypt that I might dwell among them. (Exod. 29:45-46)

Reading the Scriptures, we constantly find this emphasis. God wants to dwell with the people because he loves them. This dwelling begins with Israel, but it does not stop with Israel. God wants to dwell in the midst of all peoples — all humanity. On that note Scripture ends:

Behold, the dwelling of God is with men. He will dwell with them, and they shall be his people, and God himself will be with them; he will wipe every tear from their eyes, and death shall be no more; neither shall there be mourning nor crying nor pain any more, for the former things have passed away. (Rev. 21:3, 4, RSV)

The "tent of God" is the subject of God's conversation with Moses for seven entire chapters. Then, suddenly, it seems impossible that that tent will indeed be constructed. For as soon as God has finished speaking about dwelling in the midst of Israel, Moses is told something quite different:

The LORD said to Moses, "Go down at once! Your people, whom you brought out of the land of Egypt, have acted perversely; they have been quick to turn aside from the way that I commanded them; they have cast

THE ONE PURPOSE OF GOD

for themselves an image of a calf, and have worshiped it and sacrificed to it, and said, 'These are your gods, O Israel, who brought you up out of the land of Egypt!'" The LORD said to Moses, "I have seen this people, how stiff-necked they are. Now let me alone, so that my wrath may burn hot against them and I may consume them; and of you I will make a great nation." (Exod. 32:7-10)

"Let me alone!" Does God need Moses' consent to execute his judgment on Israel? It sounds like the story of Abraham and Sodom: God does not want to punish without Moses' involvement. But then there is something else. God makes Moses a splendid offer: He will not make Israel but Moses into a great nation.

Moses Refuses God's Offer

Moses listens to what God wants for Israel; he also listens to what God wants for him. Had he said "Yes," that is what would have happened! Israel would have been finished, and God would have made Moses into a great people! But Moses refuses God's offer. He refuses to be elected in this manner — at the expense of others! Just like Abraham, he "remains standing" before God.

> But Moses implored the LORD his God, and said, "O LORD, why does your wrath burn hot against your people, whom you brought out of the land of Egypt with great power and with a mighty hand? Why should the Egyptians say, 'It was with evil intent that he brought them out to kill them in the mountains, and to consume them from the face of the earth'? Turn your fierce wrath; change your mind and do not bring disaster on your people." (Exod. 32:11-12)

We should not overlook that here there is an additional element not found in Abraham's intercession for Sodom. In our earlier discussion we used the words "standing in the breach": Abraham "stood in the breach" for Sodom. Such words are truly applicable in the case of Moses. For here everything is at stake: Israel's entire future but also Moses' own destiny — his own share in God's salvation.

First, we notice how God speaks about Israel. He says to Moses: "Your people, whom you brought out of Egypt" — thus Moses' people, the people Moses had led out of Egypt. But Moses replies to God: "*Your* people, whom *you* brought out of the land of Egypt with great power and a mighty hand!"

Think about your reputation! What will the Egyptians say about You? This God of Israel, from whom they expected deliverance — what has he done? He has brought them out, not to bring them deliverance but to destroy them!

Then follows Moses' real argument.

> Remember Abraham, Isaac, and Israel, your servants, how you swore to them by your own self, saying to them, I will multiply your descendants like the stars of heaven, and all this land that I have promised I will give to your descendants, and they shall inherit it forever. And the LORD changed his mind about the disaster that he planned to bring on his people. (Exod. 32:13, 14)

Moses appeals to the oath that God had sworn to Abraham, Isaac, and Jacob.[9] Once again we realize: Moses does exactly what God wants him to do. God wants Moses to appeal to that promise! Notice also that Moses does not ask God to spare the righteous in Israel. He asks that all the people — the "stiff-necked people" — be spared, because of his promise to Abraham, Isaac, and Jacob. If his promise to Abraham were contingent upon Israel's loyalty — human loyalty — he should not have begun with them! Nor should he begin with Moses' posterity! It would not be long, or it would be the same story with them. And again God would have to look for another people. This search would go on and on. Thus the future salvation of all nations, which he promised to Abraham, would never come. In spite of what God says, Moses clings to the promise. And that is what God looks for. Thus Moses proves that he is the man God is seeking.

"But If Not, Then Blot Me out of the Book That You Have Written"

Moses succeeds in convincing God not to destroy his people — notice to whom the word *his* refers (32:14). But more needs to happen. After his return and his hard measures to get the wayward people back on the right track, we hear:

9. It is the oath that God swore to Abraham after the sacrifice of Isaac (Gen. 22:18). This oath gives the promise for the third time (after 12:2-3 and 18:18). But this is the first statement that "*by your offspring* shall all the nations of the earth gain blessing." This promise is repeated to Isaac and Jacob (Gen. 26:3; 28:14).

On the next day Moses said to the people, "You have sinned a great sin. But now I will go up to the LORD; perhaps I can make atonement for your sin." So Moses returned to the LORD and said, "Alas, this people has sinned a great sin; they have made for themselves gods of gold. But now, if you will only forgive their sin — but if not, blot me out of the book that you have written." (32:30-32)

We find here two words that have the same meaning: atonement and forgiveness. "If you will only forgive their sins." Moses does not make his request and then wait passively until God grants his plea. No, he gives God the choice. If God does not forgive Israel's sins, then he should blot him — Moses — out of his book. That is quite different from what God has suggested! Moses wants no future salvation for himself without that of his people, in spite of the fact that this people have committed all kinds of horrendous sins. That is what the Bible calls "standing in the breach before God." We find this expression in Psalm 106:23: "Therefore he said he would destroy them — had not Moses, his chosen one, stood in the breach before him, to turn away his wrath from destroying them." Moses is the shepherd, but he counts his life as no more valuable than that of his sheep. He insists that God forgive them, and if God does not do so, God will have to do without him!

"But if not, then blot me out of the book that you have written." Can a person say this to God? We know that Paul voiced the same sentiment. "For I could wish that I myself were accursed and cut off from Christ for the sake of my own people, my kindred according to the flesh" (Rom. 9:3). He is also concerned about the fulfillment of God's promises to rebellious Israel. We will deal with this matter more fully at some later point. But if we ask whether God allows such a thing, we must say: If Moses had not made this request, he would not have been the man God wanted — his chosen one! A person is not chosen because God is willing to accept that person but not the others. An individual is chosen because God intends to use that person to save those others. Moses was God's chosen one because he was willing to put his own salvation at risk on behalf of that of others.[10]

10. I here rely on the deeply moving exegesis of the Jewish scholar U. Cassuto, *A Commentary on the Book of Exodus,* trans. Israel Abrahams (2nd ed.; Jerusalem, 1974).

"As a Man Speaks with His Friend"

That Moses did exactly what God wanted is shown in what follows. Moses has not yet moved God to the point where he wants God to be. The only answer he receives for the time being is that God will not blot him out of his book, and that he will visit the sins of the people, "when the time comes for him to punish." There is not a word, however, about *forgiveness*. The next thing he hears is, Go toward the promised land, and God will send his angel before you. But "I will not go up among you, or I would consume you on the way, for you are a stiff-necked people" (Exod. 33:3). Twice (vv. 3 and 5) we hear the word "stiff-necked," which God already used when he threatened to destroy the people (32:9). The only way God can spare his people is by putting distance between them and him.

But Moses does not give up. He refuses to accept that *distance*. We hear that he pitched his tent outside the camp. In so doing the problem becomes visible: the distance between God and his people. Moses refers to the tent as "the tent of meeting." The same name is reserved for the tabernacle itself, as we saw; the tent for meeting with God, the place where God dwells in the midst of his people. That tent has not yet been constructed, and will not be constructed as long as this state of affairs between God and Israel prevails. This preliminary "tent of meeting" demonstrates how Moses continues to seek an encounter with God. If that cannot take place within the camp, then it will have to be outside.

Then we hear how much Moses means to God. Moses refuses to proceed without God, but God, likewise, does not want to proceed without Moses! "When Moses entered the tent, the pillar of cloud would descend and stand at the entrance, and the LORD would speak with Moses" (33:9). This Moses, who dared to say to God: "But if not, then blot me out of the book that you have written," had found the way to God's heart. "The LORD used to speak to Moses face to face, as one speaks to a friend" (33:11). God has found among humans a friend with whom he can talk, a friend who understands what is in his heart! There is not a hint that Moses had gone too far. No, *precisely because he has gone further than any other, he is as no other the friend of God*. "Never since has there arisen a prophet in Israel like Moses, whom the LORD knew face to face" (Deut. 34:10; cf. Num. 12:6-8). The words that follow make clear what this conversation between God and his friend Moses was about: God dwelling in the midst of his people. What God had told him about this on the mountain has to happen! Meanwhile we notice that so far Moses has not received an answer to his real question, for which he put his own salvation at risk. "Please, forgive their sin." Moses will not relent until he has had his answer.

> Moses said to the LORD, "See, you have said to me, 'Bring up this people'; but you have not let me know whom you will send with me. Yet you have said, 'I know you by name, and you have also found favor in my sight.' Now if I have found favor in your sight, show me your ways, so that I may know you and find favor in your sight. Consider too that this nation is your people." He said, "My presence will go with you, and I will give you rest." And he said to him, "If your presence will not go, do not carry us up from here. For how shall it be known that I have found favor in your sight, I and your people, unless you go with us? In this way, we shall be distinct, I and your people, from every people on the face of the earth." The LORD said to Moses, "I will do the very thing that you have asked; for you have found favor in my sight, and I know you by name." (Exod. 33:12-17)

We see how Moses continues to stand in the breach for Israel. He has not reached his goal until he is assured of God's presence — "his face" — in Israel. There must be a place where he can be met, in the midst of the people, and not far away, outside the camp. That is forgiveness — "finding mercy" with God. And God hears this prayer! He will do it: He will accompany Israel!

"I Hereby Make a Covenant"

But Moses still worries. What is going to happen to the relationship between God and this people? Israel had been on the brink of destruction. If in the future things would, even to a limited extent, depend on the loyalty of this people, it was bound to be a failure. It is a "stiff-necked people" — as God had said three times. How would this promise to Abraham ever be fulfilled: "And by your offspring shall all nations of the earth gain blessing for themselves" (Gen. 22:18)? How is he going to bring to fruition this promise to this stiff-necked people? What is God like? — that is what everything depends on. Therefore Moses wants to meet with God, so as to leave no doubt whatsoever regarding God's feeling towards Israel: "So that I may know you" (Exod. 33:13). That is why he wants to *see* God: "Show me your glory, I pray" (v. 18).

It is impossible to see God's face, but God will show him his glory and will proclaim the name, "the LORD" (33:19).[11] Then follows Moses' encounter with God on the holy mountain.

11. "The LORD" here refers to the name of God, YHWH. God used this name when

The LORD descended in the cloud, and stood with him there, and proclaimed the name, "the LORD." The LORD passed before him, and proclaimed, "The LORD, the LORD, a God merciful and gracious, slow to anger, and abounding in steadfast love and faithfulness, keeping steadfast love for the thousandth generation, forgiving iniquity, and transgression and sin, yet by no means clearing the guilty, but visiting the iniquity of the parents upon the children and children's children, to the third and fourth generation." (34:5-7)

We notice three things. First we learn *what God is like:* He is merciful, gracious, and slow to anger, and abounding in love and faithfulness. The word translated "steadfast love" (Hebrew: *hesed*) refers to God's acts through which he demonstrates his loyalty as a covenant partner. This leads us to the second matter: *What God does.* God demonstrates his steadfast love and faithfulness "for the thousandth generation" — there is no limit. Notice the contrast with the next statement about punishing until the third and fourth generation — there is a very definite limit. But first comes the word for which Moses has been waiting. "Forgive their sins," he had asked. The answer is proclaimed in the Name: "forgiving iniquity, and transgression and sin"; these are the same words that were used in 32:32 when Moses asked for forgiveness. The promise to the fathers can be fulfilled only because God is like that.

But then follows the third element: He does not leave the guilty unpunished, and he *visits* their iniquity. God does not pretend that nothing happened. He comes back to the evil that has been committed. Does this mean that one hand takes back what the other hand has given? Is forgiveness merely temporal — a postponement of the final reckoning? That would not have been an answer to Moses' prayer. Moses receives what he has asked for, for he has found mercy in the eyes of the Lord. That God visits the sins does not contradict his forgiveness of sins. The God who visits the sins is the Merciful and the Gracious One. That determines his intentions in visiting the sins. It is not a matter of exacting payment for these sins. His purpose is mercy. Sin thwarts his purposes, and he visits the sins in order to eliminate them, so that he can show his love to those he visits. Later Paul

he revealed himself to Moses (Exod. 3:13-15). Out of reverence for God the Jews refuse to pronounce that name; they say "Adonai" which means "Lord." But in our Bibles this name is written as LORD. (See the introduction "To the Reader" and the notes on Exod. 3:14-15 in the NSRV).

was to phrase this purpose in these words: "For God has imprisoned all in disobedience so that he may be merciful to all" (Rom. 11:32).

Learning that God had answered his prayer of forgiveness for Israel, Moses "quickly bowed his head toward the earth, and worshiped":

> "If now I have found favor in your sight, O LORD, I pray, let the LORD go with us. Although this is a stiff-necked people, pardon our iniquity and our sin, and take us for your inheritance." He said: "I hereby make a covenant. . . . (Exod. 34:9-10)

Once again the main goal is expressed: God is to dwell in the midst of Israel, in spite of the stiff-neckedness of the people. He must forgive. Notice the word "our": forgive our wickedness and our sins. Moses has totally identified himself with his stiff-necked people. And he clings to what God told him about himself: "Who forgives iniquity, and transgression and sin." And: "Take us for your inheritance." That sums up everything: Israel must be God's possession from generation to generation.

Then follows God's answer: "I hereby make a covenant with you." In the Hebrew text, the emphasis is on the word "I." God himself takes the initiative — not just to please Moses but because he himself wants it: He ties himself to Israel — forever! And he knows what he does: He ties himself to a stiff-necked nation; with this people he wants to achieve his purposes. He will visit their sins, but he will be a forgiving God (Ps. 99:8). This people will be his *inheritance*. He stakes the honor of his name on it: Through this people he will achieve his purpose for his entire creation, as he once had sworn to Abraham. In so doing, God granted everything Moses had requested from him. What Moses wanted was exactly the desire of God's own heart.

Acquiescence, the Opposite of What God Wants

Thus we notice that God's purpose for Israel is not achieved automatically. It is realized only when Moses stands in the breach before God. God wants salvation for Israel, and through Israel he wants to reach all nations with his redemption. He wants to achieve this through human beings (mortals!) who share in the same aim, and who want that so eagerly that they are willing to put their own salvation at risk! We completely miss the point Scripture is trying to make if we argue that God would have done this anyway, since it had been predetermined what he would do! No, God himself puts everything at risk. If Moses had not intervened, Israel would not have received the forgiveness required for the fulfillment of the promise to the fathers. This Moses, who refuses to quit until God has assured him that he will forgive Israel and will dwell in their midst, appears as no other to be God's tool by which the divine intentions with Israel — and with all of humanity — can be realized.

Again we ask from the perspective of our tradition: Is it God's will that his children passively accept the perdition of the many? This story about Moses makes abundantly clear that this spirit of acquiescence is the complete opposite of what Scripture teaches us about the will of God. Whoever is called by him is called not to accept passively the doom people have brought upon themselves. And those who do acquiesce cannot be the tools through which God realizes his purposes.

3. The Compassion of the Father

The Parable of What Was Lost (Luke 15)

> Now all the tax collectors and the sinners were coming near to listen to him. And the Pharisees and the scribes were grumbling and saying, "This fellow welcomes sinners and eats with them."
>
> So He told them this parable, "Which one of you, having a hundred sheep and losing one of them, does not leave the ninety-nine in the wilderness and goes after the one that is lost until he finds it?" (Luke 15:1-4)

In Luke 15 Jesus tells three stories. But they belong together as "this parable." The shepherd does not want to lose that one sheep! Therefore, he does not stop searching until he has found it. Jesus makes the same point in the next story about the woman; she has no rest until that one coin which she had lost has been found.

That is what God is like, Jesus says. That is how the prophets speak about him. He is the Shepherd of Israel who searches for his lost sheep: "As a shepherd looks after his scattered flock when he is with them, so will I look after my sheep" (Ezek. 34:11-12). In Jesus, the searching Shepherd of Israel has appeared among the lost sheep of the house of Israel (Matt. 10:6). For that reason the tax collectors and sinners are now gathered around him.

The parable of the prodigal son perfectly expresses what God is like. He is the father who worries all his life about his missing son. He cannot feast until he has him back and has closed his arms around him. This parable illustrates what Jesus has to say to the Pharisees and scribes. They object to the fact that Jesus receives sinners and moves among them. We hear the same message in the story of Zaccheus, the chief of the tax collectors. But Jesus' voice echoes the joy of the shepherd who has found his sheep: "Today salvation has come to this house, because he too is a son of Abraham. For the Son of Man came to seek out and to save the lost." Compare this joyful statement with the reproach: "All who saw it began to grumble and said, 'He has gone to be the guest of one who is a sinner'" (Luke 19:1-10). This contrast between Jesus' attitude and that of his opponents is the subject of the third of these three stories.

The Father and His Lost Son

This story is silent about any *searching* by God. The father has not gone out to search for his son. Yet this is the starting point of the entire story, as is clear from the two previous stories. It begins with God's search. The publicans and sinners gather around Jesus, the searching Shepherd. And the son returns to his father because there had been a search for him. This fact is clear from the words of the father: "He was lost and is found."

The stories of the lost sheep and the lost coin do not refer to sin and conversion — only to a searching God. But now Jesus turns to these themes. Of course we should not forget that this is *one* parable. The parable of the lost son applies to the same people as the stories of the lost sheep and the lost coin. Now we see what was wrong with them.

The son is confronted with his life's failure. He is stuck. He has lost everything and no one is interested in him.

> But when he came to himself he said, "How many of my father's hired hands have bread enough and to spare, but here I am dying of hunger! I will get up and go to my father, and I will say to him, 'Father, I have sinned against heaven and before you; I am no longer worthy to be called your son; treat me like one of your hired hands.'" So he set off and went to his father. (Luke 15:17-20)

He comes to his senses. The story is not about what others have done wrong, but what he himself has done. *I* have sinned! Then he remembers his father's house.

But notice the father! "But while he was still far off, his father saw him and was filled with compassion; he ran and put his arms around him and kissed him" (v. 20). That is what God is like! Now everything gets moving:

64

the best robe is found, which he puts on; a ring is placed on his finger and shoes on his feet. The fatted calf is prepared. There is music and dancing. " 'For this son of mine was dead and is alive again; he was lost and is found!' And they began to celebrate" (v. 24).

The Attitude of the Elder Son

There is happiness, celebration, in all three parts of the parable. Only now, however, do we find a descriptions of the feast. And only now do we hear about something else — the reason why Jesus tells this parable: the disruption of the feast!

> Now his elder son was in the field; and when he came and approached the house, he heard music and dancing. He called one of the slaves and asked what was going on. He replied, "Your brother has come, and your father has killed the fatted calf, because he has got him back safe and sound." (vv. 25-26)

From the father we hear words of excitement: lost and found, dead and returned to life; from the servant we only hear: he is back safe and sound. What else would the servant say? That the son of the boss is back is hardly his problem. He did not miss him; he has not been looking for him, every day, year after year. But now follows the distressing part: neither has the elder son! Worse still: he gets angry and refuses to join the festivities.

No, the elder son had not missed his brother. He was gone, and as far as he was concerned, it could stay that way. What has come over his father? Music and dancing because his son has come back! The elder son refuses to participate. And he blurts it out to his father when he comes outside:

> "Listen, for all these years I have been working like a slave for you, and I have never disobeyed your command; yet you have never given me even a young goat so that I might celebrate with my friends. But when this son of yours came back, who has devoured your property with prostitutes, you killed the fatted calf for him!" (vv. 29-30)

Look at all the contrasts and notice how the elder son finds his father totally unreasonable! I have served you for many years; he went to prostitutes to waste your money; for me there is not even a goat for a party with my friends; for him you kill the fatted calf and everybody celebrates. Why did I work so hard? If this is how it can be done, I would have done things differently too! We know this objection: Live it up, and still make it to heaven!

THE ONE PURPOSE OF GOD

What about the father? As soon as the elder son has vented his rage, we hear these precious words:

> "Son, you are always with me, and all that is mine is yours. But we had to celebrate and rejoice, because this brother of yours was dead and has come to life; he was lost and has been found." (vv. 31-32)

Note the word "son" — everything the father has is at the son's disposal. He has no other interest than the joy of his children. Compare that with the words of our tradition about a God who demands that his justice be satisfied (Heidelberg Catechism, Q. 11). That is not the God about whom Jesus speaks!

The father and the son are outside the house; the feast has been disrupted. That is where the story breaks off, and we are left asking: How will it end? From what we know about the father, the story will not end before the elder son also enters the house. For one thing is clear: This father does not want to continue without his elder son, just as he does not want to go on without the younger! "Son, all that is mine is yours" — these words are spoken after his refusal to enter. This does not change because of the son's attitude: This is the relationship between the father and his elder son, and this is how it continues!

The Elder Son and the Church

In this parable Jesus addresses the Pharisees and the scribes, who were grumbling because he received tax collectors and sinners. The parable does not deal with a passing matter, for it focuses on the contrast between the attitudes of Jesus and of the Jewish leaders of his time — the contrast that would lead to the rejection of Jesus by the majority of the Jews.

But why would Luke include this parable in his Gospel? The answer is that he wrote for the church! He did not include it to criticize a specifically Jewish problem. No, the parable is in the Bible as a challenge to the *church*. The church is called not to acquiesce in the perdition of fellow human beings — not one of them — *since God himself does not passively accept that.*

The Laborers and the Harvest

This fact is confirmed when we note the calling of the church as outlined by Matthew. As Jesus travels through the towns and villages of Galilee, we keep hearing the words *all* and *every:* all towns and villages; he cures every disease and illness. And then we read:

When he saw the crowds, he had compassion for them, because they were harassed and helpless, like sheep without a shepherd. Then He said to his disciples, "The harvest is plentiful, but the laborers are few; therefore ask the Lord of the harvest to send out laborers into his harvest." (Matt. 9:36-38)

"He had compassion for them" — we hear the same from the father in the parable. It is the compassion of the Father — he came himself, in Jesus Christ, to the lost sheep. The word used by the Gospel writers is uncommonly strong: "moved with compassion." It tells us that Jesus' heart, yes, everything in Jesus, is and remains agitated about the fate of these people: He will not rest before they have been saved from this fate — even at the cost of his own life!

Through the image of the harvest we are told what relationship the disciples of Jesus have to his compassion. Jesus sees the human multitudes as a harvest that might be lost because of a lack of workers. The entire church is called to be workers in this harvest; called to share in his compassion and to serve him in realizing his intentions. Many workers are needed, for the harvest is large, and the Lord of the harvest wants the entire harvest to be brought in. The workers must keep that in mind. Those who are called by him but feel that it would be sufficient if only part of the harvest were saved do not share their Lord's perspective and are disloyal to the task he has committed to them. Jesus warns the church against this danger in the story of the lost sheep and the lost coin: Not one of them should remain missing.

But Does the Father Also Show Another Face?

But is this compassion of the Father a *full* description of him? For where is this compassion in the harsh words of Jesus about the judgment? We hear those words when he speaks about the many and the few: Someone asked him, "Lord will only a few be saved?" He said to them, "Strive to enter through the narrow door, for many, I tell you, will try to enter, but will not be able" (Luke 13:23-24).

Some people feel that in this text Jesus rejects the concern for the salvation of the many as something wrong: We must make sure that we are saved ourselves, and the destiny of the many is not our business but God's. Is that what Jesus teaches? No, Jesus does not rebuff the questioner. In fact, Jesus does not directly address him. He uses the plural: You people, you must strive to enter. The emphasis is on the idea of *strive*. He gives a solemn warning to be aware of the danger that one could be left outside: Listen therefore to what I say, and act accordingly; for many will try to enter and will not be able to. The Lord will have to reject them: "Go away from me, all you evildoers" (v. 27).

The same message about the many and the few is found in Matthew's well-known words about the broad and the narrow road:

Enter through the narrow gate; the gate is wide and the road is easy that leads to destruction, and there are many who take it. For the gate is narrow, and the road is hard that leads to life, and there are few who find it. (Matt. 7:13-14)

Not everyone who says to me, "Lord, Lord," will enter the kingdom of heaven, but only the one who does the will of my Father in heaven. On that day many will say to me, "Lord, Lord, did we not prophesy in your name, and cast out demons in your name, and do many deeds of power in your name?" Then I will declare to them, "I never knew you; go away from me, you evildoers." (vv. 21-23)

Then there is this frightening word when the last judgment is announced and when the sheep are separated from the goats: "You that are accursed, depart from me into the eternal fire prepared for the devil and his angels . . ." (Matt. 25:41). How can one maintain that this leaves room for compassion? Here Jesus is no longer the Savior, but the Judge! If this is true, then his compassion for the many is merely of a passing nature! His compassion will end on the judgment day! It may look that way, but it is not like that.

Two Sets of Statements?

It has been argued that there are two sets of statements in the Bible. One series deals with the lostness of the many, while another series gives hope for the salvation of all. We are supposed to let those two series stand side by side without attempting to harmonize them. It would be a way to concede the traditional belief that Scripture indeed teaches that eternal damnation while maintaining that Scripture also contains other statements, such as, "that God may be all in all" (1 Cor. 15:28).[12]

12. The view that there are two sets of statements was discussed in 1920 at the Synod of the Reformed Gereformeerde Churches in the Netherlands. J. B. Netelenbos, a minister, faced charges because of his views of Scripture. Regarding the eternal nature

But the parable of the searching shepherd and the compassionate father lose their meaning if Scripture teaches both! For in these stories Jesus tells his disciples not to accept passively the perdition of the many, not even of one of them. The shepherd and the woman keep on searching until they have found what was lost — the one sheep and the one coin. How can we follow that example if, simultaneously, we are told that God has destined most people to perdition? What keeps us from giving in to despair even in apparently hopeless situations? It is the certainty that there can be no case in which he does not fully support us; he is the One who desires the salvation of that particular individual, and he will never stop wanting it. We serve him in what he desires! That certainty empowers us never to regard a person as hopeless, not even after his death. Jesus gives us that certainty! The Father of whom he speaks is the father of the prodigal son and of his brother — and nothing else! There are no other statements in the Bible that attribute another attitude to the Father. "For the Son of God, Jesus Christ, whom we proclaimed among you, . . . was not 'Yes and No', but in him it is always 'Yes'" (2 Cor. 1:19).

What does it mean to hear that in the judgment Jesus will say to many, "You that are accursed, depart from me into the eternal fire prepared for the devil and his angels . . ." (Matt. 25:41)? It does not mean that there he is a different Jesus, and not the One full of compassion. *For even at the time of judgment he continues to desire their salvation!* But does the Bible indeed speak in those terms of the divine judgment? We will deal with that later.

---

of divine punishment he had argued that "over and against the pertinent statements in the New Testament about the eternity of punishment, we have the incomparably deep word of Paul, which appears to open unlimited perspectives, when he pictures the final goal of Christ's rule as God being 'all in all.'" "Since *both* of these arguments are found in the Holy Scriptures, and since I regard the Holy Scriptures as God's Word, I submit to both." The study committee stated: "that brother N. explains the words of 1 Cor. 15:28: 'that God be all in all,' in such a way, that the apostle therein denies the eternal nature of God's punishment. Brother N. does admit that eternal punishment and the reality of hell are scriptural teachings, but, on the basis of the text just referred to, he also accepts — and this text he considers to be the clearest — that the Holy Scriptures also teach the opposite, which causes him to end with a *non liquet* [it remains unclear]. According to him, God's Word teaches two things, which seem mutually exclusive, and he does not know which of the two to choose." See the report of the committee: *Acta van de Generale Synode der Gereformeerde Kerken* (1929), pp. 118, 121-23. For this reason, Netelenbos lost his ministerial credentials. The view that there are two distinct sets of statements, however, is still held by many theologians; this prevents them from stating that the doctrine of eternal punishment is contrary to the Bible. We will return to these "two sets" in IV, 3.

Now we will limit ourselves to just a few of Jesus' statements. How did he talk about the coming judgment?

Did Jesus Teach a Never-ending Punishment?

Several times Jesus referred to the final judgment in terms that clearly imply that this judgment is to have an end. Let us look at a few examples.

1. Jesus refers to a differentiation in judgment. The slave who knew what his master wanted, but did not do accordingly, will receive "many stripes." "But the one who did not know and did what deserved a beating, will receive "few stripes" (Luke 12:47-48, AV). "Few stripes" surely have an end! And the same applies even to "many stripes." The text does not speak of an eternal or endless beating. Thus Jesus here refers to a punishment that has an end. This also implies that the punishment has a *purpose;* when that has been reached, sooner or later the punishment ceases.[13]

2. We are told that there is forgiveness for all sin and blasphemy except blasphemy against the Spirit (Matt. 12:31).[14] Let us limit ourselves to the sins Jesus lists in Matthew 25:31-46. Verse 46, in particular, has always been cited as undeniable proof that Jesus taught eternal punishment. Yet it is clear that the sins Jesus lists in this passage do not constitute the blasphemy against the Spirit. Assuming that Jesus did not utter this severe word with the intention of contradicting what he said moments before, we must accept that the sins mentioned in this passage will eventually be forgiven. *This means, however strange this may sound to us, that this statement of Jesus about eternal punishment is not the final word for those who are condemned.*[15]

13. We have quoted the AV because of the literal translation, "stripes." S. Greijdanus, *Het evangelie naar de beschrijving van Lucas* (Amsterdam, 1940), I:627ff. "Even if he did not know of an unambiguous command or prohibition by his lord, there are also things which he knew, or should know, without that. . . . To be lost forever is in itself already horrible. But even in that eternal lostness there will be a gradation in punishment." This exegesis makes even the "few stripes" eternal!

14. In the context of the blasphemy against the Spirit, nothing is said about a punishment resulting from that sin, as in Matthew 25:46 (eternal punishment). This is also true of Jesus' statement about Judas: "better for that one not to have been born" (Matt. 26:46). Some feel that this may point to annihilation. About the possibility to utter a definite "No," and to end in nothingness (annihilation), see IX.

15. This becomes more understandable when we realize that the Greek word for eternity *(aiōn)* is translated both "age" — "this *age*," and the "future *age*" (Matt. 12:32) — and *world* "the end of the world" (Matt. 13:40, 49; 28:20). In both cases a time period is intended that has an end. See also VII, 3.

3. Jesus announces the fall of Jerusalem:

Jerusalem, Jerusalem, the city that kills the prophets and stones those that are sent to it! How often have I desired to gather your children together as a hen gathers her brood under her wings, and you were not willing! See, your house is left to you, desolate. For I tell you, you will not see me again until you say, "Blessed is the one who comes in the name of the Lord." (Matt. 23:37-39; Luke 13:34-35)

Jesus speaks of this judgment as "hell" (Matt. 23:33). It is the final judgment of Jerusalem, which has rejected its Messiah. But this final judgment is not the end of God's intentions for Jerusalem. The punishment will continue, "until you say, 'Blessed is the one who comes in the name of the Lord.'" The same Jesus who announced the judgment of Jerusalem will, after the judgment has been executed, return to his city and be welcomed as the Messiah who will fulfill God's promises to Israel and the nations.[16]

4. Lastly, we mention the parable of the rich man and poor Lazarus — a story always quoted to underline the eternal nature of God's punishment. First, we hear Abraham say, "Child!" This rich man, in spite of his lostness, remains a child of Abraham! Then we hear Abraham compare Lazarus's fate during his life with that of the rich man after his death. They are judged

16. The conviction that Israel was irreversibly lost determined the exegesis. Calvin writes: "He therefore announced to them that He will not return to them except when — too late — they will shout, trembling before the sight of his fearful majesty, that he is in truth the Son of God." Again: "Him, whom you now reject as your Savior, Him you will know as your Judge" (*De Evangeliën van Mattheüs, Markus en Lukas,* translated under the supervision of A. Brummelkamp [2nd ed.; Goudriaan, 1971], 3:305). See H. N. Ridderbos for the same view (*Het Evangelie naar Mattheüs* [Kampen, 1946], 2:141). See further: Joachim Gnilka (*Das Mattheüsevangelium* [Freiburg, 1988], 2:305), who believes there can be no question of salvation. Paul, he thinks, did see some possibility of a future form of salvation, but this "strange statement" of Jesus does not point in that direction. F. W Grosheide (*Het heilig Evangelie volgens Mattheüs* [2nd rev. ed.; Kampen, 1954], p. 355) does not follow Calvin but thinks that Jesus here simply refers to a joyful *possibility.* Adolf Schlatter (*Der Evangelist Mattheüs* [5th ed.; Stuttgart, 1959], p. 691) writes: 'Israël hat den rächenden Zorn . . . verdient, aber das ist nicht das Letze; darüber steht das zur Vollendung gebrachte Werk des Christus, der im Dienst der göttlichen Gnade mit dem rettende Hilfe Gottes kommen wird.' [Israel has earned . . . the fierce wrath, but this is not the end of the matter; because there is also the completed work of Christ, who in the ministry of divine grace comes with the saving help from God.] I agree with Schlatter. For the view that Jesus here refers only to a distant posterity that will be converted, see also VI, 4.

by the same measure! But if the rich man was enduring never-ending torture, while the suffering of Lazarus was limited to his life on earth, we would not have the same measure! Admittedly, this statement does not directly refer to the end of the punishment, but Jesus would not have spoken in these terms if he referred to a punishment that would continue forever.

Why Was It Not Mentioned? Paul as Teacher

We now look back. We are searching for a solid basis in Scripture for the hope of salvation for the many. The church has taught that there is no such hope. It says that the Bible tells us that God wants not only salvation for the elect but also eternal damnation for the masses. And since he wants this, believers must simply acquiesce. Is that true? we have been asking. We hear something different in Abraham's prayer for Sodom, in Moses' intercession for Israel, and, in particular, in Jesus' teaching about the compassion of the father for his lost son: Those who are called by God are called precisely because they will not passively accept the perdition of the many. *That is the point of departure in our search for a foundation of our hope: If God calls us not to simply accept this, it is because he does not want the many to be lost.*

The statements of Jesus about the coming judgment seem to have a different tone. In the interpretation commonly held in the church through the centuries, the teaching on the judgment has been viewed as the irrefutable message of eternal perdition, to which God has predestined the lost, with the intention that this state be permanent.[17] We have argued against such irrefutability. But why did Jesus not explain himself better if the expression "everlasting punishment" does not really mean eternal punishment? If he had, all misunderstanding would have been avoided.

Could it be that the idea of everlasting punishment was so totally foreign to the thinking of the early church, that such additional explanations were not needed, in order to avoid misunderstandings? Do we not realize that the early church lived by those Scriptures, which we now call the Old Testament? And do we not realize that the idea of everlasting punishment is nowhere found in the Old Testament? Could it be that our

17. D. P. Walker, *The Decline of Hell* (see I, nn. 42 and 46), p. 19: 'The scriptural evidence for the doctrine of eternal torment is extremely strong. . . . There are two crucial texts for the eternity of hell: Christ's eschatological discourse in Matthew XXV, and the lake of fire and brimstone in Revelation XIV and XX.' Thus even Walker believes that the Bible teaches eternal torment.

misunderstandings arise from the fact that we, in contrast to the early church, do not base our thinking on the Old Testament? Is that something we should learn first, if we want to understand Jesus' words as he intended them?

But if the early church did not think of heaven and hell as the dual *finale* of history, what did she think about the end? The Gospels do not provide the answer to that question. Apparently these Bible books are not intended to enlighten us about that. With Paul things are different. He does write about this subject. In his letter to the Romans in particular, he emphatically addresses the questions of God's ultimate purpose with humanity and the connection between that purpose and the divine judgment.[18]

18. J. H. Leckie (*The World to Come and Final Destiny* [2nd ed.; n.p., 1922], pp. 162-82), emphasizes the importance of Paul: ". . . unlike St. John, he was interested in the problem of the End" (p. 170).

CHAPTER III

God Wants All to Be Saved
(Romans 1–5)

1. Rebellion and Judgment

A Journey through Romans

Just as Moses could not accept that God would destroy Israel, so Paul cannot accept that Israel would be forever cut off from the salvation God has provided in Jesus. We read in Romans 9:3: 'For I could wish that I myself were accursed and cut off from Christ for the sake of my own people, my kindred according to the flesh."

Reading the letter to the Romans, we find more statements that relate to our question. We notice immediately that Romans 5:12-21 deals with the salvation of humanity as a whole, from Adam onward. In Romans 8:19-21 we read about the deliverance of all creation from "futility" and "bondage to decay." Then we find the chapters about the salvation of Israel in its entirety (9–11).

What is the apostle's line of thought? How does the salvation of Israel relate to what he wrote in the first part of his letter regarding the salvation of humanity? To understand his line of thinking, we will make a "journey" through this letter, from beginning to end. We want to know what Paul teaches about God's intentions for humanity: about the coming judgment and the salvation that God wants to bring. In other words: we want to ask Paul what he has to say about the matter that concerns us. Is Paul's answer

74

the same as what is taught is our tradition, or not? If we could find the answer to that question, we would have the answer firsthand!

With this goal in mind, we will explore a few consecutive angles that allow us to survey what applies to our question. In order to make sure that we have correctly understood the apostle, we will also check what he said on the same topic in his other letters. At times we will also compare Paul's teaching in the letters with other passages of Scripture.[1]

Righteousness, the Saving God

The first stop on our journey is Romans 1:16-17a:

> For I am not ashamed of the gospel; it is the power of God for salvation to everyone who has faith, to the Jew first and also to the Greek. For in it the righteousness of God is revealed.

What does Paul mean when he says that "the righteousness of God" is revealed? Paul agrees fully with the way in which the Old Testament speaks of God's righteousness. In Scripture God's righteousness is always saving righteousness: God brings deliverance, peace, and life.[2]

We find a song of praise celebrating the revelation of God's righteousness in Psalm 98:

> The Lord has made known his salvation: his righteousness hath he openly shewed in the sight of the heathen.

---

1. For the study of the epistle I relied mainly on the commentaries by Herman Ridderbos *(Romeinen);* Adolf Schlatter *(Gerechtigkeit);* Ulrich Wilckens *(Römer);* and H. Baarlink *(Romeinen).*

2. From the earliest times, Israel has worshiped Jahweh as the One who directs his universal gift of righteousness to them. The idea that this would at the same time be a threat to Israel is untenable. There is no such concept as "punishing righteousness." The term "punishing" would contradict the very idea of "righteousness" (Gerhard von Rad, *Theologie des Alten Testaments* [1962], 1:389; Eng. trans. *Old Testament Theology* [San Francisco, 1962].) Cf. Schlatter, *Gerechtigkeit,* pp. 34-35. See also K. Kertelge, "Dikaiosynê, Gerechtigkeit," *Exegetical Dictionary of the New Testament,* 1:325-30. For Paul, righteousness is in harmony with the old-Judaistic tradition, which sees it "not only as an ethical attribute of God and/or of mankind; instead, with reference to humans, it is an essential characteristic of that which allows man to be what he should be in relationship to God and mankind" (pp. 326-27).

He hath remembered his mercy and his truth toward the house of
Israel: all the ends of the earth have seen the salvation of our God.

Make a joyful noise unto the Lord, all the earth: make a loud noise,
and rejoice, and sing praise. (vv. 2-4, AV)

The earth bursts forth in jubilation when God reveals his righteousness in
the sight of the nations. The meaning of the word "righteousness" is not
found by looking at the work of the judge. It is not the punishing of the
guilty; nor acquittal by the judge, nor receiving mercy or forgiveness. A
guilty individual can be acquitted, or his case can be dismissed, but that
does not make him a person who will behave better in the future than he
did in the past. This is precisely what is involved in God's righteousness.
When God reveals his righteousness "in the sight of the nations," it signals
a complete turnaround: the restoration of the relationship between human
beings and God. At last, things go the way the Creator intended. God's will
is done on earth as it is in heaven; not only by some but by all people; not
to a degree but with total dedication. That brings salvation! In this psalm
it is not a part of humanity that sings praise, but all the nations do: All the
ends of the earth see the victory of Israel's God. And everything joins in:
the sea, the animals, the rivers, and the mountains (vv. 7-8).

In writing that God's righteousness has been revealed, Paul is pointing
to Jesus of Nazareth. He met him on the road to Damascus. There the saving
righteousness of God was revealed to him: the Messiah, radiating God's
glory, God's love. Who made him into another being. Once a persecutor
of the Messiah, he became his zealous messenger, his apostle, sent out into
the world to preach his message of salvation. That message is his subject
in the letter to the Romans.

Rebellion against God's Coming to Man

Over against the revelation of God's righteousness stands his wrath over
all the ungodliness and wickedness of humankind (Rom. 1:18). Does this
wrath represent the dark side of God that we wished did not exist? What
would happen if there were no divine wrath? It would mean that God would
simply let the people do whatever they wanted with this earth. Evil would
continue and death would have the final say — with God's approval. God's
wrath signifies that he does not approve; that he does not abandon the
earth and all that lives to evil and death. He does not abandon the goal he
has for his creation. That divine purpose is all-important. It is the deliver-

ance of his creation from all that attempts to destroy it. God's wrath is an intrinsic part of this deliverance, that is, of his saving righteousness.

We are told that this wrath is directed toward humankind: against all ungodliness and wickedness of men (1:18). Human beings suppress God's truth in unrighteousness. God comes with his truth to them. He *reveals* that truth to humans (1:19). He lets them know what is good (Mic. 6:8). But humans rebel against God. Scripture records this rebellion from the beginning: God speaks to Adam and Eve, but they do not listen to his voice; they listen to another voice, that of the serpent (Gen. 3:1-7).

We must clarify what we mean when we refer to *God's coming with his truth to humankind*. Paul does not speak of a divine truth that each individual can discover by some kind of innate knowledge of God. As if, through looking at creation, or by analyzing history, or by intense contemplation, or through the discovery of a "divine spark" within himself, human beings can arrive at the conviction that there must be a Creator. It is not like that. Humans cannot "find the way" to God. No one has the ability to find out anything about God unless God *gives* him understanding. That is what it means for God to *speak* to humans.

In some unfathomable way God speaks to humans, to all people, every day; but they rebel. Continually they suppress the truth by their wickedness (Rom. 1:18). They know God's "decree," but they rebel against it, and they encourage others to do likewise (1:32). And there is no excuse for what they do. They would have had an excuse if God had not spoken to them. Had that been so, they would have been ignorant. In that case it would have been God's own fault that they did not know about good and evil. But eventually it will be clear that this was not so. God's judgment will make clear that they did know, but were unwilling: They are left without excuse (1:20).

That bring us to the crux of the matter. Why does God continue to come with his truth to people? Only that he might eventually condemn them? Tradition understood it that way. Supposedly God knew already that the people to whom he would come with his truth would not listen. But he comes nevertheless. As a result their evil-doing is revealed, and it becomes clear that he is justified in condemning them.

This line of thinking fits perfectly with the terrifying image of God that found its way into the tradition of the church, but it is at complete odds with what Scripture tells us about God! "Have I any pleasure in the death of the wicked, says the Lord, and not rather that they should turn from their ways and live?" (Ezek. 18:23). That is what God is like! He

77

continues to come with his truth, since he desires that all people will eventually listen to that truth, and share in the salvation that he intended for humankind when he created them. He does not abandon that purpose. And that he does not give up on that goal finds expression in his wrath against the ungodliness and unrighteousness of humankind (Rom. 1:18).

The Judgment and Its Dual Result

God's revelation of his will to humanity and humanity's rebellion against God will finally result in the judgment:

> . . . the day of wrath, when God's righteous judgment will be revealed. For he will repay according to each one's deeds: to those who by patiently doing good seek for glory and honor and immortality, he will give eternal life; while for those who are self-seeking and who obey not the truth but wickedness, there will be wrath and fury. There will be anguish and distress for everyone who does evil, the Jew first and also the Greek, but glory and honor and peace for everyone who does good, the Jew first and also the Greek. (Rom. 2:5b-10)

The judgment has a dual outcome. It brings both condemnation and acquittal. Who receives acquittal? Our tradition would suggest that acquittal is based on faith or on grace. But here we hear a different message: There is acquittal for those who "do good." Who, however, can be justified because of the works he has done? Later Paul will write that there is no condemnation "for those who are in Christ Jesus." In them the demand of the law is fulfilled, since they walk "according to the Spirit" (8:1, 4). The acquittal of Romans 2:7 must therefore refer to those who allow themselves to be led by the Spirit of God; the children of God for whom all creation waits "with eager longing" (8:19).

But in Romans 2 the emphasis is not on acquittal but on condemnation — it is the "day of wrath." Here everything depends on God's purpose in his wrath and judgment, as we already noted. According to the Scriptures that goal is always that humans will cease to do evil; that they cease their rebellion against God; that they return to him and listen to what he says. The Bible is silent about a divine demand that requires satisfaction, or about a payment by humankind through punishment to even the scales of justice, as the church has taught (Heidelberg Catechism, Q. 12). The sole purpose of God's wrath is that people do not remain as they are, but become what

78

God wants them to be: men and women created in the image of God (Gen. 1:26); bearers of his love in his creation.[3]

Our tradition has presented the condemnation in the judgment as the permanent destiny of those who are condemned — people remain as they are, and where they are. From what we have said so far we cannot but suspect that this cannot be true. If God's coming to the world is not a coming with evil intent, but a coming that desires the salvation of rebellious people, it cannot end in a final judgment that destines them to a perdition that he wants to be everlasting. In Romans Paul does indeed speak of condemnation, but he indicates in no way that this is God's final purpose for the condemned! On the contrary, all the remaining chapters of the letter focus on the *salvation* of condemned humanity (Rom. 5:18).

2. The Privilege of the Jews

No Difference in the Judgment

In writing about the coming judgment, Paul addresses the Jews. The church in Rome consisted of Jews and non-Jews (Rom. 9:24, called from the Jews and from the Gentiles). There were many Jews in Rome, but the majority rejected the gospel. And yet the gospel is and remains first for the Jew (1:16), for the entire Jewish people. The Messiah does not want to be without his people! When the apostle proclaims the gospel, the Jews who reject the Messiah remain Paul's first concern. They must be convinced that the Jesus of the gospel is the fulfillment of Scripture. When he arrives shortly afterward in Rome, that will be his first work (Acts 28:23).

Why did they reject the gospel? They had the law of Moses. That made them privileged above the Gentiles. In this privilege they put their trust; they boasted that they were God's people and that they possessed the law (Rom. 2:17, 23). They were sure that, through keeping the law, they would be saved from the coming judgment. Any message that told them that they would not be saved by their loyalty to the law infuriated them as a denial of that privilege.

Of course, no Jew thought he had never sinned and needed no forgiveness. But they were all convinced that forgiveness would be given only to those who had been loyal in keeping the law. For in the judgment the law

---

3. For the purpose of God's judgment, see VII, 2 and VII, 3.

of God will be the norm according to which he judges. Now if the only nation that honors the law will not be saved, whom will God have left? It would mean that God would be unable to fulfill what he had promised Israel through the prophets!

Paul writes that God will judge everyone according to his deeds, without differentiating between Jews and non-Jews. "All who have sinned apart from the law will also perish apart from the law, and all who have sinned under the law will also be judged by the law" (2:12). The law was for Israel like a protecting wall by which God had separated his people from the other nations. Paul does not deny the existence of this wall, but he stresses its relative nature. God's law is not limited to Israel. Beyond this wall are other people who apparently also know about "Honor your father and your mother" and "You shall not kill . . . not commit adultery . . . not steal." Non-Jews, who do not possess the law, by nature do what the law commands; they demonstrate, Paul writes, that the work of the law is written in their hearts (2:14-15, AV). Here we see a connection with what he earlier wrote about God's revelation to them, and about their awareness of God's "decree" (1:19, 32). This rebellion, which suppresses God's truth in unrighteousness, is therefore not the final word. Because God continues to speak to human beings, there is still some proper conduct in the world — there is not only crime and wrongdoing. God does not abandon people to total chaos.

Israel did not deny this. They believed that salvation would not be reserved for Israel only. There were righteous individuals among the Gentiles, whose way of life would bring them salvation.[4] But that was the limit. Those people were exceptions; the majority of the non-Jews would be excluded from the salvation of the coming era — the kingdom of God.

Thus, works of the law could be found outside the wall of the law. But what about inside the walls — about the Jews themselves? Alas, even among them we find theft and adultery (2:21-22; the meaning of the "robbing of the temples" is less clear). Repeatedly Gentiles would dishonor the name of Israel's God as a result of what the Jews had done. Scripture tells us that every person will be judged according to his own deeds (Ps. 62:13). The

4. On the righteous among the Gentiles, see H. Strack and P. Billerbeck, *Kommentar zum Neuen Testament aus Talmud und Midrasch* (Munich, 1922-28), 3:142; 4:1117; Ephraim E. Urbach, *The Sages,* 2 vols. (Jerusalem, 1979), 1:324, 325, 412; C. G. Montefiore and H. Loewe, *A Rabbinic Anthology* (Philadelphia, 1963), pp. 557-60.

same norm for all! The separate status of the Jews does not grant them any privilege in the judgment.

> There will be anguish and distress for everyone who does evil, the Jew first and also the Greek, but glory and honor and peace for everyone who does good, the Jew first and also the Greek. For God shows no partiality. (Rom. 2:9-11)

"Then What Advantage Has the Jew?"

If in the judgment God does not differentiate between Jews and Gentiles, what good is it for Israel to be the people that God has chosen from among the nations? "What advantage has the Jew? Or what is the value of circumcision? Much, in every way. For in the first place the Jews were entrusted with the oracles of God" (3:2).

What does Paul mean when he uses the term "oracles of God"? The law? Indeed, the law is included. In Romans 9:4 he writes: To them "belongs" the giving of the law. But that can be only a very relative privilege if the keeping of Moses' law does not give them any advantage in the judgment! But Romans 9:4 adds something: To them "belong" also the promises! There is ample reason to emphasize these promises when we refer to the "oracles of God" that have been entrusted to Israel. Traces of the law may be found in other nations, but the promises are found only in Israel. Nothing like the promise to Abraham — that with him all nations of the earth would be blessed — is found in the religions of other peoples. Where, except in the psalms and the writings of Israel's prophets, do we hear of God's intentions to deliver humanity and all of creation from perdition and death? That promise has been given to Israel only. Through this people God will realize his plans. To their city, Jerusalem, all nations will march, that they might learn the ways of the Lord (Isa. 2:1-4). There he will destroy death forever and wipe away the tears from all faces (Isa. 25:8). There the words God has spoken to Israel on behalf of all nations will be fulfilled — in spite of Israel's disloyalty!

> What if some were unfaithful? Will their faithlessness nullify the faithfulness of God? By no means! Although everyone is a liar, let God be proved true. . . . (Rom. 3:3, 4)

God's faithfulness is his faithfulness to unfaithful Israel! Some exegetes have robbed these words of their power by arguing that God proves his faithfulness by remaining faithful to the faithful part of Israel that has accepted the Messiah. But Paul is not the kind of apostle to write such self-evident things. He does not refer to a part of Israel that has remained loyal and finds its loyalty rewarded by God's faithfulness. "Everyone is a liar"!

"Then what advantage has the Jew? Or what is the value of circumcision?" That privilege is not a matter of God's giving them salvation as a reward for their faithfulness to the law. The privilege of the Jews is the promise that is anchored in his faithfulness: Israel will be the first to experience the fact that he remains faithful to the unfaithful. The salvation of the whole world rests on this loyalty to unfaithful Israel! That is his promise to Abraham: In his posterity all peoples of the earth will be blessed.

God's Purpose with Israel Not Achieved through the Law

We now return to Paul's arguments against his Jewish opponents. What he says seems quite unreasonable. "While you preach against stealing, do you steal? You that forbid adultery, do you commit adultery? You that abhor idols, do you rob temples?" (Rom. 2:21-24). There must have been many Jews who did not steal, or commit adultery, or would not have anything to do with robbing temples of idols. How can Paul address them as if they are all guilty of these things?

This is not what the apostle has in mind. The point he wants to stress is not — as we already indicated — that some Jews have impeccable behavior but that all Israel will be the people through whom God will reach the world with his salvation. "The LORD has made known his salvation . . . in the sight of the heathen; he has remembered his mercy and his truth [faithfulness] to the house of Israel" (Ps. 98:2-3, AV). The nations will see his loyalty to the *house* of Israel — that is to say: to Israel in its entirety. Therein his saving righteousness toward them will be revealed. But what was heard among the nations was something different: God's name was blasphemed among the peoples because of the things that were found in the house of Israel (Rom. 2:24). True, it was not because of the misconduct of *all* of them, but it was certainly not so that Israel answered to the purpose for which God had chosen them: That all people would burst forth in jubilation and praise because of what became visible of him in the house of Israel.

God chose Israel to be the messenger of his salvation to all nations. "Make known his deeds among the people" (Ps. 105:1). His deeds: the deeds of his faithfulness toward Israel. It is not a question of what the people of Israel did for their God, but rather of what God did for his people. The praise is not about Israel's faithfulness, but about *his* faithfulness; his loyalty to the unfaith-ful; his saving righteousness for the unrighteous. But as long as Israel is focused exclusively on the law, it focuses on its own deeds, on its own faithfulness toward God. Its message to others is the message of the law. Paul speaks no evil of the law. On the contrary: it was one of the fundamental privileges of Israel that they were given his law (Rom. 9:4). However, the law is not the first thing Israel is to proclaim to the nations, but rather the message of the saving God. "What must I do to be saved?" cries the jailor in Philippi (Acts 16:31). The law answers, "Be circumcised and join Israel, keep the law of Moses, and you will be saved." Only those who do this will receive God's salvation; together with, as we saw, a few righteous from among the Gentiles. The message of the law is a message of limited salvation, salvation for the few who keep God's commandments; certainly not salvation for all peoples. And whether these few will really receive salvation remains a question. It always depends on how an individual acts, and it always remains a question whether he has done enough. In fact, it will never be enough. For what is God's will? That people will follow God's original intentions: to be humankind after his image, his likeness (Gen. 1:26). And no amount of religious work and zeal can bring that about![5]

Scripture has a totally different message for us. First, it is the message of God's salvation for all of Israel. "In the Lord all the offspring of Israel shall triumph and glory" (Isa. 45:25). "It is he who will redeem Israel from all its iniquities" (Ps. 130:8). Secondly, through Israel all nations. All of humanity will be led to the destiny for which God created humankind. All nations will sing praise to God; the prophets and the psalms stress this fact over and over again. This is achieved in what God does for Israel and for humanity as a whole: through the redemption which he provides *as a gift* (Isa. 55:1; Rom. 3:24). Paul is about to unfold this message. But not until he has summarized what he has said so far:

> What then? Are we [Jews] any better off? No, not at all; for we have already charged that all, both Jews and Greeks, are under the power of sin, as it is written: There is no one who is righteous, not even one . . . there is no one who shows kindness, there is not even one. . . . (Rom. 3:9-20)

5. This truth applies even more to other religions. They also stipulate what humans must do to obtain redemption. God himself gave Israel its law. That cannot be said about other religions. So, if even Israel cannot be saved through its law, which it received directly from God, how much less will other religious systems be able to lead people to the salvation God has intended for humankind.

Paul starts with a word from Ecclesiastes: "Surely there is no one on earth so righteous as to do good without ever sinning" (7:20), and then continues with quotes from five different psalms and from Isaiah. This is what the law says to those who are under the law, he writes. Strictly speaking, these words are not from the law, the Torah. But in these words the law does speak to Israel: Israel — no one excepted — transgressed the divine commandments. A Jew reading the Old Testament would not find any basis for the hope that all of Israel would be saved by its faithfulness to the law. Precisely because God gave his law to Israel, the relationship between human beings and God — between all human beings and God — becomes clear. Those who listen to the law, Paul writes, will experience how their mouth is silenced: "so that every mouth may be silenced, and the whole world may be held accountable to God" (Rom. 3:19-20).

Paul spoke in this passage to the Jews who had rejected the gospel. By quoting their own law, Paul wants to convince his brothers that they are travelling along a road that simply cannot lead to the goal to which they have been called: to be the nation through which all people will eventually praise God. That goal will never be achieved as long as Israel will think it does not need to be saved from its sins and believes that it suffices to keep the Mosaic law.

3. The Power of the Death of Christ

God Saves the World in the Death of Christ

> But now, apart from the law, the righteousness of God has been disclosed, and is attested by the law and the prophets, the righteousness of God through faith in Jesus Christ for all who believe. For there is no distinction, since all have sinned and come short of the glory of God; they are now justified by his grace as a gift, through the redemption that is in Christ Jesus. (Rom. 3:21-24)

This study does not intend to deal with what the Bible says about reconciliation with God. We must limit ourselves to this one point: We will not enter the life for which God has made us through something we do ourselves, but only through what God has done for us.

Through one act of transgression, condemnation has come to all people, and, likewise, through one righteous act justification and life come to all. Through the disobedience of one man (Adam) the many have become sinners, and through the obedience of one man (Christ), the many will be justified. In these words of Romans 5:18-19 Paul summarizes the meaning of the cross of Jesus Christ. Later on we will have a look at what we are here told about Adam. Our concern here is what that one man, Jesus of Nazareth, did for all people. And in Romans 3:25 we hear what God has done: "whom God put forward as a sacrifice of atonement by his blood." We are faced with the mystery that what God did and what Jesus did are one and the same. That is also clear from what the apostle wrote earlier in another letter:

> All this is from God, who reconciled us to himself through Christ, and has given us the ministry of reconciliation; that is, in Christ God was reconciling the world to himself, not counting their trespasses against them, and entrusting the message of reconciliation to us. So we are ambassadors for Christ since God is making his appeal through us; we entreat you on behalf of Christ, be reconciled to God. For our sake he made him to be sin who knew no sin, so that in him we might become the righteousness of God. (2 Cor. 5:18-21)

These words of Paul are probably based on the confession of the Jewish church.[6] God acted in Christ: He reconciled the world unto himself through Jesus. And he desires that, through him, we become the righteousness of God.

To become the "righteousness of God" means: At last we will do what God intended us to do from the beginning. That is clear from what precedes. "We are convinced," Paul writes, "that one has died for all; therefore all have died. And he died for all, so that those who live might live no longer for themselves, but for him who died and was raised for them (vv. 14-15). The situation was: all lived for themselves, in rebellion against God. They could not do otherwise. His death put an end to that. The new situation is: following Jesus, living for him. That is: "righteousness of God in him." The world is on its way to that goal; not only the church but all people: He died for all in order that all might no longer live for themselves but for him.

---

6. It is generally assumed that the words in 2 Corinthians 5:18-22 (from "All this is from God . . .") have been strongly influenced by the Judeo-Christian tradition and the liturgy of the early church; see P. Stuhlmacher, *Gerechtigkeit Gottes bei Paulus.* (Göttingen, 1965), pp. 77-78: "a passage that strongly reflects terminology fashioned by tradition and liturgy."

God himself acted in Christ! We also hear this in the praise sung by the church, as found in the letter to the Colossians: "For in him all the fullness of God was pleased to dwell, and through him God was pleased to reconcile to himself all things, whether on earth or in heaven, by making peace through the blood of his cross" (1:19-20). What is said about Jesus cannot be said of any one else: God dwells in him, God in his fullness (see also 2:9). In him God reconciles all things to himself, not only all people but all that has been created, in heaven and on earth, things visible and invisible (1:16).

The Death of Jesus, a Mystery

How can it be that the death of that one man, Jesus of Nazareth, can bring global redemption? Nowhere in the New Testament do we find any attempt to explain this. We are told only that this *had* to happen. Why? This was the great and frightening question for Jesus himself in Gethsemane. "My Father, if it is possible, let this cup pass from me" (Matt. 26:39). But Scripture is clear that his own Father shows him this way: "How then would the Scriptures be fulfilled, which say it must happen in this way" (v. 54). But why? He is unable to see the meaning of this road that leads him into death and abandonment from God. It is the road of *faith* in the love and faithfulness of God. Jesus *obeyed* the voice of his Father without understanding him. While everything he was experiencing seemed to deny the love and faithfulness of God, he believed in that love and faithfulness, and he surrendered his life to the utter darkness and abandonment from God — believing that this was the road of God's love, which would deliver the whole creation from the power of death and would lead humankind back to the life for which God created it. This is the theme of the song of praise in Philippians 2: "He . . . became obedient to the point of death, even death on a cross." Therefore every knee shall bow and every tongue shall praise God (vv. 8-11; Rom. 14:11).

While Scripture tells us that the *why* of this "divine necessity" of his death on the cross remained completely hidden for Jesus himself, the church in later centuries did not rest until it had come up with an explanation. Christ had to be obedient to the point of death, since no other price could be paid in view of God's righteousness and truth (Heidelberg Catechism, Q. 40; regarding this "payment," see also Qq. 12-16).

The Heidelberg Catechism reminds us of Jesus' statement that the Son of Man came not to be served but to serve, and to give his life a ransom for many (Matt. 20:28). But a ransom is not a debt that has to paid. Jesus does not speak of a price to be paid to God, but tells us *at what cost God saved* humanity. "God did not withhold his own Son, but gave him up for all of us," so that he might give us all things with him (Rom. 8:32). That is something else than a God who demands satisfaction! By speaking about him in such terms, people lost sight of the One who is total love. The cross is a mystery, beyond any human explanation! For the Jews it remains a stumbling block and for the Greeks it is foolishness (1 Cor. 1:22-23). And that is how it must remain if we want to stay close to Scripture.

Whom God Put Forward — The Place of Atonement

Now we come to what Paul writes in Romans 3:23-26. There are clear indications that Paul once again borrows from the Jewish church, possibly from their hymns. For we find words he does not use elsewhere.

> . . . since all have sinned and fall short of the glory of God, they are now justified by his grace as a gift, through the redemption which is in Christ Jesus, whom God put forward as a sacrifice of atonement by his blood effective through faith. He did this to show his righteousness. (Rom. 3:23-25a)[7]

We first note some specific details in this passage. "Whom God put forward as a sacrifice of atonement." What is meant is: God has made it visible to all people that he reconciles the world to himself through the cross of Jesus Christ. Paul here uses words that are related to the sacrifice of the Day of Atonement. The term translated "sacrifice of atonement" is the word for the cover of the ark, the same word that is used in the Greek text of Hebrews 9:5. This cover was called "the mercy seat" or "the place of atonement" because there the high priest once a year offered the blood as

---

7. As in 2 Corinthians 5:18-22, we find in Romans 3:25-26a terminology from the Judeo-Christian tradition. This is the only instance where Paul utilizes the words "put forward" with this connotation. Nowhere else does he use the words *hilastērion* (propitiation, expiation) and *paresis* ("pass over," RSV, or "forgiveness, remission," AV). He used the word "blood" only in connection with terms that were known to the church because of its Jewish background. See Wilckens, *Römer;* and Stuhlmacher, *Paul's Letter to the Romans.* See also Ernst Käsemann, *Commentary on Romans* (Tübingen, 1980), pp. 91-101. Georg Eichholz, *Die Theologie des Paulus im Umriss* (5th ed.; Neukirchen, 1985), pp. 190-97.

an atonement for himself and for the sins of the people (Heb. 9:3-7; v. 5 margin: "place of atonement").

Paul here establishes a link between the death of Christ on the cross and Israel's sacrificial system, in particular the Day of Atonement. The central feature of Israel's sacrificial system was the substitutionary sacrifices. They offered animals. However, "it is impossible for the blood of bulls and goats to take away sins" (Heb. 10:4).[8] Israel's sacrifices anticipated the real sacrifice, one that would in reality take away sins.

The death of Christ fulfills Israel's sacrificial service. His death was the sacrifice that took away the sins not only of Israel but of the whole world. This opened the way to the blessings for all nations that God had promised to Abraham (Gal. 3:13-14). What happened once a year behind the veil of the Holy of Holies of the Jerusalem temple to atone for the sins of Israel is now "put forward" to the whole world — the atonement of the sins of all humanity. "For there is no distinction; since all have sinned and fall short of the glory of God, they are now justified by his grace as a gift, through the redemption which is in Christ Jesus."

The gospel is the message of reconciliation with God through Christ's atonement. The rebellion that caused separation between God and humankind, and all the consequences of that separation, are removed by what God has done in Christ. And humankind answers to God's original intention: to bear the "glory of God," to be men and women after God's image (Gen. 1:26), manifesting the love of God in the midst of creation. Humanity lost this as a result of his rebellion (Rom. 3:23). Through him "whom God put forward as a sacrifice of atonement by his blood," this glory is given back to humanity — humanity in its entirety.

That glory is *life!* "All will be made alive in Christ" (1 Cor. 15:22). In the atonement God deals with our death. As sin is removed, death loses its hold on humanity. In his death he destroyed "the one who has the power of death" (Heb. 2:14). This is, therefore, not a redemption of our soul after death, leaving behind an earth where death continues. This is how many

---

8. That the sacrifices are substitutionary is clear from the story of the sacrifice of Isaac (Gen. 22). Abraham found a ram "and offered it up as a burnt offering *instead of his son.*" On that place (Mt. Moriah) the temple and the altar for the burnt offerings will be built (2 Chron. 3:1). Thus Israel's sacrificial system must be seen in the light of Abraham's sacrifice, offered at the place to which God directed him (cf. Deut. 12). The sacrifices in the temple are, just as Abraham's sacrifice of the ram, substitutionary sacrifices: *instead of the real sacrifice.* The real sacrifice has not yet been offered! Throughout Old Testament times that sacrifice remained in the future.

of us think — we find it difficult not to. But the gospel points to something different: redemption from death. All will be raised: all the dead of all ages. There will be no more death on the earth. Creation shall be set free from its bondage to decay (Rom. 8:21)

John tells us the same thing as we heard from Paul: "He is the atoning sacrifice [the expiation] for our sins, and not for ours only but also for the sins of the whole world" (1 John 2:2). In his Gospel John writes: "And just as Moses lifted up the serpent in the wilderness, so must the Son of Man be lifted up, that whoever believes in him may have eternal life" (John 3:13, 14). When in the desert Israel rebelled against God and Moses, God sent poisonous snakes and many died. The people realized that they had sinned and they cried for deliverance. God then commanded Moses to make a serpent of brass and to put it on a pole. Those who had been bitten and looked at the serpent of brass remained alive (Num. 21:4-9). Believing is simply a matter of looking — not of doing. It is a matter of looking to the One God "put forward"; looking up just as the people in the desert did: "Here is the Lamb of God, who takes away the sin of the world" (John 1:29). Look only to Him. There is no other way of salvation. It is that one event at that one place in the Jewish land in the days of the Roman governor Pontius Pilate: the crucifixion of Jesus of Nazareth near Jerusalem. For the whole world this cross is the place of atonement with God. This event has broken the power of death over the world and has put the whole human race on the road to the future of God's salvation.

The Power of the Cross Is Revealed

"For I decided to know nothing among you except Jesus Christ and him crucified," Paul writes to the Corinthians as he looks back to his first stay among them (1 Cor. 2:2). He then writes about the power of the cross: "For the message of the cross is foolishness to those who are perishing, but to us who are being saved it is the power of God" (1 Cor. 1:18). We heard the same message at the beginning of his letter to the Romans: "I am not ashamed of the gospel; it is the power of God for salvation to everyone who has faith, to the Jew first and also to the Greek. For in it the righteousness of God is revealed" (Rom. 1:16-17). The focus is on something *visible:* God's power that saves the world. He wants to make the same point in what he now writes: "the righteousness of God is manifested" (Rom. 3:21, AV; RSV). And: "He did this to show his righteousness" (3:25). Here Paul points to the source of that power: the cross of Christ. His work as an apostle has a single purpose: to direct attention to the One "whom God put forward."

This power became visible in the transformed lives of the believers. He who had conquered death was with them through the Holy Spirit whom he had given to them. They could not but speak of what they had experienced (Acts 4:20; 5:32). And the gospel of the crucified Savior spread, irresistibly. Opponents tried to silence this foolish message through persecution. But the persecuted believers remained loyal, in spite of torture, and gladly accepted even death.[9] This joy finds an echo in their hymns, such as the one from which Paul borrowed the words of this text. We also hear this joy in the words of Origen, already quoted (I, 5), who himself belonged to those who suffered torture: "But we maintain that the power of Christ's cross and of his death . . . is so great that it will be sufficient for the healing and restoration not only of the present and future ages, but even for those of the past."

4. Through Faith — A Limitation?

The Message of Unlimited Salvation

The hymns in Philippians 2 and Colossians 1 quoted above extol the salvation God offers to all people through the cross and resurrection of Jesus Christ. They do not refer to the role of faith. But here, in his letter to the Romans, Paul does refer to faith: all have sinned and fall short of God's glory, and all who believe are saved (1:16; 3:22, 25). "All who believe" — is that a limitation? Does Paul intend to say that salvation comes only to those who believe and not to those who do not believe?

In writing about faith, Paul does not want us to think of any limitations.

9. The early Christians caught people's attention through their care for the sick and fellow human beings in need, but also through the miracles that accompanied their preaching of the gospel: "God added his testimony by signs and wonders and various miracles and by gifts of the Holy Spirit" (Heb. 2:4). See Adolf von Harnack, *Die Mission und die Ausbreitung des Christentums in die ersten drei Jahrhunderten* (4th ed.; Wiesbaden, 1924), pp. 11-239; Evelyn Frost, *Christian Healing: A Consideration of the Place of Spiritual Healing in the Church of Today in the Light of the Doctrine and Practice of the Ante-Nicene Church* (3rd ed.; London, 1954), pp. 48-110. But this did not continue; "Towards the end of the third century a change had come over the Church" (Frost, *Christian Healing*, p. 68).

Paul has encountered God's love in Jesus Christ, and this encounter has awakened in him a limitless hope. If God is able to save him, a persecutor of the church, God can save all people! And that is what he wants: Along with the other apostles, God has called him (Paul) as a messenger of the gospel, the joyous message that in Christ God has reconciled the world to himself (2 Cor. 5:18-20). Who can still think of limitations?

> Or is God the God of the Jews only? Is he not the God of the Gentiles also? Yes, of the Gentiles also, since God is one; and he will justify the circumcised on the ground of faith, and the uncircumcised through the same faith. (3:29-30)

The words are precise. Paul does not say: God will justify the Jews and the Gentiles *if* they believe, or *to the extent that* they believe. He stresses two aspects: First, God will justify all people — the Jews and the non-Jews. And, second, God will do this through faith. In other words: God will bring both the Jews and the Gentiles to faith in Jesus as their Savior!

The Limitation We Have Been Taught

Paul's message of "only through faith" is not a message of limitation, but rather a message that — contrary to the law — does away with all limitations. What does this mean for what we have been taught, about salvation being limited to believers? We mention two things. First, it did not take long before the church taught that the Jewish people had made themselves unacceptable in God's eyes by their rejection of the Messiah; Israel was unworthy any longer to be considered as God's people. The church of the Gentiles had accepted Christ in faith and had thereby replaced Israel. Her faith made her worthy to be the people of God. Then, secondly, it was not long before it was generally taught that there is no salvation except through the church. Judaism required the keeping of the law and circumcision. Without these there was no salvation. The church did the same with regard to baptism and orthodoxy. It boasted that it possessed the true doctrines, just as Judaism boasted its compliance with the law of Moses and its insistence on circumcision. The "true faith" had become a required work. Thus one kind of work was replaced by a different kind of work, one restriction by another. But if God is the God of all people, any such limitation is impossible. He is not only the God of Christians, but also of non-Christians.

There is, however, a problem. *Right before our eyes we see the reality of*

91

that restriction. We see that most people do not become believers. They hear the gospel that urges them to be reconciled with God, but they do not want to be reconciled with God. And they die without having accepted the salvation that was offered to them. If God wants to save all people through faith, why does he not lead all people to this faith? So what do we do? We restrict salvation to the living. But God is not only the God of the living but also of the dead! How can he possibly be the God of living unbelievers, and not of those who have died in their unbelief! Did they cease to be his creatures after they died? If he is the God of all people, then this word of Paul must also apply to them: He will justify even the dead through faith. But, it is argued, the Bible is silent on that point. We will deal with that objection when we continue our journey (when we come to Rom. 5:12, 21). Our preliminary response is: Where does the Bible exclude this possibility? If he is said to justify all people through faith, we are not at liberty to exclude the dead. For the gospel is the message of God for whom death is no insuperable boundary. He is the God who "gives life to the dead" (Rom. 4:17).

Abraham Believed — The Temptation of the Long Wait (Gen. 15:1-6)

Paul writes the above words when he uses Abraham's faith as an example. Abraham receives the promise "as a gift"; not through keeping the law of Moses, for the law did not even exist at the time. But this "gift" does not come cheap! That is what Paul's Jewish opponents accused him of: he cheapened salvation by preaching that the Gentiles would be saved by faith alone, "without the works of the law" — that is, without obedience to the law of Moses. Abraham lived before God gave the law to Moses. When God called him, he called him to faith in his promise. That did not mean that it was easy for Abraham. For faith in God is a faith that is constantly challenged. It means clinging to what God has promised, while his everyday experience tells him that it is an illusion. God had called him and had given him the promise that he would become a great nation, and that in him — or, as we are told later, in his people (Gen. 22:18) — God would bless all nations on earth. But nothing happens. At last, Abraham is faced with the fact that nothing can happen anymore. His own age and his wife's age preclude that there will yet be a child. He is disappointed. God has given him a world-encompassing promise, and then lets everything continue as it is! Abraham does not give up on the promise, but the painful fact that God does not act leads him to despondency.

92

In that situation God appears once more to him — in a vision — and says, "Do not be afraid, Abram, I am your shield; your reward shall be very great." Abraham's answer reflects his despondency: "What will you give me, for I continue childless. . . ." And then it happens!

> He brought him outside and said, "Look toward heaven and count the stars, if you are able to count them." Then he said to him, "So shall your descendants be." And he believed the LORD; and the LORD reckoned it to him as righteousness. (Gen. 15:5, 6)

It is an unforgettable scene. The clear, moonless sky. A heaven dotted with innumerable stars. Abraham, an old man, how small he looks. He stands beside God. "Look above you," says God. And Abraham looks up and sees the starry skies. "Count them, if you can," says God. "So shall be your posterity." And Abraham believed God.

God did not yet do what Abraham wanted. He remained childless for years to come. But he believed God. He believed, Paul writes, that he would "inherit" the world (Rom. 4:13). He believed that God had called him to be the father of many nations (v. 17). How this "many" is to be understood is clear from God's reference to the starry skies. "So shall be your posterity." Too large to count — limitless. Abraham believed God, "fully convinced that God was able to do what he had promised. Therefore his faith was reckoned to him as righteousness" (Rom. 4:21, 22). "The LORD reckoned it to him as righteousness" (Gen. 15:6). Let us make sure that we do not misunderstand this word "reckoned." Abraham is not merely called righteous by God, while in reality he is still his old self. No, from this moment onward, Abraham is for God the right man to bring his plans to fruition, because he believed God's words. So he did what God wanted him to do. And in so doing, he brought joy to God's heart!

Abraham and the History of Israel

What did this faith imply? It would all begin with his "very own issue" (Gen. 15:4). And it would continue from generation to generation. He would become a great nation. But that is not the essence: The people of Abraham will be God's people! God himself will go with this people, from generation to generation. The ties between him and this people are never to be broken.

And this promise is for all Israel, not just for a "remnant" from this people, or from the many nations. "So shall be your descendants" — like that entire starry sky. If part of these stars were to fall into endless darkness, this would run contrary to what God had promised. Abraham believed that God was able to fulfill the promise in its entirety. It could not turn out to be less because God had said so! Abraham truly believed God.

Abraham built his faith on him "who justifies the ungodly," Paul writes (Rom. 4:5). Was Abraham an "ungodly" person? Had he led an "ungodly" life? That is not what Paul says. He says: God would do what he had promised, and — this is very important — this was not contingent on his works, nor on the works of his posterity. It only depended on the faithfulness of God, who is able to do what he has promised. This people often will be unfaithful and disobedient, but this unfaithfulness and disobedience will never be the last word.

> For the promise that he would inherit the world did not come to Abraham or his descendants through the law, but through the righteousness of faith. . . . For this reason it depends on faith, that the promise may rest on grace and be guaranteed to all his descendants, not only to the adherents of the law but also to those who share the faith of Abraham, for he is the father of us all. . . . (Rom. 4:13, 16)

Be guaranteed is the terminology Paul uses. The promise would not be guaranteed if it depended upon Israel's faithfulness and obedience, and — let us not overlook this either — on the faithfulness and obedience of the believers from the Gentiles.

We now turn to the history of Israel that follows. Abraham is in heaven with God. He sees what is happening. He sees Israel in Egypt; Israel liberated through the ministry of Moses; the encounter with God near the mountain in the Sinai desert; the giving of the law. Then he sees something terrible: his children dancing around a golden calf. If it now depended on works, on the obedience of his posterity, it could only end in disaster. But Abraham looks to God. He believes his promise. Whatever evil is committed by Israel, it does not come unexpected as far as God is concerned. He knew what he was doing when he called him. And nothing will make him abandon what he promised Abraham. Then Abraham sees the day of the Messiah. He had longed for that day (John 8:56). For *he* will save his people from their sins (Matt. 1:21). God has given his children everything he could give! But *then* there comes the day of Calvary. Abraham looks intently. What is it God is doing? God takes his Son, his only one, whom he loves, and sacrifices him — the Lamb of God that takes away the sin of the world (Gen. 22; John 1:29). What, however, are his children doing? "But they kept urgently

94

demanding with loud shouts that he should be crucified; and their voices prevailed" (Luke 23:23). This is the moment of truth: Will God justify the ungodly? On this Abraham has built his faith. And it happens: God raises Jesus from the dead — as Israel's Messiah! Now nothing can stop the fulfillment of the promise: All nations will be blessed through his posterity. This posterity does not drop its resistance against the Messiah. But the Messiah does not give up on his people — never! It is a matter of waiting — for many centuries. But Abraham believes God, "fully convinced that God is able to do what he has promised" (Rom. 4:21).

Following in the Steps of Abraham's Faith

Paul has described what God is going to do. God will justify the circumcised through faith in Jesus (3:30). Paul thought it would not take long before God would bring the Jews to faith in Jesus. But we live almost two thousand years later. Nothing suggests that Israel regrets its rejection of Jesus as the Messiah. Has history not shown Paul to be wrong? And what about the promise that God will justify the uncircumcised through faith in Jesus. Who in the world believes that all people will come to be reconciled with God? We live in a church that has grown used to the fact that most people will not accept the gospel and has simply learned to accept that.

But look at Abraham. When God gives Abraham his promise, and when Abraham believes, the fulfillment is nowhere in sight. All has yet to happen. Nothing suggests that it is about to happen. Then Isaac is born. The name means: *he laughs.* Abraham and Sarah had to laugh when God spoke to them — it was simply impossible (Gen. 18:17; 18:12)! Again and again the path of the promise is marked by the ridiculous — "this simply cannot be."

But is there no limit to waiting? Is it not absurd to keep on waiting when nothing happens for over nineteen centuries? No, there is no limit. It is an essential aspect of faith that there is no such limit. There are two options if, after nineteen centuries, the promise of Scripture has not yet been fulfilled: We stop believing what the Bible says and admit that we were chasing an illusion, or we keep on expecting what has been promised. Believing in God means: If something he has promised has not yet happened, then it will happen in the future; even if it takes so long that this in itself would make it ridiculous to continue believing — keep on believing that God's promises are true, and that we will not be disappointed in that confidence. That is what following in the footsteps of Abraham's faith means. It implies that we will not escape the temptation of the long wait

95

by focusing our expectation on something we find easier to believe in — the salvation of our souls after death, or some other form of continued existence, while on earth death still has the final word. Abraham did not tone down God's promise. "Count the stars, if you can — thus will be your posterity," God had said. And he truly believed. He believed that God would bless all nations through him. God's blessing would deliver the earth from the curse, from death and corruption, and God would lead all humanity to the life for which he had created man. It was impossible to exaggerate what God would do for humanity. Think of the starry sky! To such a faith we have been called. For, Paul concludes, what was written about Abraham's faith was written for the sake of us, "who believe in him who raised Jesus our Lord from the dead, who was handed over to death for our trespasses and was raised for our justification" (Rom. 4:24-25). For *our* trespasses and for *our* justification — does that mean that it is limited to the church? Indeed, in this passage Paul writes about the church: We are justified through faith and enjoy peace with God (5:1). But in what follows we shall see even more clearly that for Paul believing in God has nothing to do with limiting God's salvation as something that is only for the church. For faith is following in the footsteps of Abraham's faith. That kind of faith is limitless hope.[10]

10. A proponent of this hope is J. C. Blumhardt (see IX): "He will cover all generations of the earth with his grace of forgiveness. And because he is the Judge over both the dead and the living, He can be a merciful Judge of the dead who have passed away in blindness. For He is the Compassionate One. Let us entrust everything to his mercy! For, when we burn with desire for his compassion, nothing will be too great to expect from Him, nothing too daring to ask Him or to seek from Him" (sermon, 1875, in *Predigtblätter aus Bad Boll,* 1180, p. 232). Witnesses of an entirely different tradition have said the same. H. U. von Balthasar (*Schwestern im Geist, Therese von Lisieux und Elisabeth von Dijon* [3rd ed.; Einsiedeln, 1978], p. 319) writes about Teresa of Lisieux (1873-1897): " 'Believe my words, for they are true: We can never have too much confidence in God's love, which is so powerful and compassionate. We get from Him as much as we expect to receive.' And that is only the minimum, for Teresa knows what the Lord spoke to St. Mechthild: 'I say this in truth, that I am extremely delighted, when men and women expect great things from me. . . . In actual fact, it is impossible that someone will not receive, what he has believed and hoped for in view of my power and compassion.' "

5. Adam, the Abiding Unity of the Human Race

Adam and Christ

In this section of his letter (Rom. 5:12-21) Paul refers back to the first chapters of the Bible, which tell us about the creation of the human race. *Adam* (v. 14) is the Hebrew word for "humanity." Humanity shares the same origin, and this origin is portrayed as the first human being. This origin teaches us that everything human on this earth, from the earliest beginning, is a divinely ordained unity. It also tells us that humanity has one destiny in this unity: to live amid all that God created as people who are "God's image, his likeness" (Gen. 1:26-27), as bearers of his salvation for all creation. This was the task of the human race, and it was against this assignment — as we learned in the first part of this letter — that the first humans rebelled. Thus they became bearers of misery: their disobedience caused death to rule on earth — contrary to God's intentions!

Paul's argument is far from simple. He interrupts himself in verse 13, and picks up the thread again in verse 18. Therefore, we do well first to read verses 12, 18, and 19.

> Therefore, just as sin came into the world through one man, and death came through sin, and so death spread to all because all have sinned. . . . (Rom. 5:12)

> Therefore, just as one man's trespass led to condemnation for all, so one man's act of righteousness leads to justification and life for all. For just as by the one man's disobedience the many were made sinners, so by the one man's obedience the many will be made righteous. (vv. 18-19; we will return to "the many")

We discover that Paul relates the history of Adam to what God has done in Jesus Christ. In so doing, he makes clear that the salvation God has realized in Christ encompasses all humanity, from the beginning. All who lived on this earth and died, and all who will live and die in the future, are united, and together they will be delivered from the power of death and will be brought to the destiny for which God created the human race. This has been revealed by Christ's resurrection.

A few years prior to Romans Paul wrote the same to the Corinthians:

> But in fact Christ has been raised from the dead, the first fruits of those who have died. For since death came through a human being, the resur-

rection from the dead has also come through a human being; for as all die in Adam, so will all be made alive in Christ. (1 Cor. 15:20-22)

This concise wording points up the sharp contrast with our tradition. We hear it in the words of the Heidelberg Catechism:

Are all men, then, saved by Christ, as they have perished by Adam? — No; only such as by true faith are ingrafted into him, and receive all his benefits. (Q. 20)

Thus a restriction: "No." Some editions of this catechism make reference to Matthew 7:14 to support this "No": "For the gate is narrow and the road is hard that leads to life, and there are few who find it." They also cite Matthew 22:14: "For many are called, but few are chosen." Twice we find the word "few." These references are then followed by some texts that indicate that human beings can be saved only by faith. There is no attempt whatsoever to explain what Paul says about Adam and Christ! Does Scripture contradict itself? Or did Paul not intend to say that the salvation through Christ covers all human beings?

The Other Law

Strangely enough, Paul first takes up the subject of the law of Moses and, in particular, that of the period before the giving of the law.

Sin was indeed in the world before the law, but sin is not reckoned when there is no law. Yet death exercised dominion from Adam to Moses. . . . (Rom. 5:13-14a)

Why does the apostle want to speak about the time before Moses? His motive is the same as when he exclaimed: "Or is God the God of Jews only? Is he not the God of Gentiles also. Yes, of Gentiles also" (3:29). Of Gentiles also: God's work does not begin with Israel, nor is it limited to Israel. It begins with the first human being and comprises all humanity.

Paul here refers to God's law before the law had been given to Moses. We saw in Romans 1:19 already that God spoke to human beings from the beginning. He made his will known to them. In some sense or another, this is his *law:* "The LORD God commanded the man . . ." (Gen. 2:16). Some interpreters argue that God did not "reckon" sin in the period from Adam to Moses because there was no law. That, however, is not Paul's line of thought. Sin was "reckoned." That is evident from the fact that death ruled over humankind from the days of Adam. Because they had sinned, they were subject to death (Rom. 5:14). And this fact implies that there was a law. For "sin is not reckoned when there is no law" (v. 13).

We agree with the the authors of the comments in the margin of the Dutch Statenvertaling. Paul believed, they write,

> . . . that there was indeed another law, and by disobeying that law all people in that time were also sinners; and that not only the natural law. . . , but the law which God had given to Adam . . . to all . . . is "reckoned. . . ."

The first humans knew God's will. That was true not only for Adam, the first human, but for humanity in general: all humanity that issued from the first human. This is true not because God's will was, from the beginning, communicated from father to son, but because God himself unceasingly communicated his will. This "other law" somehow reveals the same will of God that is made known in the law of Moses. "He has showed you, O man *(adam)*, what is good" (Mic. 6:8, AV).

Because God communicates his will, Cain knows he has committed a crime too great to bear. Thus the crime is "reckoned" to him: "And now, you are cursed . . ." (Gen. 4:13, 11). And when subsequently, in the story of Noah, we are told that the earth was filled with violence (Gen. 6:11, 13), it is not because they did not know any better! No, they had no excuse (Rom. 1:20). Therefore it was "reckoned" to them — what other reason could there have been for the Flood? We also encounter this other law in Noah's story:

> For your own lifeblood I will surely require a reckoning: from every animal I will require it and from human beings, each one for the blood of another, I will require a reckoning for human life. (Gen. 9:5)

"Thou shalt not kill." Cain was the first to kill another human being; Lamech enjoyed killing people (Gen. 4:23-24). That caused the earth to be filled with violence. The right of the strongest prevailed, and this is what God's commandment addresses. He keeps on emphasizing this commandment, and he continues to "reckon" when it is being trespassed: He will continue to exact the life of the one who was killed from the hand of his brother who took his life.

The story of Sodom also shows that Scripture assumes that people know the difference between good and evil; the destruction of Sodom is like the Flood: a "reckoning" of the evil that has been committed.[11] This "other law" might be called "the law for the nations." It is not a different law, in the sense that it announces a divine will that differs from the law given to Israel. But there is a significant difference.

In speaking to Abraham, God makes himself known to him. He is the God who wants to bless all nations, and he calls Abraham to serve him with that purpose in mind. That is the content of God's promise to him (Gen. 12:3). In this respect God makes a distinction between Israel and the other nations.

The Ten Commandments begin with the self-revelation of God. He is the God who delivers his people: "I am the LORD your God, who brought you out of the land of Egypt, out of the house of slavery." And this law, given through Moses, calls all Israel to the service of his promise to Abraham; Israel is the people through which he will lead all peoples to his salvation. Therefore Israel is not allowed to "have other gods before him" (Exod. 20:1-2).[12] But is this "law for the nations" a law without promise? No, God never gives a law without promise; his promise is also for the nations of the earth. But the promise was embedded in Israel!

The "Reckoning" Not a Fate — Hereditary Sin

God made his will known to human beings and they rebelled against him. But humans are unable to free themselves from this rebellion. They caused sin to enter the world, and through sin death came. We are all born under that dominion: No one can avoid it "because all have sinned" (Rom. 5:12). Following Augustine, tradition speaks of original sin or hereditary sin. It says: Because Adam sinned, humankind sinned even before birth, and as a result all must die! This line of thinking is at odds with what Paul wrote

11. Calvin (*The Epistle of Paul the Apostle to the Romans* [Edinburgh, 1961], p. 112) writes: "The punishment of Cain, the deluge which destroyed the whole world, the downfall of Sodom . . . testify that God has laid men's iniquities to their charge." We will not discuss the difference between Adam's sin and that of his posterity ("not like the transgression of Adam," v. 14).

12. In Galatians 3:19 we read that Moses' law was added to the promise, "until the offspring would come to whom the promise had been made." Here, in Romans 5 we find: "But law came in" (v. 20). Here, too, it must refer to the promise. Paul points to the purpose of the Mosaic law: the rule of sin — with death as its final result — is annulled, to be replaced by the rule of grace, with eternal life in Christ as its final result (Rom. 5:21). In other words, the purpose of the law is the fulfillment of the promise to Israel.

earlier. All evidence suggests that in speaking about God's "reckoning" of sins, Paul refers to sins committed by the individual himself and does not speak in terms of hereditary sin as a guilt of the first human, which is "reckoned" as the sin of all his posterity.[13]

Yet, there is this link with that first sin, which we cannot fathom. All human beings are born slaves to sin (Rom. 6:6, 17). They do not commit sin because they are forced to do so; they are the ones who sin and they themselves bear responsibility for what they do. That is the element of truth in the doctrine of hereditary sin. But tradition has burdened this doctrine with other implications. It suggests that, because of this link with our ancestors, hereditary sin is a matter of inescapable fate! And its final consequence will be that the vast majority of humankind will end in perdition. That is the opposite of what Paul is arguing!

Here we return to our exposition of Romans 1:18 and 19: God comes with his law to all people, from generation to generation, without any exceptions, and he holds them accountable for their sins. This fact demonstrates, first of all, that he insists on the unity of the entire human race; and, next, that he has not abandoned his purpose for any of them. It is his only purpose: that all will eventually do the good for which he has created them. If we were to speak of another purpose, we would speak about another God than the Scriptures talk about. For it is *utterly impossible that God reveals his will to human beings, and simultaneously wills that they should not reach the point of doing God's will.* Yet, this is what tradition tells us. It suggests that he would reveal his will to people who were destined not to comply with it. Presumably, he would have no other purpose than to let all, except for a few elect, end up in eternal suffering as a punishment for their sins. That is what the doctrine of hereditary sins implies.

In contrast I contend that if God continues to make his will known to people, and *if he continues to hold them accountable for their sins, then he has not abandoned his purpose for humankind.* In his judgment he says "No" to the evil committed by people, because he wants them to be different and to act differently.

13. The Vulgate renders Romans 5:12 as: "in quo omnes peccaverunt." Augustine understood these words as a reference to hereditary sin: "in Adam all have sinned" (*Enchiridion,* 26). He taught that because of original sin unbaptized children will be eternally lost; nevertheless they will suffer the lightest degree of punishment (*Enchiridion,* 93).

THE ONE PURPOSE OF GOD

Romans 5:19 states his purpose: that all may be made righteous, that all will do justice, that all will be messengers of salvation in his creation. There we are also told that this purpose will be achieved! That is the message of the gospel: Through the cross and resurrection of Jesus Christ God demonstrates that he did not subject humankind to a blind fate, but rather that he has no other purpose, and never had any other purpose, than that all might inherit the life for which he created them.

A Unity from Which No One Can Be Excluded

In pointing back to Adam, Paul speaks, as we saw, about the beginning of humanity as given and intended by God. Through this beginning humanity is a unity, indivisibly united, members of one family. It is a unity from which no one can be excluded. Cain apparently can do without his brother, but this precisely shows his rebellion against God. He does not want to be his brother's keeper, but God does want him to be that. God has created man with the intention that all should love one another, as he loves them. This love allows of no exception: One is even to love one's enemies, since God loves them all (Matt. 5:44-45).

If God had, and continues to have, such intentions for humankind, it is impossible that he would want the human race to be divided into two eternally separated categories. Yes, we hear about the twofold result of God's judgment: a saved humanity and a lost humanity. But because of this unity he has intended, he himself will never acquiesce in this division. What he intended as a unity when he created it, he *continues* to intend as a unity. He continues to consider it a unity from which no one can be excluded, and this remains the content of his law for humankind. For that reason his children cannot, yes, are forbidden to, accept the eternal absence of their fellow human beings: an eternal separation between those who are saved and those who are lost. *In God's law, the single command of love, given to all human beings, we find the answer to the doctrine of eternal punishment.* This law makes it crystal clear that we are dealing with a doctrine that clashes with God's commandment. But, as we will yet see, it is not the complete answer.

More Than Compensated

In Romans 5:15-17 Paul emphasizes a "much more." God's gift in Jesus Christ far exceeds what was lost in Adam. We already saw that through him

God's goal for humanity has been reached. That could not be said about the first people. They were told to till and keep God's creation (Gen. 2:15). That creation was threatened by powers of evil, in enmity with God. Adam was called to conquer those powers — to be a blessing for creation. But he failed. Through his disobedience he brought the rule of death over all. The new Adam God has given is, through his obedience, conqueror of sin and death. Thus he does not simply bring humanity back to the situation of the beginning, where the victory was yet to be gained. If so, he would simply provide compensation for what had gone wrong at the outset. Humanity would once again face the task of conquering evil, and what happened in the beginning could happen again! But the gospel offers more: Not only has the evil caused in creation by the first Adam been overcome; through him, the new Adam, everything is more than restored. No longer is there an enemy to be defeated — he has been defeated once and for all.

That is the joyous message of Jesus Christ of which Paul is the bearer. Not less than in Adam, all of humanity is comprised in him. Nor does he compensate only for what humanity lost in the beginning: through him God's purpose for humankind is fulfilled. Through one act of transgression death came to rule as king, but through the One, Jesus Christ, much more is received than was ever possessed: They will live and exercise dominion through the One, Jesus Christ (Rom. 5:17). God created the human race that it might rule over his creation, as beings created in his image, after his likeness; as bearers of his blessings for all creatures, just as the One who went through Galilee, healing all kinds of sickness and diseases of the people — "conformed to the image of his Son" (8:29). That must be the "glory of God," of which we now "fall short" (3:23). We will hear more about this glory when Paul writes about the children of God as deliverers of his creation (8:19-21).

6. All the Living and All the Dead

Church Tradition Clashes with Scripture

In its response to Question 20, the Heidelberg Catechism denies that just as all are condemned in Adam, all will be saved through Christ. Salvation is restricted to those who, *through true faith,* are included in him. Here we encounter the main objection of our tradition against the interpretation of Romans 5, as we have just outlined: Not all people believe, and therefore, whatever Paul writes in Romans 5, it cannot mean that all people will be saved through Christ.

Commenting on this verse, Calvin writes that Paul here compares Christ with Adam to clarify that he

> was not privately righteous on his own account, but the righteousness with which He was endowed was more extensive, in order that He might enrich believers with the gift conferred upon Himself. Paul makes grace common to all men, not because it in fact extends to all, but because it is offered to all. Although Christ suffered for the sins of the world, and is offered by the goodness of God without distinction to all men, yet not all receive Him.[14]

Presumably, Paul's only suggestion was that God *offers* his grace to all people, but since only few accept it, only a few are saved. The authors of the notes in the margin of the Dutch Statenvertaling follow Calvin in this view. In their comment on "justification for all," they write: "That is to say: For those who believe in Him; or, those who accept this gift." If that is what Paul means to say, how he could say what he says is something these commentators do not deal with. Apparently they did not see a problem here.

But later exegetes did see the problem. Twice Paul refers to "all," "just as all were condemned, so all will be justified." The first time he means all people, but the second time presumably, only believers. S. Greijdanus comments on the words "just as": "This refers to the similarity between the relationship of Christ to all his own, and that of Adam to all mankind." He explains "all his own" as "all who have been given by the Father to Christ, and which He bought with his blood."[15] Herman Ridderbos agrees with this view: "The final question is, what is meant by this twice-repeated word 'all'? In the first instance, no doubt all Adam's descendants are intended. . . . The same cannot be said about the one act of righteousness that leads to justification and life for all. For that is limited to those who (through faith) have accepted that gift of justification." Here he refers to v. 17: "those who receive the abundance of grace." The words that Ridderbos places between parentheses are crucial: through faith. For only through faith will they receive this abundance. He continues: "The essence of the similarity be-tween Adam and Christ is not that in both cases the same categories of

14. Calvin, *Romans*, pp. 117-18.
15. Greijdanus, *Romeinen*, 1:288.

people are intended, but rather that, not only in the sin of the one, but also in the righteousness of the Other, all mankind that belonged to them was involved."[16] Thus, for Ridderbos, "all humankind that belongs to Christ" is restricted to that part of humankind that believes in him.

If this exegesis is correct, it is not true that Christ, through his obedience, more than compensates for the havoc wreaked by the first human's disobedience. If Paul writes "much more," it surely must be understood in terms of much more grace, but much more grace for far fewer people. Paul's omission of "far fewer people" is simply due to the fact that it was self-evident for him and the church that it affected far fewer people. Thus we arrive at an explanation that harmonizes with the pessimism of our tradition. These commentators expend considerable energy in their attempts to convince us that these words of Paul cannot possibly mean what they appear to say: that God in Christ wants to save the entire human race.

The Present of the Church and the Future of Humanity

Calvin argues that Paul compares Christ with Adam in order to prove that he was not just righteous for his own sake, but for the sake of others. The two other exegetes take a slightly different approach: Paul wants to stress that the salvation of Christ is for all believers, not just for some of them. Were these the questions the believers in Rome wanted to be answered? Did Paul, when writing about the reconciliation that God brought about in Christ, leave the church in the dark as to whether he did this for his own sake or for the sake of others, and whether this does include *all* who believe in him? That was his opening statement! "The gospel . . . is the power of God for salvation to everyone who has faith" (Rom. 1:16)! This was the constant theme in what he had written so far. The argument about Adam and Christ was not needed to shed any further light on this point.

But what does Paul intend to say when he compares Christ with Adam? We must pay attention to the context. Paul begins as follows: "Since we are justified by faith, we have peace with God through our Lord Jesus Christ,

---

16. Ridderbos, *Romeinen*, p. 121. W. Hendriksen (*Romans* [Grand Rapids, 1981], 1:182-83) defends the view that "all" in this case applies only to believers. He adduces the following reason: "Paul is combatting the ever-present tendency of Jews to regard themselves as being better than Gentiles." Thus: not all people, but all believers from the Jews and from the Gentiles, without any distinction. This is just another example of explanations that are devised all the time.

through whom we have obtained access to this grace in which we stand" (Rom. 5:1-2). And: "We boast in our hope of sharing the glory of God" (v. 2); and: "the hope does not disappoint us, because God's love has been poured into our hearts through the Holy Spirit that has been given to us" (v. 5). And: "God proves his love for us in that while we were still sinners Christ died for us" (v. 9). Paul here refers to "us" and "we," the believers: what the church has received through faith in Christ.

Then he continues his discourse on Adam. In fact, he describes the hope of the church. This hope extends to all humanity. Paul thus makes a distinction between the church, which believes in Jesus, and the world, which does not. He writes about the church in the present tense: We are justified by faith, we have peace with God, God's love has been poured into our hearts, we are reconciled to God, we now have received reconciliation (vv. 1, 5, 10, 11). Then he writes about the whole of humanity in the future tense: All people will be justified, and the many will be made righteous (vv. 18-19). Therefore: *What we already have, all people will have in the future.* To make sure that this "all" is without any limitation, Paul here compares Christ with Adam: It applies to all people of all times, from the beginning of creation.

We note that verse 18 refers to "all," whereas verse 19 refers to "many," or, more precisely, "the many." This word "many" does not imply a restriction: many people, but not all. Paul in no way weakens what he said in verse 18, where he emphasized that *all* will be justified. We encounter the same phenomenon in verse 12 and verse 15. First of all, death has spread to all; second, the many die through Adam's trespass. Obviously, in the latter case no one is excluded from "the many." Paul uses the word "many" to indicate the extension of the "all" mentioned in verse 18: all people who have ever lived and have died on this earth, and all who are yet to follow — the great multitude that no one can number (see VII, 5).[17]

---

17. In the *Theological Dictionary of the New Testament* (under *polloi*, 6:536-46) Joachim Jeremias points to the inclusive use of "many" in Hebrew parlance. The term *kol* ("the entirety") serves to express totality, whereas the word *rabbim* expresses the fullness of that totality. Cf. Isaiah 2:2-3: All *(kol)* the nations shall stream to it. Many *(rabbim)* peoples shall come. This reference to "many" peoples does not mean that some are excluded; the idea is that the nations cannot be numbered. We regularly encounter the same usage in the New Testament. Therefore, the ransom for "many" in Matthew 20:28 is identical with the ransom for "all" in 1 Timothy 2:6. And here, in Romans 5:18-19, we find (just as in Isa. 2:2-3) that in the same breath "many" and "all" are mentioned. (Of course, this does not apply when, as in Matthew 7:13-14 and 22:14, the few are put *over against* the many.)

By means of the comparison between Christ and Adam, Paul develops what he wrote previously: "All have sinned and will be justified by his grace as a gift, through the redemption that is in Christ Jesus" (3:23-24). The evil that has been brought about by Adam extends to the whole of humanity, without any exception. And the salvation that Christ brings extends to the whole of humanity without any exception, comprising everyone, just as Adam's fall did. What God intended with the creation of humanity and what was not achieved because of the disobedience of "the man from the beginning," that is achieved through the One who was obedient, Jesus Christ. Only when this has been said has Paul set forth the full scope of the gospel.

The Dead Will Believe

This, however, does not yet fully answer our question. What we now possess, we have through faith in Jesus Christ: "Since we are justified by faith . . ." (Rom. 5:1). Just as it can already be said of us, it will have to be said of all people that they are justified by faith! Paul earlier wrote along the same lines: "Since God is one; and He will justify the circumcised on the ground of faith and the uncircumcised through that same faith" (Rom. 3:30). Considering that most people die without having come to faith in Christ, this must mean that they will come to believe at some time after their death. Where does Scripture give us reason to entertain that hope?

Note that Paul emphatically refers to death: "and death came through sin, and so death spread to all because all have sinned" (Rom. 5:12); "yet death exercised dominion from Adam to Moses . . ." (v. 14); "if because of the one man's trespass, death exercised dominion . . ." (v. 17); "so that, just as sin exercised dominion in death . . ." (v. 21). And in verse 15 he writes about the dead. Let us take a closer look at that text: "But the free gift is not like the trespass. For if the many died through the one man's trespass, much more surely have the grace of God and the free gift in the grace of the one man, Jesus Christ, abounded for the many." Of those "many" who have died it is said that for them the grace of that one man, Jesus Christ, has abounded. What else can this mean than that the salvation God offers in Jesus Christ covers all who died from the beginning of the world?

But — remember our question — is it possible that someone can come to believe in Jesus Christ after his death? Note first of all that even during this life no one can decide to believe. The real question is: Is God able to bring a person after his death to faith in him? Well, just as surely as he can bring the living into an encounter with him, he can do that with the dead. And just as surely as in this encounter he can give the living faith in him, he can do the same with the dead. He is the God who gives life to the dead and calls into existence the things that do not exist (Rom. 4:17). For him death poses no limit to what he can do.

The basic question is: Does God *want* this? Where in the Bible do we read that God intends to bring the dead to an encounter with him, so that they may be saved? We read it here! God's grace has abounded for the many who have died (v. 15). And: For all who have been led to condemnation, there is justification and life (v. 18). This reference to "life" also indicates that this verse deals with the dead. They were dead as a result of God's condemnation. In this passage Paul does not retract what he wrote about the judgment in Romans 2:5-11. No, rather he wants to clarify God's intentions with regard to those who have been condemned: they might yet be justified unto life. And since God justifies people through faith (Rom. 3:30), he will also justify them through faith. That death is no obstacle for him in the realization of his plan of salvation, is confirmed by Paul's words in the conclusion of his letter, which we will now discuss.

Kingship over the Dead and the Living

> For to this end Christ died and lived again, so that he might be Lord of both the dead and the living. (Rom. 14:9)

We notice that the emphasis is on the dead: they are mentioned first. That the dead fall under Christ's kingship means that he can reach them. They are just as reachable as the living! Through his resurrection he has broken through the boundary of death for good so that it no longer matters! The dead now have the Victor over death as their king! A divinely given king has as his task to assure the salvation of those who are under his rule:

> For he delivers the needy when they call, the poor and those who have no helper. He has pity on the weak and the needy, and saves the lives of the needy. (Ps. 72:12-13)

If a king has conquered death and he is appointed to rule over the dead, what else can this mean for those dead than their salvation? What purpose would his victory over death have if he would not use it to free his subjects from the archenemy who keeps them prisoners? What other reason could there be why he was resurrected by God?[18] His kingship brings salvation for all who have died, for it does not apply only to some of the dead, while the rest remain subject to the old ruler. That ruler has lost his power (2 Tim. 1:10)! Therefore 1 Corinthians 15:22 tells us that all who die in Adam will be brought back to life in Christ. Not all at the same time — this will be the subject of our next chapter — but all, nonetheless.

As we said before, Paul takes back nothing of what he said earlier about the coming judgment. What he writes in Romans 14:10 about Christ's lordship over both the living and the dead also applies to the judgment: "For we will all stand before the judgment seat of God." The dead are not excluded from this. We should beware not to take away from the seriousness of standing before God's judgment seat. But the final word is: "Every knee shall bow to me, and every tongue shall give praise to God" (vv. 10-12). Or, as we find it in the hymn of praise in Philippians: "At the name of Jesus every knee should bend . . . and every tongue should confess that Jesus Christ is Lord," to the glory of God, the Father.

We now repeat our question: Will God bring even those who died without having come to faith in him to the point where they will believe? Well, if every knee bows to the name of Jesus, and every tongue confesses his lordship, that is *the confession of their faith*. They praise him from the bottom of their heart. For God's grace, and the gift of that grace through that one man, Jesus Christ, has abounded for them — the many who had died (Rom. 5:15)!

18. To the early church it did not seem strange that Jesus should have gone to the dead. The *Odes of Solomon* (end of the first or beginning of the second century) are considered to be a collection of very early Christian hymns. In *Ode* 42 — the last — we hear Christ speak about his victory over death. Sheol — the realm of the dead — has been conquered. The dead hasten toward Christ and cry: "Son of God, have mercy on us; deal with us according to your kindness and lead us from the chains of darkness. . . . Let us also be redeemed with You, for You are our Redeemer." Jesus hears their plea: "And I heard their voice, and placed their faith in my heart. And I placed my name upon their head, because they are free and they are mine." It is clear that they want to be his (J. H. Charlesworth, *The Old Testament Pseudepigrapha* [London, 1985], 2:771). Walter Bauer translates (in E. Hennecke, *Neutestamentliche Apokryphen* [4th ed.; Tübingen, 1971], pp. 623-25: "und Ich nam mir zu Herzen ihren Glauben" (And I took their faith to my heart). According to Charlesworth, most scholars now believe that the *Odes* in their present form are not of Gnostic origin (as Bauer thought), but are "plainly Christian" (note p. 725).

A Misguided Hope

We have found what we were looking for in what Paul writes in these verses. Here we have discovered the foundation for our hope for the many — even hope for the dead.[19] We are now assured: God wants all people to be saved, and that remains his desire even after their death. We therefore know that he cannot possibly desire their eternal destruction, not even in the judgment. That is what these words tell us.

This brings us to a major question. Does it make sense to continue our journey through Romans? What else do we need? We already said: In what Paul writes about Adam and Christ, we find our answer to the doctrine of eternal punishment. But there is more to say. Strange as it may seem, this conviction that eventually God will save all people can be accompanied by a sense of despondency. If our expectation cannot get beyond this, we are compelled to accept the status quo. We must simply accept that now most will reject the gospel: now we get nowhere, now everything goes wrong with the world, and nothing can be done about it. But, so we tell ourselves, eventually, in the hereafter, everything will come out all right. That, however, is a misguided hope! That kind of hope can easily become an excuse to let evil have its way. That is not the living hope proclaimed in the gospel.

The hope of the gospel calls the church to gospel service. The Lord of the harvest wants the entire harvest to be gathered in. That is a message of joy! But the harvest does not get saved automatically. It is saved through

---

19. Some have tried to build hope for the dead on the puzzling words of 1 Peter 3:19-20. This passage tells us that Christ preached to the "spirits in prison" who lived at the time of Noah. We cannot be sure that this text refers to dead *people,* but even if that were so, it does not include *all* who have died. This is not Peter's concern — note that nothing is said about the salvation of these spirits. For our present study 1 Peter 4:6 has more relevance. There the apostle clearly deals with the dead to whom the gospel has been preached for their salvation (cf. n. 18). Peter looks back and mentions this aspect in the context of the future judgment. He is not dealing here with what Christ means for all who have died in the past and will die in the future. That, however, is Paul's concern in Romans 5:12-21; 14:9; and 1 Corinthians 15:20-28.

Of special interest are the attempts by Augustine, and subsequently many others, to prove that Peter cannot have meant that Christ wants to save those who have died without salvation; those attempts are so unconvincing that they tend to suggest the opposite (e.g., H. Bavinck, *Dogmatiek,* 3:479-80; 4:608; S. Greijdanus, *De Brieven van de Apostelen Petrus, Johannes en Judas* [Amsterdam, 1929]). For the history of this exegesis, see D. A. du Toit, *Neergedaald ter helle* (Kampen, 1971), pp. 131-35, 164-65, and 186-87.

the service of workers called by the Lord to labor in his harvest (Matt. 9:37-38). We therefore note that Paul, as soon as he has held out the salvation of all humanity, writes about this call of believers to be instruments of righteousness (Rom. 6:13, 17-23). The service to which they are called is to advance God's saving righteousness; it is a service rendered to him who wants to save this world. Only where this task is taken up, does the church become what God wants her to be: a light, radiating hope for this world! That is clear from what Paul writes about the delivery of all creation and the task of God's children (Rom. 8:19-22).

CHAPTER IV

The Salvation of the Church and of the World (Romans 8)

1. The Deliverance of the World Lost in Sin

The Deliverance of Creation in Scripture

Paul concluded his argument about Adam and Christ by stating that, as sin has ruled through death, so grace will rule through justification, leading to eternal life through Jesus Christ, our Lord (Rom. 5:21). What this dominion of grace entails we discover in Romans 8:19-22: It is the deliverance of creation from the power of death. Why does Paul write about the deliverance of creation? Does Scripture mention this elsewhere? Scripture begins with it! God made everything "very good," and what we experience now is far from "very good." There is a power of evil that has put itself between God and his creation. As a result the relationship between creation and Creator has been disturbed. A curse has come over creation and, with that curse, the rule of death. Humankind, in turning away from God, is the cause of all this: "Cursed is the ground because of you" (Gen. 3:17). But God will not rest before this curse has been lifted from his creation. God wants all the nations of the earth to be blessed (Gen. 12:3). The call of Abraham is the call to the deliverance of creation!

The prophets were looking forward with keen anticipation to that time.

112

Read, for instance, Isaiah 55:12-13: "The mountains and the hills before you shall burst into song, and all the trees of the field shall clap their hands. Instead of the thorn shall come up the cypress; instead of the brier shall come up the myrtle. . . ." The thorn and the brier remind us of the curse on the earth in Genesis 3:18: "Thorns and thistles it shall bring forth for you." Even though the Hebrew text does not repeat the very same words, this prophecy will be fulfilled when all misery that then began is over. We heard this already when, in discussing Romans 1:17, we quoted from Psalm 98: The righteousness of God will be revealed and all the ends of the earth will see the salvation of our God. The earth will break forth into joyous song and will sing psalms; the sea, and all that fills it, will roar; and so will the world and those who live in it; the streams will clap their hands, and the hills will sing together for joy, for he is coming. . . . It is a psalm about the deliverance of creation, like Psalm 65, 96, 104 and others. In speaking about the deliverance of creation, Paul is at one with the prophets and the psalms.

Once Again: The Limitation We Have Been Taught

It is crucial to understand that here Paul does not write about the deliverance of creation without humanity, but in the first place about the deliverance of lost humanity. It is also important to recognize that there is a clear distinction between the salvation of lost human beings and the salvation of the church. For it is a salvation that is realized through the children of God, and Paul clearly refers to the church when he refers to God's children: ". . . You have received a spirit of adoption. When we cry, "Abba, Father!" it is that very Spirit bearing witness with our spirit that we are children of God" (Rom. 8:15-16). These children of God will be revealed: "When Christ who is your life is revealed, then you also will be revealed with him in glory" (Col. 3:4). When that happens, their salvation has been completed. Then follows the deliverance Paul is here describing. But what we need to show is that he refers to *the deliverance of those who are not yet saved.*

Our tradition dismisses the idea that the term "creation" here refers to people. It denies the possibility of salvation of the human race apart from the church. Calvin therefore thinks that Paul here writes about "the dumb creatures," that is, animals, plants, and minerals. They will not possess the same kind of glory as God's children, but in their own way they will have a part in the restoration of God's creation. There is no problem with that explanation other than that it limits the deliverance to believers and these

113

"dumb creatures," while that part of humanity which does not belong to God's children is tacitly excluded from this deliverance.[1]

This is also true, openly, in S. Greijdanus's commentary on Romans 8. The creation is to be understood as the sum total of what was created. "And this in an all-embracing fashion . . . the dumb animal and all of nature . . . except, of course, the devils. . . . The plants grow, the trees blossom, the animals procreate. But why, what purpose does it serve? Soon everything will wither, it dies, it disappears." This creation will be delivered. But what is meant by this "all-embracing fashion"? "Not only the believers (vv. 17-18, but also the rest of creation . . . the created things . . . in its totality." But not a word about a lost humanity that is also part of this totality, and that longs for deliverance. This lost humanity exists and yearns for deliverance, but that longing is not to be fulfilled. It is not included in this deliverance. "Believers will share in this glory. It is reserved for them. But it cannot be received where there is no faith or where it is rejected."[2] This exegesis is entirely in line with the interpretation followed by our tradition with regard to Paul's argument about Adam and Christ. We shall see how our rejection of that interpretation is here confirmed.

Jesus and the Suffering of Humanity

That the suffering creation has to do with *people* is instantly clear when we read the story of Jesus in the Gospels. Traveling through Galilee, he preaches the gospel of the kingdom and heals all kinds of sickness and disease among the people. These multitudes that approach him with their illnesses, what else do they represent than the suffering of creation? Jesus is moved with compassion for them — and not just for some of them but, without exception, for all: He heals all kinds of sickness and disease among the people. His healing miracles are acts of deliverance for suffering people. We hear of no other kind of deliverance. Nature and the animals are not beyond his care, but he came for

---

1. Calvin, *Romans*, pp. 172-74.

2. Greijdanus, *Romeinen*, pp. 374-75, 377, 373-74. The intended meaning is: whoever has not come to believe before his death will be excluded. William Hendriksen shares this view (*Romans* [Grand Rapids, 1980], 1:266) ". . . 'the whole creation' . . . cannot include . . . all those people who will never be saved, the non-elect" (2 Thess. 1:8-9). The author then refers to that "glorious day" when there will be no more disease in the plant and animal kingdom (p. 268). We do not deny this aspect, but it is unthinkable that Paul would speak of a deliverance of "the whole creation," and of "a glorious day," if most of humankind ("the non-elect") continues to suffer.

the sake of suffering humanity. And when he calls his disciples, and gives them authority over unclean spirits, and to cure every disease and every sickness (Matt. 9:35–10:1), we see again the ministry of deliverance and restoration of human life. These are the signs of the coming kingdom of God. We are told about these signs in the context of the ministry of his apostles. How can it possibly be that, all of a sudden, Paul speaks of a totally different kind of deliverance, a deliverance of those who have been called by Jesus — God's children — but with the exclusion of suffering humanity? For this is precisely their calling: to serve their Master in the work that has begun through him.

A Meaningless Existence

That Paul is speaking here of people is also clear when we take a closer look at this suffering: What kind of suffering is it? Creation is subjected to "futility." The New English Bible says: "It was made the victim of frustration." Both terms, "futility" and "frustration," are good renderings of what Paul intends to say. Another synonym would be "meaninglessness." We find the same expression in the Old Testament word "breath" (Heb. *hebel*); it is found in the name "Habel," or "Abel." "You have made my days a few handbreaths, and my lifetime is as nothing in your sight. Surely, everyone stands as a mere breath" (Ps. 39:5). This is said of every person, "everyone." In Ecclesiastes this word plays a major role. There it is translated "vanity":

> Vanity of vanities, says the Teacher, vanity of vanities! All is vanity. What do people gain from all the toil at which they toil under the sun? . . . I saw all the deeds that are done under the sun; and see, all is vanity and a chasing after wind. (1:2, 3, 14)

> For the fate of humans and the fate of animals is the same; as one dies, so dies the other. They all have the same breath, and humans have no advantage over the animals; for all is vanity. All go to one place; all are from the dust, and all turn to dust again. (3:19, 20)

Nothing reaches its ultimate goal — that is what we hear in the word "vanity." All diligence, all zeal and hard work, ends in nothingness. The end is inescapable: die and be buried. All you have achieved is gone. Others may continue for a while, but they will face the same end: death. The Teacher of Ecclesiastes feels distressed. We receive life without asking for it. We find it worthwhile. But in the end there is only death!

To exist and to know at the same time that this existence ends in nothingness — that is the human predicament, not the worry of "dumb creatures." Human beings cannot live without a longing that things were different.[3] God himself put this longing in us; that is how he created us. He created all things "to Him" (Rom. 11:36).[4]

Therefore, since God created humans "to Himself," this desire will not be in vain. The Creator will not rest until the human race has reached the destiny for which he created it. That is the message of the Bible. From beginning to end it is the *message of hope*.

"Cursed Is the Ground Because of You"

Creation is subject to futility or frustration, "not by its own will but by the will of the one who subjected it" (Rom. 8:20). "Not by its own will": It goes against the grain of its existence, and that is how it is experienced by all creation. It comes from an alien power, an enemy. Let us look a little more closely at these words. Paul once again alludes to the book of Genesis. When Adam and Eve refused to listen to God's voice, he said:

> Cursed is the ground because of you; in toil you shall eat of it all the days of your life; thorns and thistles it shall bring forth for you. . . . By the sweat of your face you shall eat bread until you return to the ground, for out of it you were taken; you are dust, and to dust you shall return. (Gen. 3:17-19)

"By the will of the one who subjected it," Paul writes. To whom does Paul refer? God, humans, or the power of death? This remains unclear.[5] For our present purpose it suffices to note three things. First of all, as a result of humanity's guilt, the earth is subject to the power of death. Second: Human beings themselves are the victims of this subjection: they must toil and will return to the earth. That will be their fate. Not only people, but all of creation is subject to this power. The emphasis, however, is on people.

3. Ridderbos speaks in this connection about "the vague sense of homesickness that vibrates, as it were, through all creation. . . . The term 'creation' is here used in the sense of all creaturely, transitory existence, that is subject to death, cf. vv. 20-21. The resulting yearning for life is, of course, most clearly visible in human beings . . ." (*Romeinen*, p. 185). Thus, in contrast to the authors we mentioned earlier, Ridderbos emphasizes human suffering.

4. "Our hearts are restless till they find rest in Thee" (Augustine, *Confessions*, 1.1).

5. Wilckens (*Römer*, 1:154): "Eine eindeutige Entscheidung jedoch scheint mir nicht möglich." This sentiment is echoed by Ridderbos: "not of decisive significance for the understanding of these words" (*Romeinen*, p. 186).

Third: There is hope! This subjection to death is linked to hope! Even before God pronounced the curse, he declared war against the serpent — against the power that brought death. "Cursed are you," said God. The posterity of the woman will "strike" the head of the serpent (Gen. 3:15). And humans understood this word of hope. For immediately after Adam hears that he will return to dust, he cries: "Life!" He calls out the name of his wife: "Eve," which means "Life" (v. 20).

This reflection on Genesis 3:17-19 indicates the emphasis Scripture places on the essential unity between humanity and the totality of creation. We just referred to God's judgment: God is acting here. He could have done it differently. He could simply have eradicated the human race from his creation. If He had done so, creation would have remained undefiled: "pure" nature. But without human beings, creation is not what God intended it to be. It would be a decapitated creation! To be the creation God intended, it must include humans as God intended. And when they prove to be disloyal, we see how the Creator does not "forsake the work of his hands." He remains loyal to his creation. Not by leaving them out, but by demonstrating his faithfulness to unfaithful people! To all people! For in Adam we are confronted with "original humanity," which comprises all of humankind, all his posterity — as we saw in Romans 5:12-21. This earth will only be blessed when all of lost humanity has returned to its Creator. Then, as a result of their redemption there will be *peace on earth* — a creation that is no longer ruled by brute power but by divine love. We catch a glimpse of this in Isaiah 11:1-10: "The wolf shall live with the lamb, the leopard shall lie down with the kid" — the strong and the weak! — "for the earth will be full of the knowledge of the LORD as the waters cover the sea."

The Deliverance

In writing about the suffering creation and its future deliverance, Paul does not think only of human beings, but he certainly does not think of "nature" without humans. That he refers to the suffering of humans is also clear from what the apostle writes about the freedom for which creation is set free. It is freed to obtain "the freedom of the glory of the children of God" (Rom. 8:21). What is this glory of the children of God? Paul earlier stated that all "fall short of the glory of God" since all have sinned (Rom. 3:23). This freedom and this glory are the gifts God intended them to have: the honor and the glory of being created in his image and after his likeness. It is his ultimate goal for humanity. The "futility" and "frustration" they suffer from is nothing else than the fact that this goal is beyond their reach. And the deliverance is that they now reach that destination. For them, humanity, God gave his Son, and they are the ones for whom that day of freedom will dawn which he has obtained for them. That glory is not God's gift for the trees and the animals.[6] It is his gift to humankind. But, as we already saw, that freedom and that glory bring the peace of God for the entire creation (Isa. 11:1-11).

In this passage Paul writes about what humanity outside the church will receive, not what the church will receive. The church receives its part prior to this. When the Messiah appears, they, the children of God, will appear with him in glory (Col. 3:3; cf. Rom. 8:17-19; Phil. 3:21). The entire human world awaits that moment. As yet it does not belong to "God's children." But when they "appear," all will enjoy the same freedom that God's children have already received.

It is the deliverance from the rule of futility and corruption. That means the resurrection of the dead! The dead! Were they no longer part of God's creation as soon as they died? If death continued to rule over those who died, how can it be maintained that creation is delivered from the rule of death?[7]

---

6. "But neither trees nor animals will have the freedom and glory which the children of God will receive. That is only for humans, created as persons" (Schlatter, *Erläuterungen,* 5:163).

7. The early church cared about the destiny of the dead — through the baptism for the dead (1 Cor. 15:29). M. Rissi (*De Taufe für die Toten* [Zurich, 1962]) believes that this baptism must have been restricted to cases where believers had died without being baptized. But we are here clearly dealing with a concern about the lost state of those who had died, and not with the question: Who among the dead has a right to baptism? K. McAll, an English psychiatrist, describes (in *Healing the Family Tree* [London, 1986]) experiences from his practice that led him to request eucharistic celebrations for deceased family members of some of his patients. He remarks that it made no difference whether the deceased had been Christians or not. A friend of mine, a member of the Dutch Order of St. Luke, told me a similar story. Some inexplicable, highly disturbing experiences led him to the conviction that he should pray that a deceased member of the family would receive forgiveness for something that person had done to him. After the prayer these disturbing experiences no longer occurred. These experiences were not sought, but just came. They were not restricted to family members, but also concerned nonrelatives. This I learned from what another friend confided to me. They confirm what the Bible says about the anguish of the unredeemed dead, and about God's will that they should not remain unredeemed (see III, 6; IV, 2; VII, 5). But I must admit that I have no answer to the many questions these strange experiences raise (nor about a possible connection with 1 Cor. 15:29).

This deliverance must mean the end of the anguish and distress that have come as the result of God's judgment of humanity (Rom. 2:9). The coming of the Messiah is indeed accompanied by the judgment. But the judgment is not the end of his work; the end has not been reached until the deliverance of creation is complete. When at last the entire creation has been delivered, then the anguish and distress have forever ceased to exist.

We already heard that through Christ all will receive justification and life (Rom. 5:18). And we saw that the tradition of the church denied this: Only believers will be saved. Paul's statement in Romans 8:19-21 confirms that salvation is not limited to believers. In fact, it allows for no doubt whatsoever on this point — not only because the deliverance of humankind *follows* upon the deliverance of the church, but also because it will be the *work* of the delivered church. What exactly does this mean?

2. Each in His Own Order

The Order in 1 Corinthians 15

We have not been taught that there will be a redemption of the world subsequent to the redemption of the church. We must therefore make sure that we have not misunderstood the apostle. We already noticed that 1 Corinthians 15:20-22 as well as Romans 5:12-21 draws a parallel between Christ and Adam. We now focus on what follows.

> For as all die in Adam, so will all be made alive in Christ. But each in his own order: Christ the first fruits, then at his coming those that belong to Christ. Then comes the end, when he hands over the kingdom to God the Father, after he has destroyed every ruler and every authority and power. For he must reign until he has put all his enemies under his feet. The last enemy to be destroyed is death. For God has put all things under subjection under his feet. . . . When all things are subjected to him, then the Son himself will also be subjected to the one who put all things in subjection under him, so that God may be all in all. (1 Cor. 15:22-28)

After Paul has stated that in Christ all people will be made alive, we hear that there is an "order" in this resurrection. First Christ. Christ is the first-fruits, that is to say, the first who is brought back to life; the others follow after him — not all at the same time, but in a certain order or sequence. "Then at his coming those who belong to Christ." That represents the second stage. It is limited to those who "belong to Christ," that is, those who believe in him and follow him; this cannot be said of all people. The resurrection of all "who belong to Christ" does not fulfill the words of Paul that all who died through Adam would be made alive through Christ. Something is yet to follow — the word "order" also indicates this. What follows is *the end,* the completion of Christ's work. When that has been achieved, he transfers the kingship to the Father. But first he has to dethrone all rule, authority, and power. For "he must reign until he has put all his enemies under his feet." These are numerous! The last one in this series of enemies is death itself. Only when death has been despoiled of its power can it truly be said that all his enemies have been destroyed. Then all people who died through Adam will be made alive. Here we encounter the same message as in Romans 5:18; all will come to justification and life. But in 1 Corinthians we are told something we had not heard in Romans: "Each in his own order" (v. 23). Salvation does not come to all at the same time.[8]

Once Again: At Odds with Our Tradition

Looking at how these words have been interpreted within our tradition, we find once again that salvation is limited to the church. What we discover is almost a repetition of what we found when we dealt with Romans 8:19-21. Calvin in his commentary simply ignores the possibility that others than those "who belong to Christ" will be among the saved. He believes that at Christ's coming everything is completed: All his enemies are defeated and death has been robbed of its power. The time when he puts all enemies under his feet is the time prior to his second coming: the time in which we now live. He is convinced that those who died as unbelievers will not be delivered from the power of death; they are lost forever. But if those who are lost remain in the power of death, death is not the last enemy to be destroyed! This simple fact in itself makes it clear that Christ's coming is not the same as "the end" to which Paul refers in 1 Corinthians 15:23.

We find this same interpretation in F. W. Grosheide, but he does react

---

8. For this topic see A. Schlatter, *Paulus der Bote Jesu, eine Deutung seiner Briefe an die Korinther* (2nd ed.; Stuttgart, 1956), pp. 409-20 (1st ed. 1934). See also: O. Cullmann, *Köningsherrschaft Christi und Kirche im Neuen Testament* (Zollikon-Zurich, 1950); H. Bietenhardt, *Das Tausendjährige Reich* (Zurich, 1955), pp. 52-67; M. Rissi, *Was ist und was geschehen soll danach* (Zurich, 1965), pp. 119-30.

to the explanation of other exegetes who argue that the resurrection of "those who belong to Christ" will be followed by the resurrection of those who do not believe in Christ. That is the interpretation we have adopted, but Grosheide rejects it. He believes that "Paul deals only with the resurrection of those who are Christ's. He further adds: "This means in other words, that in this chapter Paul refers only to believers." He is absolutely convinced "that in no way does the apostle teach that all people will be saved through Christ." "In fact," he writes, "this is not what the text says. It tells us that all will be made alive." For Grosheide this does not necessarily imply salvation. Those who are lost will indeed be resurrected, but not to salvation, for, according to Grosheide, the letters of Paul clearly teach the eternal damnation of the lost. He refers to Romans 2:5 and to a series of texts in 1 Corinthians, beginning at 1:18. Admittedly, in these passages Paul speaks about "being lost," but we read nowhere that this state of being lost is the final phase of God's dealings with the lost. With regard to the resurrection of the lost this interpretation refers to John 5:19, Acts 24:15, and Revelation 20:15.[9] In the first two texts we hear about a "resurrection of condemnation," but we are not told that this judgment brings *eternal* damnation, as Grosheide believes. This interpretation entirely ignores the fact that Paul writes that all who will be made alive, will be made alive "through Christ"; this contrasts with death "through Adam" and cannot refer to a resurrection in order to be lost!

The Destruction of Death

1 Corinthians 15 does not refer to the judgment. But we will have to understand the period of Christ's kingly rule as the era of the judgment. He comes to judge the living and the dead (Acts 10:42; 1 Pet. 4:5). There is no indication that this judgment will occupy only a short period. Here, in 1 Corinthians 15, the enemies are dethroned, one by one, death being the last one. Those who do not "belong to Christ" will not be made alive when he comes.[10] They continue to be subjected to the rule of death. Will they remain in that state? According to the doctrine of eternal punishment, that is the case. There is a

---

9. F. W. Grosheide, *De eerste brief van den apostel Paulus aan de kerk te Korinthe* (Amsterdam, 1932), p. 511.

10. All unredeemed are dead, waiting for deliverance from the power of death, which is the last enemy to be destroyed. There is no question of a "surrealistic" future, when people are resurrected in the midst of people who must still face death.

resurrection of unbelievers, but this resurrection is not a deliverance from the power of death. In the book of Revelation (20:6, 14) we hear that they will experience a "second death." The doctrine of eternal punishment refers to this death as eternal. Whatever one might think of this "second death,"[11] as long as it rules over most people, it cannot possibly be maintained that death, as the last enemy, has been robbed of its power. Notice the triumph that echoes from the final verses of this chapter about the resurrection:

> Then the saying that is written will be fulfilled: "Death has been swallowed up in victory." "Where, O death, is your victory? Where, O death, is your sting?" (1 Cor. 15:54-55)

Paul bases his thoughts on one of Isaiah's prophecies:

> On this mountain the LORD of hosts will make for all peoples a feast of rich food. . . . And he will destroy on this mountain the shroud that is cast over all peoples, the sheet that is spread over all nations; he will swallow up death forever. Then the Lord GOD will wipe away the tears from all faces. (Isa. 25:6-8)

That the prophet here refers only to believers is not a possibility. All peoples outside Israel (i.e., worshipers of other gods) are gathered "on this mountain" — Mt. Sion.[12] For all of them death is destroyed, and God wipes away all tears from their faces. "Death is swallowed up in victory," Paul writes. The real meaning of the word that many translations render as *forever* is *victory* (Heb. *nētsach*; Isa. 25:8, AV). It is the victory that forever ends the power of death over the dead. How then could there be another death that will continue eternally? If there were such a death, death would not be swallowed up in victory; on the contrary: in that case death would be the final victor over the human race that God created — the only exception

11. See Rissi: "Here we should also think of God's disciplinary love, which allows the lost creature to fall into the abyss of condemnation and rejection, that he may lead it in infinite compassion to repentance and thus to salvation and re-creation" (p. 127). Rissi points to the similarities between the last part of the book of Revelation and 1 Corinthians 15:20-28. About the second death, see also W. Michaelis, *Versöhnung des Alls* (Gümlichen [Bern], 1950), pp. 97-121, 183-87. Cf. VII, 5.

12. The margin of the Dutch Authorized Version limits the words "all peoples" to: "The Gentiles as well as the Jews, which He will call to a knowledge of Him, through the preaching of the holy gospel"; the word "feast" to "the abundant grace in Christ which God will give to his elect"; and "all tears" to "tears from the faces of his people."

being the few who "belong to Christ." If God wipes away the tears from all eyes — of all people — then suffering and sorrow cannot be the final end of them. Referring to the judgment, Jesus speaks of "weeping and gnashing of teeth" (Matt. 13:42, 50). But this prophecy of Isaiah makes it very clear that Jesus never intended this to go on forever and ever.

"That God May Be All in All"

As soon as Christ has fully completed the establishment of his kingly rule, he will transfer everything to the Father, so "that God may be all in all" (1 Cor. 15:28). God's love will be "all in all" for his creatures. But notice what is left of this promise if we cling to what the church has always taught about eternal punishment.

First Calvin:

> "That God may be all in all." Will He also be everything in the devils and in the ungodly? No, unless one wants to understand the word *be* as *be acknowledged,* or as *will be visible.* In that case the meaning would be: Now, while the devil resists God, and while the ungodly disturb and upset the divine order of things . . . it cannot be clearly discerned that God is all in all; but when Christ will have completed his judgment, which the Father has charged Him with, and will have subjected the devil and the ungodly, the glory of God will be visible in their perdition.[13]

We find the same trend in Grosheide's comments on verse 28: "All people, the godless and the God-fearing, all devils must through the work of Christ come to the recognition that God is the only One. The apostle does not refer to God's blessed presence, but as is evident from repeated use of *hypotassein* ("to subject") to God's authority. His rule will be universal and will be recognized by all." Commenting on verse 24, Grosheide links this subjection to ". . . powers which refused to subject themselves to God's kingly rule, *but now have no choice but to recognize this.* . . . Verse 23 indicates that this will happen at his parousia."[14] This enforced recognition, not only by the "powers," but also by all ungodly people, according to this explanation, presumably is the meaning of God being "all in all."

13. Calvin, *Uitlegging op den eersten en tweeden zendbrief van Paulus aan de Corinthiers,* Dutch trans. A. M. Donner (2nd ed.; Goudriaan, 1972), p. 262.
14. Grosheide, *De eerste brief te Korinthe,* pp. 520, 515. The term "parousia" refers to the Second Coming. For this forced obedience, see VII, 4.

In this study we carefully distance ourselves from any theory about
the possible destiny of Satan. As we stated earlier: We do not know what
the power of evil is, and we have not been asked to make it our concern.
Colossians 1:19-20, just like 1 Corinthians 15, refers to "powers." Christ's
redemption somehow will also include them.[15] But we will also refrain
from speaking about the ultimate fate of these powers. Our concern is the
destiny of humankind: all those who died through Adam and will be made
alive through Christ (v. 22). They will all be brought by Christ to the
destiny for which they were created by God: "that God be all in all" (v. 28).
This can mean only: All are filled with God; there is no room whatsoever
for anything but the joy in his goodness — "All your works shall give
thanks to you, O LORD" (Ps. 145:10). This cannot be reconciled with a
forced recognition of God's rule over people who continue to exist as his
enemies while undergoing eternal torment. As long as there is enmity
against God, he is not all in all; there is something alien to God, something
against God, that continues to exist in man. Here again it is clear that one
had to take recourse in specious explanations to maintain the doctrine of
eternal punishment.

Resurrected for Service in the Kingdom

In Romans 8:19-21 Paul writes that creation is waiting for the revelation
of the children of God. They accompany Christ as the deliverers of the
unredeemed creation (including unredeemed humanity) from the power
of death and perdition. In 1 Corinthians 15:23-28 he refers to the resurrection of those "who belong to Christ," and then to the deliverance of lost
humanity, through the kingly rule of Christ. But we read nothing about
any service rendered by those who "belong to Christ." Nonetheless, that is
God's intention. We will understand this when we pay attention to what
Paul subsequently writes about those who partake in this resurrection (vv.
35-49).

The question is asked: "How are the dead raised? With what kind of
body do they come?" In answering this, Paul draws a comparison with a
grain of wheat that is sown and grows into a plant. The resurrection will
be similar. We cannot express in words what the resurrection body will be
like; it will be characterized by "glory." It will radiate the glory of God,

---

15. These powers should not be identified with Satan! See H. Berkhof, *Christ and
the Powers* (Scottdale, PA, 1977).

which had become visible in Jesus' victory over death. The glory is described in the following words:

> So it is with the resurrection of the dead. What is sown is perishable, what is raised is imperishable. It is sown in dishonor, it is raised in glory. It is sown in weakness, it is raised in power. It is sown a physical body, it is raised a spiritual body. (1 Cor. 15:42-44)

It will be a "spiritual body"; not a "spirit," but a body filled with the Spirit of God. Those who are raised will be filled with the love of God and the victorious power of the Messiah over the powers of death and destruction. But for what purpose do they receive all this? Not simply to be spectators of what their Lord does! They are resurrected as "belonging to Christ" — to serve him in what is about to happen: the subjection of the hostile powers, in particular of the last enemy — Death (1 Cor. 15:25-26). They are now fully equipped for this task. Romans 8:17-21 tells us that they receive this glory so that they may serve God in the deliverance of the 'groaning' creation.

3. Salvation: First for the Church, Then for the World

"Do You Not Know That the Saints Will Judge the World?"

An earlier passage in the letter to the Corinthians clearly indicates that Paul did not for a moment view the resurrection as a prelude to idleness. The context is the court cases between members of the church about which Paul had heard. They bring their problems to the court rather than to the wise in the church, even though they have been "called to be saints," as he wrote in the introduction of this letter (1 Cor. 1:2). Are they ignorant of the task to which they have been called?

> Do you not know that the saints will judge the world? And if the world is to be judged by you, are you incompetent to try trivial cases? Do you not know that we are to judge angels — to say nothing of ordinary matters? (1 Cor. 6:2-3)

We should note that the word here translated "to judge" has a much broader meaning than to preside over a court case. It also means "to govern" (see, e.g., Matt. 19:28). It is the work of the king: bringing justice to the oppressed, to right what was wrong, and thus to create peace for his people (Ps. 72).

This is the kind of kingship referred to in Matthew:

> Truly I tell you, at the renewal of all things, when the Son of Man is seated on the throne of his glory, you who have followed me will also sit on twelve thrones, judging the twelve tribes of Israel." (Matt. 19:28)

Paul reminds the fighting and suing members of the church of their calling. Why would they, as people who are "called to be saints," turn to a pagan judge! As the church of the Messiah they have been called to judge the world when he comes. Their service will consist of bringing unredeemed humanity to its intended destiny.[16] Now they are unable to even deal with their personal problems and turn to a pagan judge. Court cases against each other! If they persist in that kind of attitude, they risk their future in God's kingdom — it will make them useless for the task that awaits them (1 Cor. 6:7-9)!

Kingship and Discipleship

This passage of Paul about the future task is not an isolated statement. This service is repeatedly referred to in the New Testament as ruling with Christ as kings. We encounter this kingship for the first time in the book of Daniel: "The holy ones of the Most High shall receive the kingdom" (Dan. 7:18). In Jesus' statement, which we just quoted, we also hear of the twelve thrones on which the twelve apostles will sit to judge the twelve tribes of Israel. We hear the same in Romans 5: '. . . much more will those who receive the abundance of grace and the free gift of righteousness reign in life through the one man, Jesus Christ" (Rom. 5:17, RSV).[17] Again: "If we endure, we

16. Commenting on 1 Corinthians 6:2, the margin of the Dutch Authorized Version says: "That is, as assessors of Christ, the primary Judge, whose verdict they will approve and vindicate" — with reference to Matthew 19:28 and Luke 22:30. See also Grosheide (*De eerste brief te Korinthe*, p. 195): "Here, those who have been glorified, i.e., those who have already been pronounced free by Christ, are the *spectators*, in whose midst Christ, in his final judgment, will judge the world. In that sense, the saints will partake in Christ's judgment" (italics added).

17. Romans 5:17 has the same Greek word that is used in the following quotations (*basileuein*, "to reign as kings"). Here Paul does not explicitly say that *all* (or: *the many*) will live and rule as kings. Rather, he describes them as: "those who receive the abundance of grace and the free gift of righteousness." Does that not include all? We may find the answer in what has been said about the order of the resurrection. All will receive that abundance, but not all will rule as kings. That privilege is reserved for those who are

will also reign with him" (2 Tim. 2:12). Finally, we hear this in the book of Revelation. In the hymn of praise in chapter 5 Christ is described as the one who ransomed for God saints from every tribe and language and people and nation; "you have made them to be a kingdom and priests serving our God, and they will reign on earth" (Rev. 5:10; see also 20:6 and 22:5).

We should note how Paul links this future kingship with the life of the church in the present. The manner in which church members interact is decisive for their position in the kingdom. If they do injustice, they will not inherit the kingdom of God; in other words, they will not share in this kingly rule (1 Cor. 6:7-11). We find the same link in Romans 8. The creation waits for the revelation of God's children — those who are now being led by the Spirit. Those who refuse to be led by the Spirit are not heirs, and they will not inherit the kingdom (Rom. 8:12-17; see also Gal. 5:16-22).

We hear about this same relationship between our obedience and the future kingship in Jesus' words, which we quoted above: those *who followed him* will sit on twelve thrones to judge the twelve tribes of Israel (Matt. 19:28). Being led by the Spirit is simply being a disciple of Jesus; it is a matter of doing what he says. He calls his disciples to that kind of discipleship when he sees the crowds and is moved with compassion for them, because they are chased around and exhausted, like sheep without a shepherd. He calls them to a service of compassion — as laborers in a harvest that threatens to be lost (Matt. 9:36-38; see II, 3). To be his disciple is to follow him in his compassion. As he was moved with compassion, so they will have to be moved. This compassion will be the main test in the judgment: what they have done to the least of their brothers and sisters will be the qualifying test for the service that awaits them in their future kingship (Matt. 25:35-36).

This discipleship is nothing but a preparation for that task. This is what Jesus wants to instill in the hearts of his disciples in the parable of the loyal and intelligent servant, whom the lord puts in charge of all his possessions, and in particular in the parable of the talents (Matt. 24:45-47; 25:14-30). Only those who have been faithful in small things will enter the kingdom and will be put in charge of important things. "Well done, good and faithful

---

Christ's at his coming (1 Cor. 15:23). This is their service for the deliverance of the many who do not yet belong to Christ. Once this deliverance has been completed, all will have received this abundance — all will then have been restored to life in Christ. This marks the end of the service of kingship. The Son will then submit himself to God, and God will be all in all (v. 28).

servant; you have been faithful over a little, I will set you over much; enter into the joy of your master" (Matt. 25:21). "I will set you over much." That is what this kingly rule means. Luke puts it even more precisely: "Take charge of ten cities," to another, "rule over five cities" (Luke 19:17, 19). The parable also mentions a lazy servant. He did nothing at all; he had no compassion for the lost sheep. Therefore, he has no task in the kingdom in which *all* lost sheep must be found and be brought home. His future is in "the outer darkness" (Matt. 25:14-30).

Entering the kingdom is not simply a matter of one's individual salvation. It implies that God's children share in Christ's kingship. Together with him they will rule the world as good kings: judging, even condemning. But in so doing they will manifest compassion and seek to liberate from the powers of death, with one purpose in mind: to bring back a lost world to the house of the Father. That is what it means to bring in the harvest — the harvest in its entirety. The service of their kingship is not complete until that purpose has been achieved.

Two Salvations

"Do you not know. . . ?" Paul asks (1 Cor. 6:2, 3). Had the Corinthians forgotten what they had been taught? We note that the coming ruling as kings belonged to the basic principles Paul had taught the church. When Christ comes, those "who are Christ's" will share in his resurrection. They are saved, but at that time that is not yet true of the world. Unredeemed people must wait for the kingship of God's children, who as servants of Christ will deliver and restore them. That is the sequence of 1 Corinthians 15:23 and Romans 8:19-21. We realize that this kingly rule and this sequence are foreign to the faith tradition in which we were taught.[18] We saw how exegetes have tried very hard to show that Paul *could not* possibly have

18. Schlatter comments: "The traditional teaching of the church rejected the statement of Paul. . . . The motive for this opposition to Paul was the aversion against the so-called Chiliasm and against a promise reaching out beyond the church." Schlatter further answers the objection that this view of the future (those who are Christ's have been resurrected, while others have not) is a "fantasy": "The fact that we find this scenario of the future difficult to imagine does not entitle us to eliminate the *epeita-eita* [Greek: the order of 'then . . . then' in vv. 23-24] and the plural of *tagmata* [orders in v. 23]. . . . The idea that the work of Christ is limited to the churches that have been established by the apostles and that outside these there is only destruction is emphatically denied by Paul, not only here but also in Romans 8:19-22" (*Paulus, der Bote Jesu*, pp. 414-15 on 1 Cor. 15:20-28).

believed that those who have remained outside the church can be saved. Others recognize, however, that this is what Paul does teach in these passages. But they point to the difficulty that there are so many texts that seem to indicate that only believers can be saved. We have already referred to this: the view that allows for two separate series of statements which we should not attempt to harmonize (II, 3). We now return to that problem in the light of what Paul says about this "order": his distinction between the salvation of the church and the salvation of the world.

We begin with Jesus' statement about the broad and the narrow road. Jesus says that few will find the narrow road that leads to life. This refers to the salvation of the church. Many follow the broad road leading to perdition. This refers to the lostness of the majority of humankind, the many who will be condemned in the divine judgment. They face perdition. Jesus also uses other terms for their destiny: the outer darkness, weeping and gnashing of teeth, the eternal fire. Paul teaches the same thing. The disobedient face anguish and distress (Rom. 2:9). But there is a difference! The church maintained there is no future salvation for those who are lost. Paul, however, writes that they will be liberated by God's children; that they, in their proper order will be restored to life in Christ (Rom. 8:19-21; 1 Cor. 15:23-28).

So this order, in actual fact, speaks of two separate salvations — one following the other: first, those who are Christ's at his coming; and then the redemption of the many, who are not yet Christ's, when he comes. They will experience the distress and anguish of God's judgment. Their redemption is the ultimate salvation of the nations proclaimed by the prophets: forever death is destroyed, and God will wipe away the tears from all faces (Isa. 25:8).[19]

This does not mean that all our questions have been answered, but it should be clear that this alleged contradiction between the "two sets of statements" is caused by ignoring what we are told about the salvation of those who are condemned in the divine judgment. In a later chapter we will deal in more detail with the prophetic utterances about the seriousness

---

19. In order to emphasize, contrary to tradition, that there is more than the redemption of the church, I use in this case the term "second salvation" (or "second resurrection"). The Bible does not use this phrase. We hear about a "first resurrection" (Rev. 20:6), but the resurrection that follows the first resurrection (and thus, in fact, is the second) is not referred to as the "second resurrection." This is the main, or "general" resurrection of the dead, which achieves God's final purpose for humanity. The resurrection of those who are Christ's is just the prelude; they are resurrected in order that they may serve Christ in the achievement of that purpose.

of the judgment, but also with the *purpose* of the judgment and the meaning of the word "eternal" (VII, 2 and VII, 3).

Why This Gulf between Paul and Us?

From early times the church fathers taught that there is no salvation outside the church. They abandoned hope for the salvation of all humanity, which the prophets proclaimed. Why? Could they not understand Paul's words? No, the problem was not that they did not grasp what the text said, but rather that they did not believe what it said. What prompted Augustine to interpret the text "God desires everyone to be saved" in such a way that God does not want the salvation of all? What prompted Calvin, and many other commentators after him, to explain the prophecy of God's salvation of Sodom in such a way that God does not save Sodom? What prompted them to restrict Paul's statement that in Christ all people will be restored to life, to be believers? They clearly sensed the tension between their interpretation and the text — why else would they have gone to so much trouble in attempting to defend their exegesis? Their problem with the actual wording of the text was rooted *in the deep conviction of the church that it was simply impossible that the Bible should teach that there would be salvation for the many who did not experience conversion before their death.*[20] Therefore, the real question is: How did the church come to the conviction that there is no possibility of salvation outside the church, in spite of the clear words of the Bible? What caused this deep chasm between Paul's teaching and that of the church of the ages?

This question leads us to the next section of Paul's letter to the church in Rome. The apostle writes about his great sorrow and continuous anguish: The great majority in Israel have rejected their Messiah. He writes driven by a deep concern for a church that does not seem to share in his sorrow and anguish about his kinsfolk — a church that feels no need for the return of these Jews to the Messiah, a church that is willing passively to accept the perdition of Israel! This brings us to the core of the matter: How do we find a biblical answer to the doctrine of eternal punishment, an answer that will lead us to this hope for the world that was so prominent in the thoughts of the prophets and the apostles?

---

20. The doctrine that there cannot be any salvation after death, and that the judgment marks the end of God's compassion, originates in the horrifying image of God that we found in the apocryphal book 2 Esdras (see I, 5). It is a marked example of what has been called an "unbiblical presupposition"; cf. I, n. 47.

CHAPTER V

Great Sorrow and Unceasing Anguish (Romans 9 and 10)[1]

1. Paul's Sense of Loss and the History of the Church

The Catastrophe and the Exegesis of Romans

In all likelihood, no chapter of Scripture has been so much misunderstood by the church throughout the ages as Romans 9. In this chapter the church has read that God rejected Israel forever. It has also been interpreted as the cornerstone of the traditional doctrine of predestination. "I have loved Jacob, but I have hated Esau" (v. 13, RSV), and "He has mercy on whomever he chooses, and he hardens the heart of whomever he chooses" (v. 18, RSV). The idea that God does not want to save all people began with the conviction that God does not want to save Israel.

---

1. In my study of Romans 9–11, I not only consulted the commentaries already listed (III, n. 1), but also read Origen's commentary (*Ad Romanos*, 1137-1202); Barth's exegesis, which he wrote in the context of his work on the doctrine of election (*C.D.*, II 2, pp. 222-26, 235-56, and 294-336); Bertold Klappert, "Traktat für Israel (Römer 9–11)," in *Jüdische Existenz und die Erneuerung der christlichen Theologie*, published by Martin Stöhr ([Munich, 1981], pp. 53-137); and Bertold Klappert, *Israel und die Kirche: Erwägungen zur Israellehre Karl Barths* (Munich, 1980).

131

What has this doctrine of Israel's rejection brought about? The great catastrophe of our century tells us: The murder of almost six million Jews from 1940 to 1945 in post-Christian Europe would not have been possible without the preparatory work of this ecclesiastical tradition. Here the exegesis of Romans 9–11 played a major role. In his commentary Wilckens pays much attention to this aspect. From the beginning, he writes, the church failed to understand what Paul tried to say in these chapters. It was not long before the church had become accustomed to view the Jews as dangerous outsiders. That is, in fact, what they were in times when the church was persecuted. The Jewish religion was recognized and protected by the pagan state, whereas "the new sect" — the Christians — was not. Usually the Jews supported this persecution by the pagan authorities. But the tables were turned when, in the early part of the fourth century, Christianity was officially recognized by the state. Thus, almost imperceptibly, a vast arsenal of hatred against the Jews could enter the church, and could develop into a systematic discrediting of the Jews in Christian society and lead to a multitude of collective crimes against them. Christian theology did little to counteract this fatal error. The church developed an ecclesiology and a soteriology in which any linkage with Israel disappeared. In fact, the church more and more acquired a "Gentile-Christian" character. It was the danger of this development that Paul so emphatically warned against in Romans 11. Aside from the attempts of a few to correct it, it was only the systematic genocide of the European Jews by the Nazis that changed this and led to the tide of revulsion in the world, which forced the church to rethink the "Israel problem."[2]

Wilckens's arguments had already, as early as in 1959, been voiced in a brochure published by the Dutch Reformed Church: It was not the Scriptures that opened the eyes of the church to the significance of Israel in the divine plan of salvation. Rather, as a result of the mass murders of the Jews by the Nazi state, the realization dawned that something must have gone wrong in the history of the church — namely, in what she had taught, almost from the beginning, about the Jews. The genocide was not committed by Christians, but by pagans who had rejected faith in Jesus. However, this would not have happened in Europe if through the centuries the church had taught the people to see Israel as the apple of God's eye; if the church had learned to focus her expectations on the great salvation that God would give to the world through Israel.

2. Wilckens, *Römer*, 2:190, 267.

In his letter to the Romans Paul had sufficiently impressed this on the church. For nineteen centuries the churches had read chapters 9–11 of that letter. But only now the realization dawned that people had not been listening. Brutally the church was confronted with the disastrous consequences of this teaching.

In its "Sketch of a New Reformed Confession," *Fundamenten en Perspectieven van Belijden* (Confessional Foundations and Perspectives), the Dutch Reformed Church had initiated a discussion about this matter as early as 1949.

> Since the gifts of grace and the divine calling are irrevocable, we believe that the people of Israel, through whose service God had intended to bless all nations, are not rejected and abandoned by him. . . . It remains the people of the promise and the people of the Messiah. . . . The church of Jesus Christ is not full-grown, nor has the kingdom of God been fully realized, until Israel, in the way and at the time known to God, has been brought back to its Messiah, so that both Israel and the nations learn to confess the free grace of him who has put all under disobedience, in order that he might be merciful to all.[3]

For the first time in the history of the Christian Church, this document affirms the significance of Israel in the confession of the church. The confession concerns a matter that is important for another reason too: the trustworthiness of what the church has traditionally taught. Could it be, we asked, that for many centuries the church taught a doctrine of eternal punishment that was untrue? If this was an error, would not the Holy Spirit have led her to correct this? In this case, however — Israel as a people rejected by God — it has become crystal clear that an ecclesiastical tradition of centuries provides no guarantee that the teaching of the church agrees with Scripture.

3. *Fundamenten en Perspectieven van Belijden* (The Hague, 1949), Art. 17. Art. 3 of this confession is titled "The Election of Israel." See, for the full text of both articles, H. Vreekamp, *Zonder Israel niet volgroeid* (Kampen, 1988), pp. 29-31. Vreekamp offers a short, well-documented survey of developments in the Dutch Reformed Church during the last fifty years. He also discusses the 1959 publication *Israel en de Kerk (Israel and the Church)*.

Paul in the Breach for Israel

> I am speaking the truth in Christ — I am not lying; my conscience confirms it by the Holy Spirit — I have great sorrow and unceasing anguish in my heart. For I could wish that I myself would be accursed and cut off from Christ for the sake of my own people. (Rom. 9:1-3)

The chapter divisions in our Bibles should not mislead us: Paul's statement in Romans 9:1-3 about his sorrow for Israel is not a new topic, but the direct consequence of the love of God, about which he wrote at the end of Romans 8. Without any transition, he affirms his absolute certainty that nothing can separate him from the love of God in Jesus Christ, and his great sorrow and unceasing anguish, which made him willing, even eager, to be cut off from Christ. It is the love of Christ that compels him (cf. 2 Cor. 5:14). Those who do not allow themselves to be led by the Spirit of Christ are not troubled by this sorrow. It is a mark of the bond with Christ himself. That is expressed in the empathic affirmation: He is speaking the truth in Christ, and it is confirmed in his conscience by the witness of the Holy Spirit. The same Spirit that bears witness with our spirit that we are children of God (8:16) bears witness that this sorrow is of divine origin. It is not just a personal feeling of sadness that wonders how God would feel about all this, but something that God works in the heart of his children! Schlatter writes: As a result of "Christ's communion with him the stirrings of his soul are worked by the Spirit."[4] It is the sorrow Jesus experienced, as we read in the Gospel:

> As he came near and saw the city, he wept over it, saying, "If you, even you, had only recognized on this day the things that make for peace! But now they are hidden from your eyes. Indeed, the days will come upon you, when your enemies will set up ramparts around you and surround you, and hem you in on every side. They will crush you to the ground, you and your children within you . . . because you did not recognize the time of your visitation from God." (Luke 19:41-44)

Paul shared in this anguish. For the anguish Christ suffered has not ended. It will continue as long as his people are trodden down — until the day of which he speaks in the preceding verses: the day when Jerusalem welcomes him as Deliverer with these words: "Blessed is he who

---

4. Schlatter, *Gerechtigkeit*, p. 293.

comes in the name of the Lord" (Luke 13:34-35; Matt. 23:37-39). The abiding nature of this sorrow is manifest in the continuous sorrow of the apostle Paul.

Mere Words?

"For I could wish that I myself were accursed and cut off from Christ for the sake of my brethren." We are reminded here of the very similar words of Moses: "But now, if you will only forgive their sin — but if not, blot me out of the book that you have written" (Exod. 32:32). It has been said that here Paul went too far, and that he knew he went too far. For God had already told Moses: "Whoever has sinned against me I will blot out of my book" (v. 33). But then we saw the miracle happening: "The LORD used to speak to Moses face to face, as one speaks to a friend" (Exod. 33:11). Moses, who did not want salvation from God without his people — the same Moses had found the way to God's heart. For that reason the words of Paul in this passage must have deep meaning. Paul, who does not want to enjoy Christ's redemption without his people, is close to the heart of God's love. And God leads Paul to an understanding of the mystery of Israel's history and Israel's redemption (Rom. 11:25-26).

The significance of what is being said in these verses would escape us completely if we were to assume that the future redemption of Israel was secure, even if Paul had been totally unconcerned about the fate of his people, since all was predetermined by God. If that were so, these would have been mere words, devoid of meaning. But in some way, the salvation of Moses as well as Paul was at stake! They firmly refused to accept the possibility that their people would be lost, and they themselves be saved. And as we saw in Moses' case, this is precisely what God is looking for in the people he has called. God has called them to service, and he does not want to achieve his purpose with Israel without their involvement.

A Voice from the Early Church about Paul's Sorrow

It would be difficult to find a greater admirer of the apostle Paul than the church father Origen. This is certainly the impression one gets from reading his commentary on Romans. He felt that one could never be serious enough about anything Paul had written. Thus he took with utter seriousness these words about Paul's readiness to be cut off from Christ for the sake of his own people. We read in his commentary that Paul was aware that what he was going to say about this topic could well appear to contradict what he had just said about his joy that nothing could separate him from the love of Christ. Did he really desire to be cut off from Christ? Did he want to be lost in order to save others?

No, he says, it is not like that; but I have learned from my Master and Lord that whosoever will save his soul, will lose it, and whosoever will lose it, will find it. So, why should it amaze us if the apostle is willing to be cursed for the sake of his brethren, since he knows that he, who was in the form of God, emptied himself thereof, and took the form of a servant, and became cursed for our sake? Why should it amaze us if — since the Lord has become cursed for the sake of his servants — the servant is cursed for the sake of his brethren? This is, I think, in fact what Moses said to the Lord, when the people had sinned: "But now, if you will only forgive their sin — but if not, blot me out of the book that you have written." What then? Do you want Paul to be inferior to Moses? Moses asked to be blotted out from the book of life for the sake of his brethren. Should then Paul not want to be cursed for the sake of his brethren? But possibly someone might object that Moses by making this offer, deserved to be the instrument of salvation for his people, whereas Paul had this desire, but his prayer was not answered. What would you say if I were to show you that Paul was answered more concretely than Moses? For all who, through Moses, left Egypt, died in the wilderness. And the descendants of those who received the land of promise are still wandering around, having been ejected and banned from it. But listen to what Paul says about Israel. I do not want, brethren, he says, that you remain ignorant about this mystery, that a partial blindness has come over Israel, until the full number of the Gentiles has come in, and so all Israel will be saved (Rom. 11:25-26). Thus, you see how Paul's request was answered, and that he earned the salvation for his brethren through his offer of being cursed for them. And for that reason, it would seem to me, did he begin by saying all these things: that is, that no power would be able to separate him from the love of God. . . . But, as he who through his very essence cannot be separated from the Father, and in spite of his immortality entered death and descended in the realm of the dead, likewise he [Paul], following the example of his Master, since he could not be separated from Christ's love, was cursed for the sake of his brethren. . . .[5]

5. Origen, *Ad Romanos*, 1138-39.

It is not our intention to defend this exegesis of Origen in every detail. That Paul earned the salvation of his people through his willingness to be accursed for their sake is open to misunderstanding. The church father believes that salvation is found only in the cross of Christ, and that the power of the cross, as we heard earlier, suffices for the healing and the restoration of all things (I, 5). That Paul's prayer was answered in a more concrete way than Moses' request is difficult to maintain. Moreover, in the case of Moses eternal redemption and not temporal salvation was at stake. Finally, does Origen intend to say that Paul was indeed cursed for the sake of his people? We discern the full meaning of these words in the importance Origen attached to Paul's readiness to be cut off for the sake of his brethren. It is this willingness, which we also find in Moses, that God is looking for in his servants. We should also note that, in the same breath, Origen links these words with Paul's final argument: All Israel will be saved (Rom. 11:26). Because he took Paul's sorrow utterly seriously, Origen understood that all that Paul had written, from the beginning of chapter 9 — and not just starting from chapter 11 — dealt with God's way of saving Israel.

Origen: All Israel Will Be Saved

Origen was convinced that Israel would be saved. This is clear from the following four observations in his exegesis of these chapters.

1. Israel, he writes, may have been rejected because of its unbelief, but that does not mean that God's promises to them have been withdrawn or invalidated (on 9:9).[6]
2. They have zeal for God. That is not worthless zeal, for it is better to be zealous for God — even when the right understanding is absent — than to have no zeal for God at all! To those who have (and this applies to Israel), to them, Scripture says, shall be given. That will also happen to Israel in the last days, when all Israel shall be saved (on 10:2; referring again to 11:26).[7]

---

6. Origen, *Ad Romanos*, 1142: "quod licet repudiatus sit populus Israel per infidelitatem, non tamen eae promissiones Dei quae erga eos habitae fuerant, deciderint et frustratae sint."

7. Origen, *Ad Romanos*, 1160: "Melius enim est habere zelum Dei, licet non secundum scientiam, quam penitus non habere. 'Qui enim habet,' sicut scriptum est, 'dabitur ei' vel in novissimis cum omnis Israel salvus fiet. . . ."

3. The Jews, admittedly, have denied their Savior, and they have stoned and persecuted those who were sent by him. But they still have a lot left — meditation on the law even though they lack faith and understanding; and they have zeal for God, even though without the right insight. So, they have erred, but not in such a way that their fall is irreversible; that would have been the case if they had completely turned away from meditation on God's law. Therefore, they will rise again (on 11:11).[8]

4. What Origen says about the relationship between the Jews and the church is significant: "As long as Israel persists in its unbelief, the fullness of God's inheritance cannot be said to be complete. For the people of Israel is missing from it. But when the fullness of the Gentiles will have entered, and Israel at the end of time will through faith have reached salvation, it will be the same people it was at the beginning, and . . . it will make the fullness of God's inheritance complete" (on 11:12; referring to 11:25, 26).[9]

After the parable of the olive tree, we hear Origen join Paul in a warning against the pride of the Christians from the Gentiles. Bragging and boasting against the branches that had been broken off — that is: against the Jews of the synagogue — they believed, "that it was not because of God's goodness and the unspeakable decree of his wisdom, but because of their own merit," that the Jews were rejected, and that they, as the shoots of a wild olive tree, had been grafted onto the good olive tree. It was for this reason, he writes, that Paul says to the church: I want you to understand this mystery, so that you will not follow your own wisdom. "For insulting the fallen branches and boasting against the branches that have been broken off, does not stem from God's wisdom,

8. Origen, *Ad Romanos*, 1185-86: "tamen habent adhuc aliquid residui. Est apud illos meditatio legis, licet non credant, nec intelligant. Est apud illos et aemulatio Dei, licet non secundum scientiam. Et propterea dicit Apostolus, quia non 'sic offenderunt ut caderent'; hoc est, ut ab omni legis Dei observantia, vel meditatione penitus declinarent."

9. Origen, *Ad Romanos*, 1187: "sed donec Israel in incredulitate persistit, nondum plenitudo portionis Domini dicetur esse completa. Deest enim ad integrum populus Israel. Cum vero plenitudo gentium subintraverit, et Israel in novissimi tempore per fidem venerit ad salutem, ipse erit populus qui prior quidem fuerat; sed novissimus veniens ipsam quodammodo haereditatus et portionis Domini plenitudinem complebit."

but from reprehensible human wisdom that is ignorant of the divine mystery" (on 11:25).[10]

With his fellow believers, Origen was convinced that the call to announce God's saving acts among the nations had been transferred from the Jews to the Christians. In other words, the Christians had replaced the Jews![11] When the Jewish people, through their disobedience, had been rejected as the special people of the Lord, it became necessary that there be another "special people" on the earth that would take upon itself the glory and the covenants and the law and the service of the Lord, and that would be the special people of God, to replace the people that had misbehaved.[12] Though not forever, Origen views the privileges of Israel, which Paul summarizes in Romans 9:4 as transferred to the church. Paul, however, did not intend it that way. But even in what Origen writes, we note that the term "replacement" is not the final word: God's promises to Israel have not been invalidated; their zeal and their meditation on the law are important in God's sight; and, more importantly still, at the end of time they will come to believe in Jesus and be saved, for without them God's people is not complete! This salvation not only comprised later generations of Jews who would eventually be converted, but, in particular, those Jews who in his time persecuted the Christians. Then they would once again be God's

---

10. Origen, *Ad Romanos*, 1195: "quasi elatos superbientes adversum ramos qui fractisunt, et putantes quod hoc non Dei bonitate et ineffabile dispensatione sapientiae ejus, sed suis meritis consecuti sunt . . . quia insultare lapsis, et gloriari adversus ramos qui fracti sunt, non fit per Dei sapientiam, sed per humanam notabilem et ignorantem mysterium Dei."

11. For exemple, *Contra Celsum* 2.5; 4.3, 42; 5.48 (concerning Matt. 21:43); 2.8, 13; 4.32; 8,42 (concerning the destruction of Jerusalem). See Henry Chadwick, *Origen: Contra Celsum* (Cambridge, 1965; paperback ed. 1980); Marcel Borret, *Origène, Contre Celse* (Paris, 1967-69, 4 vols., in Sources Chrétiennes). For more information, see N. R. M. de Lange, *Origen and the Jews* (2nd ed.; Cambridge, 1976), pp. 75-87: "The Church and the Jews" (in my view it could have dealt more fully with Romans 9–11); Hans Bietenhard, *Caesarea, Origenes und die Juden* (Stuttgart, 1974), pp. 61-73: "Das Verständnis von Röm. 11 bei Origenes."

12. *Ad Romanos*, 1186: ". . . necessarium fuit ut illa refutata et repudiata, esset alia pars Domini super terram, quae gloriam, et testamenta, et legislationem, et obsequia cultus Dei . . . susciperet, et pars Domini pro illa parte quae offenderat vocaretur." We should remember that in Origen's time the "substitution" and the calling to belong to "this other part of the Lord" meant persecution. His father died as a martyr. He himself was severely tortured during the reign of Emperor Decius (249-251). See Eusebius, *Ecclesiastical History* 6.2 and 39.

people, as they had been before. God has not abandoned them as his people, as the later replacement doctrine of a "spiritual Israel" argues.

Note the strong warnings against anti-Semitic sentiments in the church. Origen enlarges upon *insulting* the branches that have been broken off. He believes that God will punish Christians from the Gentiles who are guilty of this more severely than he has punished the Jews.[13] Origen has indeed listened to Paul. Had the church heeded his advice, the later anti-Jewish development of the church would not have been possible.

2. All Israel Must Become Israel

A Source of Despair

We now come to some words of Paul that until our time have been a source of despair for many believers: "I have loved Jacob, but I have hated Esau." These words became one of the cornerstones for the doctrine of predestination, which we referred to earlier: Out of the many God chooses a certain number of people he wants to save, while he does not want to save the rest. It does not depend on what you make of your life. From before his birth, before he had done anything good or bad, it had been decided that Esau had not been chosen by God: "As it is written: I have loved Jacob, but I have hated Esau" (Rom. 9:11-13). This is what Scripture says. And this had to be taken into consideration, whether one liked it or not. That was done in the Canons of Dort, the confessional document cited earlier in this book. There it says of God's "pleasure":

> . . . that he was pleased out of the common mass of sinners to adopt some certain persons as a peculiar people to himself, as it is written, "For the children being not yet born, neither having done any good or evil," etc., "it was said [namely, to Rebecca], 'The elder shall serve the younger; as it is written, 'Jacob I have loved, but Esau have I hated'. . . .'" (I, 10)

We shall consider whether these words of Paul are explained here as he meant them, beginning with what he says about Israel's rejection of the Messiah:

13. *Ad Romanos,* 1194-95.

Not as though the word of God hath taken none effect. For they are not all Israel, which [are] of Israel: Neither, because they are the seed of Abraham, [are] they all children: but, In Isaac shall they seed be called. That is, They which are the children of the flesh, these [are] not the children of God: but the children of the promise are counted for the seed. (9:6-8, AV; brackets inserted by translators)

It is not as though the Word of God has failed, Paul says. Why does he say that? The Messiah has come, but Israel has not been saved! So, God does not do what he has promised through the prophets!

What is Paul's answer? No, this is not contrary to what God promised. For not all who are descendants of Jacob truly belong to Israel, and not all who are born of Abraham are truly Abraham's children. These words have been interpreted as follows: God never indicated that his promise would be for all Israel; his promise to Abraham applies only to that part of Israel which he chooses from among all the Israelites. That, it is assumed, is what Paul makes clear through the story of Ishmael and Isaac. Both are descendants of Abraham, but the promise is only for Isaac.

In Ishmael's case it would be possible to think that the problem was with the mother: Hagar was merely Abraham's concubine. But when we come to Esau and Jacob, it becomes clear that this is not the point. Even though you have the same mother; yes, even when you are twin brothers, the promise seems to apply only to one of the two: not to Esau, but only to Jacob. There is something else. In the case of Esau and Jacob we also see that it does not depend on one's conduct: before they had done anything, even before they were born, God already said that his choice would be only Jacob and not Esau. Therefore, what we now see happening to Israel is in full agreement with Scripture. God has always acted like that. So, why does the greatest part of Israel not share in God's salvation? God does not count them as true Israelites; true Israelites are only those who belong to that part of Israel that has been elected. They are those who accepted the Messiah when he came, and possibly a few more in later times.

So this is a letdown! Paul and the other Jews had hoped that Jesus would save all Israel, but in retrospect it appears that God never intended to do so. Their expectations about God's promise to Israel were too high, and they will have to adapt them to reality, for the hope that all Israel would be saved is not grounded in Scripture. It may be a great sorrow, but however great it is, the disappointment must be accepted. This is the explanation that has become generally accepted in the church.

Why This Interpretation Is Impossible

We now list four reasons why Paul's line of thought makes this interpretation impossible.

1. *Paul does not accept it.* If it were true that Scripture offers no promise for the Israel that rejects its Messiah, Paul would have to accept that. But like Moses, Paul does not passively accept the lostness of Israel. And he is sure that God does not do this either! What he subsequently writes can therefore not be taken as an explanation why he should resign himself to the lostness of his "kindred according to the flesh."

2. *Israel's privileges have not been annulled.* Paul refers to his "kindred according to the flesh"; the descendants of the patriarchs have rejected the Messiah. But he says about them: "To them belongs the adoption" and "to them belong the promises" (Rom. 9:4). He does not declare: "Once upon a time the promises belonged to them." Such a thing can never be said of God's promises. God does what he has promised — nothing will cause him to annul his promises, for he knows what he has promised and to whom he has made his promises. Moreover, in the cases of Ishmael and Esau, this would not apply because right from the start God had stated that the promise was not for them. When Paul first says that the promises belong to disobedient Israel, he cannot later turn around and say that they are only valid for the loyal part of Israel. That is also clear from what follows.

3. *God's faithfulness to the unfaithful:* The unfaithfulness of Israel will not destroy God's faithfulness, Paul wrote earlier in his epistle (3:1-3). In the same passage he already mentioned the privileges of unfaithful Israel, which he enlarges upon in Romans 9:4-5. If he is convinced that God remains faithful to unfaithful Israel, he cannot here intend to say that God has abandoned them as his people.

4. *All Israel will be saved.* ". . . And so all Israel will be saved," Paul writes at the end of his argumentation (11:26). He says this in writing about the Israel that has been "hardened" (11:25), that has become an enemy of the gospel (11:28), and he stresses that "the gifts and the calling of God are irrevocable" (11:29) — just as he had argued in Romans 3:1-3. He continues: "God has imprisoned all in disobedience so that he may be merciful to all" (11:32). This is what Paul intended to affirm from the beginning: all! Therefore it cannot be true that Paul begins by suggesting that only part of Israel will be saved.

Jacob and Esau: What It Means to Be "Israel"

But what *did* the apostle intend to say when he used these peculiar words: "They are not all of Israel, which are of Israel" and "They which are the children of the flesh, these are not the children of God"? Let us look at these words a little more closely. In both cases the emphasis is on "they" and "these." Paul, in fact, puts it even more succinctly: "They not all Israel" and "These not the children of God."[14] The emphasis is upon what it really means to be *Israel*, what it really means to be a *child of God*. All Israelites are descendants of Israel, the new name God gave to Jacob (Gen. 32:28). But being children of Jacob in itself does not make them what God intended them to be. Not yet! — for they must come to the point where they are what God intended them to be! Herein lies the crucial difference with the interpretation we discussed above. That interpretation simply does away with those who are descendants of Israel but do not belong to Israel, and no longer recognizes them as the people of God: In rejecting its Messiah the Jewish people put itself at the same level as other nations. But that is not what the Bible teaches. All who have been born as descendants of Jacob are intended by God to become true Israelites in the fullest sense of the word. Of this Jacob is the shining example.

From his birth the promise was for Jacob. But he did not automatically become what God wanted him to be! Jacob is pictured for us as the man who wanted the blessing at the expense of his brother Esau. And that is not what God has in mind for Israel. Israel has not been called to have the blessing for itself, but to be a blessing from God for all nations. For Jacob this means: to be first of all a blessing to his brother Esau. That he becomes in the night of his wrestling with God. In that night Jacob must fight for the blessing: "I will not let you go, unless you bless me." There God gives him the name Israel, and there he receives the blessing: "And there he blessed him" — the word "there" receives the emphasis (Gen. 32:22-32). Now the past evil has been taken care of and the way is open for an encounter with his brother. In that night God makes him a different person. He has become

---

14. T. Baarda pointed to this emphasis in his essay "De aanwijzende voornaamwoorden (demonstrative pronouns) in Romeinen 9:6 en 8." For the Semitic background of Romans 9:6-9, see *Amsterdamse Cahiers voor exegese en bijbelse theologie*, ed. K. A. Deurloo (Kampen, 1986), pp. 101-13. This Semitic coloring (with the omission of the verb "to be") results in a special emphasis of these demonstrative pronouns in the Greek text (AV: *they* and *these*) on the objects to which they refer, which is of great importance for the exegesis. In the NRSV this remains unclear.

Israel: a blessing for his brother Esau. We read about this in the story of his encounter with his brother that follows. He accompanies the gift, which he had sent to Esau, with the words: "Take, I pray thee, my blessing, that is brought to thee" (AV). The Revised Standard Version refers to a "gift," but the literal meaning is "blessing" (Gen. 33:11).[15]

We needed this excursus about Jacob and Esau because we have been conditioned to see Esau as the brother whom God had written off. But in fact the story teaches us that he is the brother who receives the blessing when Jacob has truly become *Israel*. And so, the people of Esau — Edom — is not written off; it is "written in"! After Jacob and Esau together buried their father — the problem between them had been solved for good! — we find an entire chapter (Gen. 36) about Esau's posterity. God wanted them to be included in the book of his Word for Israel.

This story teaches us what it means to be *Israel*. Jacob was born to be Israel, to be a blessing to his brother Esau, a blessing to all nations. But he does not become that until his struggle with God. This is closely related to our next theme: the children of God.

Israel, the People of God

"Not the children of the flesh are the children of God." Earlier in Romans we learned who are God's children: "All who are led by the Spirit of God are children of God" (Rom. 8:14). In them the law is fulfilled — "the fruit of the Spirit is love, joy, peace . . ." (Gal. 5:22). But something must precede! Paul describes this in Romans 7 — the struggle with our own inability to obey God's law and our cry for help: "Who will rescue me from this body of death"? Human beings receive that redemption through what God did for them in Jesus Christ (7:24-25). In Christ God reconciles us with himself, and in Christ he gives us his Spirit — the spirit of adoption as children of God (Rom. 8:15).

All Israel must become God's people. For to them "belongs the adoption" (Rom. 9:4). In writing these words, Paul is referring to his "kindred

15. I owe this insight to a lecture by Frans Breukelman: God is here engaged in a struggle with Jacob to solve the matter concerning Esau; Jacob, who wanted the blessing at the expense of his brother, becomes Israel, the bearer of God's blessing on behalf of his brother. Now God will be with him as he meets Esau. Genesis 33:10 indicates the link between the two encounters: "For truly to see your face is like seeing the face of God."

according to the flesh," the Jews who rejected their Messiah. The word that is here rendered as "adoption" may also be translated "sonship." We do not read: To them *belonged* the sonship or adoption, but it *belongs* to them. This present tense is also used with regard to the promises (see also 9:4). This implies that this continues to be God's intention for the Jewish people. It will yet be: the people of God, the people for whom creation "waits with eager longing" (8:19-21).

Only God's Faithfulness — No Hidden Election

To them "belongs the adoption" — but God's intention for them has not become reality. There is an obstruction. First of all, there is the problem of trust in *descent*. We already saw that descent from Abraham does not automatically make people children of God; we also saw it in Ishmael's case, and, even more poignantly, in that of Esau. The second aspect Paul points to plays an even more significant role in his letter: *trust in the law;* by obeying the law a person would presumably be worthy to be a child of God. This is the situation for Paul's "kindred according to the flesh." They depend on the law (Rom. 2:17); they have zeal for God, and they seek to establish their own righteousness (10:3). Paul reacts to this by enlarging upon the example of Jacob and Esau; the promise had already been made before Jacob's birth, before he had done anything. This underlines, he writes, that the future must depend solely on God's purpose of election (9:11), regardless of human deeds. Had election depended on Jacob's deeds, it would all have ended in nothingness. But in spite of his conduct, God made him the bearer of his promise. Thus it becomes clear that Israel is God's people not on the basis of what it does for God, but on the basis of what God does for it.

This truth applies to all Israel. This is how God promised election to his prophets. In Jeremiah we read: "'For they shall all know me, from the least of them to the greatest,' says the LORD." Immediately follows the assurance that God will not reject Israel's posterity because of its many sins (31:34-37). Moreover in Isaiah 45:25 we read that "all the offspring of Israel" will be justified.[16] Here we find the basis for Paul's expectation that his

16. The margin of the Dutch Authorized Version once again introduces a restriction. Israel's seed in Jeremiah 31:36 is explained simply as: "That is, the church." And "all the offspring of Israel" in Isaiah 45:25 is understood as: "All the children of Israel, that is, the believers from the Jews and from the Gentiles." People read Romans through these spectacles, and this prevented them from grasping what Paul meant.

"kindred according to the flesh" will be saved: the prophetic promises of God's faithfulness to unfaithful Israel. These he has in mind from the beginning of his argument.

It is therefore a tragic mistake to think that God continues to make a separation among Jacob's posterity in the manner of Ishmael and Esau, as if all the time part of them is chosen, while part is rejected.[17] If that were true, no one in Israel would be able to depend on God, and the question would always be: "Am I like Esau?" Here is the source of despair in the traditional doctrine of election: a secret choice of God that predestines — even in the church — the one as a child of God, while rejecting the other. But that is not how God deals with his children! God's choice of Isaac and Jacob was no secret; it was announced from the beginning. And the choice of Jacob means that all his posterity is destined to be God's children. A secret election, which predestines part of Israel to become the real Israel, while rejecting another part, has nothing to do with what Scripture teaches about election.

Is God Unjust?

Nonetheless, when Paul discusses Israel's rejection of the Messiah, he says: "But I have hated Esau." It is impossible to soften the word "hated"; the prophetic words here quoted by Paul do not allow that. Edom, the people of Esau, is described as "the people with whom the LORD is angry forever" (Mal. 1:2, 4).[18]

17. Thus it was taught: "In the same manner as the blessing of the covenant created a separation between the people of Israel and all other nations, God's election makes a distinction between those who belong to this people, as He predestines some to eternal life and others to eternal doom" (Calvin, *Romans*, 198-99. Calvin refers to this as the "secret election"; see VI, n. 1.

18. It does not help to point to Genesis 29:31, where we are told that Leah was *hated* (AV), and then to turn to other versions, such as the RSV, where the word *unloved* is used. Indeed, "to hate" can here be understood as "to put in second place." This also applies to the words of Jesus: "Whoever comes to me and does not hate father and mother . . ." (Luke 14:26). But Malachi connects this hate with wrath! When speaking about *Israel*, other prophets also use the word "hate": "My heritage has become to me like a lion in the forest; she has lifted up her voice against me — therefore I hate her" (Jer. 12:8). Yet, this same prophet tells us that God loves Israel with an everlasting love, and that he will have compassion on his people (Jer. 31:3, 20, 31-37). Cf. Hosea: "Every evil of theirs began at Gilgal; there I came to hate them. Because of the wickedness of their deeds . . . I will love them no more" (9:15). Yet also for Hosea the final word is: the divine love for Israel (1:9-10). We will see in a later chapter (VII, 3) that the eternal anger to which Malachi refers (1:4) is not to be understood as a wrath without end.

Israel, even though it is not Esau, will become the object of God's wrath. Paul now broaches this subject: Israel is the object of God's "wrath" (Rom. 9:22). But that is not true of all Israelites: Out of their midst the Messiah calls his church. Not on the basis of their better conduct. Not because they are better people. That is clear from Paul: Jesus transforms a persecutor of the church into a chosen instrument! So, even within Israel, we discover God's election at work. Thus we are faced with an unfathomable mystery. If God wants to show mercy to all Israel — and that is what he wants! — why does he not do this to all Israel *at the same time?* Why does he makes this distinction? Is this not injustice?

Could God be unjust? No, that is impossible, Paul says. For he is the God who has mercy. Paul here refers to what God said to Moses: "I will have mercy on whom I have mercy. . . ." If God wants to show mercy, no one is going to stop him. His favor does not depend on human effort: "So it depends not on human will or exertion, but on God who shows mercy." Note: Romans 9:15-16 speaks only of his mercy. His reason for calling the church of the Messiah from the midst of Israel, and for leaving the rest in their disobedience and bringing them to judgment, is solely that he might show mercy to all. This is what Paul believes about God. To him it is impossible that there might be injustice in God. And with that conviction he faces the perplexing question of the "hardening" of Israel.

Pharaoh, the Hardening

Paul now points to Pharaoh. Pharaoh receives the command from Israel's God to let his people go in freedom. But he responds: "I do not know the LORD, and I will not let Israel go" (Exod. 5:1-2). The next thing we hear is that God "hardens" Pharaoh. Does God incite a human being to do evil? No, Pharaoh is not a good king who is provoked by God to do evil things. He is the ruthless oppressor of a powerless people. For that reason God sends Moses to him with the command: Stop the oppression and let my people go.

Pharaoh belongs to that part of humanity which does not listen to God's voice and serves other gods. He continues unperturbed in his rebellion against God, without knowing against whom he rebels. Now God calls this king to an encounter with him, and he demands obedience. Pharaoh must make up his mind. He must choose: Either do or refuse what God commands. His answer is, "No." As long as God allows a person to go his own way, he can avoid a clear choice; and his rebellion then remains invisible. But when God confronts a person with his commands — what else can be expected than rebellion against his will, rebellion that has characterized humankind from the beginning?

What is God's plan for the Pharaoh and for his people? Their destruction in the Sea of Reeds? That is indeed the result. But it is not God's final intention for them. He has promised Abraham that he wants to bless all nations through him (Gen. 12:3). Did God expect something different from what now happens with Pharaoh? His people is one of the peoples whom he wants to bless through Abraham and his seed! This route of "hardening" and of divine judgment over Pharaoh and his people — for this "hardening" leads directly to God's judgment — is the route God chooses in order to lead them eventually to that blessing.[19]

Pharaoh does not know the Lord and refuses to obey. But God will not rest until Pharaoh, with all his heart, will know him and will do what he commands! This is God's purpose in the way he takes with Pharaoh. The road of "hardening" and of judgment has only one goal: a healing of his rebellion. We find a prophecy about hardening and healing in the book of Isaiah: "The LORD will make himself known to the Egyptians; and the Egyptians will know the LORD on that day. . . . The LORD will strike Egypt, striking and healing. They will return to the LORD, and he will listen to their supplications and heal them" (Isa. 19:21-22).[20] This does not explain why God chooses this route. But it does emphasize what God's ultimate goal is in choosing it. Like our excursus about Jacob and Esau, this discussion about Pharaoh's fate was necessary, since our tradition pictures his "hardening" as the end of all hope for him. But, as we see, Scripture does not support that idea.

God "Hardens" Israel

Paul now continues to write, not about the disobedient Pharaoh, but about disobedient Israel. He argues: The fact that Israel has rejected the Messiah is due to God's "hardening" of Israel! This is what we hear in chapter 11:

19. Origen deals extensively with God's purpose in "hardening" Pharaoh. He does not, however, take the promise to Abraham as his point of departure. See *De Principiis*, 3:1, 7-12. For the "divine therapy and the death of Pharaoh," see also Origen, *Philocalie 21-27, Sur le libre arbitre* (Paris, 1976), pp. 279-87, published in Sources Chrétiennes, no. 226.

20. The objection that this is now impossible for Pharaoh and his people, since they are dead, does not hold! For the rule of the Messiah over the dead, cf. III, 6.

Israel failed to obtain what it was seeking. The elect obtained it, but the rest were hardened, as it is written, "God gave them a sluggish spirit, eyes that would not see, and ears that would not hear, down to this very day." And David says, ". . . Let their eyes be darkened so that they cannot see, and keep their backs forever bent." (Rom. 11:7-10)

Hardening, blinding! Only the "rest" will be excluded from this fate. And God himself does this! He wants to harden them at the same time that he shows mercy to other Jews, who are just as disobedient. Paul himself is a prime example. But is God's wrath over their disobedience just? — if he wanted to, he could change their conduct! We hear the uneasiness in the question: "You will say to me then, 'Why then does he still find fault? For who can resist his will?'" (9:19). This repeats the question, posed after the example of Jacob and Esau, in a more intense form: "Is there injustice on God's part?" (9:14). Paul simply replies: "But who indeed are you, a human being, to argue with God?" (9:20). The meaning of this statement is explained in what follows: the parable of the potter.

3. The Parable of the Potter

Two Kinds of Objects

> Will what is molded say to the one who molds it, "Why have you made me like this?" Has the potter no right over the clay, to make out of the same clay one object for special use and another for ordinary use? (Rom. 9:20-21)

A potter makes many kinds of objects. The word here rendered "object" is also used for "vessel," "cup," or "tool." At issue here is what the potter makes: various kinds of vessels. Just as the potter uses clay to produce what he wants, so God uses people. Paul writes that God wants two things. First of all, he wants to show his wrath and to reveal his power. God's wrath is directed toward the evil deeds of humankind; his power destroys that evil and eliminates it from his creation. Second, God wants to make known the richness of his mercy for all who have sinned.

God thus makes a distinction. We noticed that distinction in his treatment of Jacob and Esau, and subsequently in the mercy for Israel and the hardening of Pharaoh. That is what Paul deals with in this parable: From the same clay the potter produces two kinds of vessels. The interpretation of this parable has had a far-reaching influence on what we have been taught about God. Our tradition wants us to believe that these two kinds of vessels represent an eternal separation that God wanted between "the objects of his mercy" and "the objects of his wrath." He wants to save a small number of people, but the great majority is destined to eternal damnation. Those who demurred were rebuffed in the Canons of Dort (I, 18):

> To those who murmur at the free grace of election and just severity of reprobation, we answer with the apostle: "Nay, but, O man, who art thou that repliest against God?" (Rom. 9:20); and quote the language of our Savior: "Is it not lawful for me to do what I will with mine own?" (Matt. 20:15)

These last words are taken from the parable in which Jesus speaks of the goodness of God, who is at liberty to show goodness to those who do not deserve it. But here, in this confessional document, these words are used to prove that God is at liberty to send people to eternal perdition, and that he will indeed do so with the great majority of those he created! What does the parable of the potter look like if we assume that that is what Paul meant?

Has He No Right . . . ?

Imagine a potter who has made a number of vessels and who, upon their completion, takes a sledgehammer and beats some of them to pieces. Why would he do that? To show his strength! All must know how strong he is. To provide further proof, he thinks of something else: a process to harden his pottery so much that no one can destroy it. See, he is strong enough! He reduces the pottery to pieces! With great satisfaction he looks at the pieces: This was exactly what he wanted! For this very purpose he made these "objects of wrath." It is truly a demonstration of his power. Moreover, he is at liberty to do so, for he can do with his own property as he chooses!

But there is another side to him. For there is another product line: He also makes vessels of exquisite delicacy and beauty. These he keeps with great care and love. But we feel uneasy. Is this delicate artwork in safe hands? For he seems to need these acts of destruction. But why should he care? He can do with these objects whatever he wants. From the same lump of clay he can make something new and beautiful again! No, this man should not have become a potter.

It is an absurd example. But it shows at least one thing: God is not like that! It is not, however, superfluous to stress this fact once more. We referred (in I, 5) to the objections raised in 2 Esdras against God. If God destines most people to eternal perdition, it would have been better if he had not created the world at all. So our absurd example is not without foundation: God has been said to be like that. Now we return to Paul. God indeed does these two things: He has mercy on whom he wills, and he hardens whom he wills. But what is his purpose in making this distinction?

Why Does He "Carry" Them?

The objects of his wrath are "made for destruction." That is their future — the judgment: "anguish and distress for everybody who does evil" (Rom. 2:9). But this does not achieve God's ultimate purpose for them! What does Paul say about these objects of his wrath? He says: God carries them with much patience. Our translations use the word "endure," but the word Paul uses is the common word for "carry." It may mean "endure," but here that meaning is misleading. Enduring has to do with awkward things. We endure the rudeness of other people, but our endurance has limits! This also seems to be the case in this passage, for it ends with "destruction." And that presumably is what God had in mind all along. He bears with them for a while, but he has already determined that he is soon going to destroy them. He is like the strange potter we described above, who intended all along to destroy the objects he had made. When Jesus, however, envisages the destruction of Jerusalem — no stone would be left upon another — he weeps over the city (Luke 19:41-42). This is not what God intended for Jerusalem!

Precisely because he has other intentions for Jerusalem, he "carries" the Jews who rejected their Messiah — the objects of his wrath — with infinite patience. Why does He "carry" them? In order that he may reveal the riches of his glory over "the objects of his mercy." To whom does he want to reveal this? To the objects of his mercy? He would not need these objects of wrath for that purpose. In that case he would not need to continue "carrying" them with so much patience. No, he "carries" them because he wants to show these objects of his wrath something: his mercy for the disobedient, for the heathen; for "not my people," "not my beloved" (Rom. 9:25-26). Once they were "objects of wrath" — "children of wrath," as we read in Ephesians 2:3. And see what God did with them: He made them children of the living God! He wants to do the same with those who are now the objects of his wrath. He wants to make them *jealous,* in order that they, too, will want for themselves the same mercy he gave to those objects of

151

mercy. This, and nothing else, is the purpose of his wrath (Rom. 11:32). Karl Barth put it this way: *He carries them toward his mercy.*[21]

"A Far-reaching Modification of the Original Intention"

In our interpretation of Romans 9 we followed what Karl Barth wrote in his exposition of the doctrine of divine election. We would do well also to pay attention to an exegete who clearly kept his distance from Barth. Herman Ridderbos published his commentary on Romans in 1959. Following his exegesis of Romans 9 he wrote an Appendix: *God's Sovereignty according to Romans 9*. In this addendum he gives an account of how he came to an interpretation that differs fundamentally from the Reformed tradition. This tradition, he argues, saw a dual predestination — on the one hand to eternal salvation, and on the other to eternal perdition — as the real subject of the chapter. This interpretation was found, in particular, in Calvin. But the fact that God chose not Ishmael but Isaac, and not Esau but Jacob, should not be detached from the context in which Scripture places them. The Bible indicates that the line of God's promise ran through Isaac and Jacob. Concerning the statement: "I have loved Jacob, but I have hated Esau," he writes: "That in Romans 9:13 Paul meant 'love' and 'hate' in the sense of the eternal election of Jacob and the eternal rejection of Esau, can in no way be proven from this passage, and is, as far as we can see, an arbitrary, far-reaching modification of the original meaning of these texts."

Furthermore, in Pharaoh's case Paul speaks of God's sovereignty to harden the heart of sinful Pharaoh and to destroy him, not of God's sovereignty to predestine him to eternal perdition. "If it is argued that this latter aspect must have been the ground for Pharaoh's fate, the reply must be, that 'the apostle himself, in what he says in this passage about Pharaoh, does not draw such a conclusion of a personal predestination to damnation.' He then emphasizes that *'this position of Israel in the sequence of Esau and Pharaoh'* does not point to *'a closed, but rather an open situation'*, as will become clearer in Romans 11. Even this 'hardening' of Israel by God himself (11:7-8) does not prevent it from yet finding access to God's salvation

---

21. Barth, CD, II/2, pp. 222-23. Another exegesis has, however, been proposed: God wants the damned to see his compassion for the redeemed in order to intensify their torments. In 2 Esdras (7:83) it is part of the pains of those who are punished "to see the reward of those who have believed the testimony of the Most High."

(11:11). Or to put it even more sharply: To be an object of wrath as a result of God's sovereignty does not imply that one could never become an object of mercy (cf. 11:32)."[22]

These words of Herman Ridderbos have guided us in our interpretation of Romans 9 at least as much as Barth's exegesis. In the exegesis of this chapter in particular, our tradition deviates from Scripture — with fatal consequences! Again we are face to face with the horrifying picture of God for which the church, since the time of Augustine, sought support in these words of Paul: "I have loved Jacob, but I have hated Esau." And: "So then he has mercy on whomever he wills, and he hardens whomever he wills" — "far-reaching," because the church throughout the ages has based both the doctrine of the lost masses and the doctrine of Israel's rejection on an interpretation of Paul's words that says the opposite of what he means.

The Absolute Mystery of God's Ways

Israel has become an "object of wrath." This wrath is synonymous with God's judgment:

> Though the number of the children of Israel be as the sand of the sea, a remnant shall be saved; for he will finish the work, and cut it short in righteousness. . . . Except the Lord of Sabaoth had left us a seed, we had been as Sodom, and been made like unto Gomorrah. (Rom. 9:27-29, AV)

Only a "remnant," the "rest" will be saved; the others will not. The prophecies of Isaiah here quoted by Paul all deal with judgment. "For though your people Israel were like the sand of the sea, only a remnant of them will return. . . . For the Lord GOD of hosts will make a full end, as decreed, in all the earth" (Isa. 1:22, 23; see also Isa. 1:9).

But is this judgment the end of God's mercy? The answer becomes clear in the exegesis of Romans 9–11! Paul wrote in Romans 2:5: "By your hard and impenitent heart you are storing up wrath for yourself on the day of wrath, when God's righteous judgment will be revealed." The word "hard" is related to the word "harden" that Paul uses in Romans 9. As Pharaoh was hardened and had to meet his judgment, so the people of Israel is hardened and will meet its judgment. But that is not the end of

22. Ridderbos, *Romeinen,* pp. 227-31.

God's involvement with Israel. Note what Paul writes about the "seed" among Israel (11:5), the elect from among the Jews who believe in the Messiah. Paul uses the word "seed" to indicate the future potential of this remnant; they carry the future of all Israel in them. It is a tool in God's hand, God's instrument by which, through judgment, he leads his people to his mercy. This is immediately clear from Paul's prayer: "Brothers and sisters, my heart's desire and prayer to God for them is that they may be saved" (Rom. 10:1). Paul here prays for the salvation of the "objects of wrath that are made for destruction" (9:22). We know what it means that God has made objects of mercy: They come to God with their prayers on behalf of the objects of wrath. So they answer God's purpose of election: to be chosen instruments of God's mercy for the sake of their fellow believers who are outside of God's mercy; chosen to intercede for them. It is the prayer of the hope that comes from the Spirit; the hope that reaches beyond the judgment.

But why does God act like that? If he intends to show mercy to all his people, why would he first pour out his wrath over so many? Here we encounter the utter mystery of God's ways, which are not our ways (Isa. 55:8). Paul has borrowed the image of the potter from Isaiah 45. The clay cannot say to its potter: "What are you making?" as if the object that is created could judge whether or not the potter does his work properly (v. 9).[23] The entire chapter, however, speaks only of God's redemptive activity: "Turn to me and be saved, all the ends of the earth!" (v. 22); and "To me every knee shall bow. . . . Only in the LORD, it shall be said of me, are righteousness and strength (vv. 23, 24); and: "In the LORD all the offspring of Israel shall triumph and glory" (v. 25). This saving work of God takes the people through the judgment — why it does so is not explained — but it climaxes in the hymn of praise about his judgments and his ways (Rom. 11:33). "They shall sing of the ways of the LORD" (Ps. 138:5), for, behold, all are coming home!

Now we begin to understand what Paul means when he writes: "but who indeed, are you, a human being, to argue with God?" (Rom. 9:20). The

---

23. We also find the example of the potter and the product that protests against him in Isaiah 29:16. There also we detect God's totally incomprehensible acts, whereby he makes his people, through the judgment, into what he intends them to be. Isaiah 28:23-29 describes this incomprehensible, but fully intentional, act in the beautiful metaphor of the farmer. Note the "not forever" nature of God's judgments (the plowing and the threshing)!

point here is not that God has the absolute sovereignty to do as he pleases with his creatures and that he tolerates no protest.[24] It is rather: Who are you, a mere human being, that you should tell God what he ought to do: a world that is in total rebellion against him, bound by powers so evil and strong that no human being can fathom them — to save such a world from its bonds, and to make all people, the living and the dead, want to come and be saved. Paul here deals with the ways of a loving God, who has given all he has — he did not withhold his own Son — to reach that goal (Rom. 8:32). So he simply asks: Who are you that you should argue with *this* God!

Wrathful Jealousy and the Hands of the Father

God "carries" the objects of his wrath with great endurance (9:22), because he wants them to see his compassion for the objects of his mercy. He wants to make them jealous, as we already stated. We encounter this word "jealous" for the first time in Romans 10:19:

> Again I ask, did Israel not understand? First Moses says, "I will make you jealous of those who are not a nation; with a foolish nation I will make you angry."[25]

Paul has described his brothers and sisters as zealous, but their zeal is "not enlightened." They are unfamiliar with the righteousness that comes from God, and seek to establish their own righteousness (10:2-3). At the beginning of this letter he wrote about God's saving righteousness; now he

---

24. Augustine detects nothing strange in what God does; the argument of Romans 9:19 simply reflects stupidity. For, if someone understands this, he will find no reason to object: "For then he perceives that the whole human race was condemned in its rebellious head by a divine judgment so just, that if not a single member of the race had been redeemed, no one could justly have questioned the justice of God. . . ." Then he makes clear that God *needs* the eternal damnation of the many to make the redeemed realize how undeserved their redemption is (*Enchiridion*, 99). This "understanding" led to his horrifying concept of God (see I, 3).

25. Deut. 32:21; Paul must have perceived this text as the answer to the riddle of Israel's "hardening." J. Jeremias (*Sprachliche Beobachtungen*, p. 201) writes: "Indeed, everything points to the fact that it was the phrase 'I will make you jealous of those who are not a nation' (Deut. 32:21; cf. Rom. 10:19; 11:11, 14) that opened the eyes of the apostle to God's plans with his people and solved for him the mystery of the hardening of Israel . . . : the example of a living Gentile church was in God's plan the method to call Israel back home."

returns to this theme: "No one who believes in him will be put to shame. For there is no distinction between Jew and Greek; the same Lord is Lord of all and is generous to them who call on him. For, 'Everyone who calls on the name of the Lord shall be saved'" (Rom. 10:11-12; cf. 3:21-30). However, Israel has stumbled over this. For them the gospel of Jesus has become "a stone that will make people stumble, a rock that will make them fall" (9:33).

The jealousy has to do with stumbling and falling. For it is a wrathful jealousy about which Moses wrote. That is what Paul now sees as fulfilled. We know from the book of Acts what happened when the Gentiles accepted the gospel. When the Jews saw how a multitude of Gentiles was interested in the gospel, they "were filled with jealousy" (Acts 13:45). The Jews, who all their lives zealously served God by keeping his law, hear what is being said to the Gentiles: They can be saved by putting their faith in Jesus without the prior requirement of keeping the law. It offends them and makes them angry.

We heard about this irritation and anger earlier. "Then he became angry and refused to go in" — the elder brother in the story of the prodigal son (Luke 15:28). He was angry because his lost brother had come home and because of the reception given to him by his father. His father comes outside and urges him to enter the house and join in the celebrations. On that note the parable ends. As Paul writes his letter, this is still the situation in which that part of Israel persists: it rejects the gospel. The prophets had spoken about this: "But of Israel he says: 'All day long I have held out my hands to a disobedient and contrary people'" (Rom. 10:21; Isa. 65:2). The Father stands beside his irascible son. He does not give up: his hands remain stretched out toward him. For that reason this angry jealousy will not be the last thing with the son. His jealousy will change into the envy that wants to share in the compassion of the Father for his disobedient and lost children. This is the topic Paul addresses in Romans 11.

CHAPTER VI

And So All Israel Shall Be Saved (Romans 11)

1. To Incite Them to Jealousy

Disobedient Israel Is Not Rejected

> I ask, then, has God rejected his people? By no means! I myself am an Israelite, a descendant of Abraham, a member of the tribe of Benjamin. God has not rejected his people whom he foreknew. (Rom. 11:1-2)

The apostle here quotes Psalm 94:14 verbatim: "For the LORD will not forsake his people; he will not abandon his heritage." It is "*his* people"; it is the people "he foreknew": he knew what He was in for! He made a covenant with a stiff-necked people (Exod. 34:9-10). Therefore, their disobedience cannot be a reason for him eventually to reject them.

We may not immediately be convinced by Paul's argument: "I myself am an Israelite, a descendant of Abraham. . . ." What has the fact that he himself is called to serve Jesus to do with the Jews who reject Jesus? But yet it is so: Paul considers his own calling as an apostle a guarantee that God has not rejected his people! He, a persecutor of the church, had been called by Jesus to be his servant — irresistibly. For Paul this is proof that God will not give up on his people: He will do with all what he did with him. He points to the time of Elijah. The prophet believed he was the only one left who served God. But God reminded him that there were seven thousand others who had not bowed their knees to Baal. Likewise, now, there is a "remnant, chosen by grace" (Rom. 11:4-5); this is the "seed" earlier referred to that the Lord had left — seed with a future potential (9:29).

Some interpreters have argued that God will fulfill his promise to Abraham through the salvation of this remnant. In so doing he would have fulfilled his promise: For God the part represents the whole.[1] But Paul does not refer to the salvation of the "remnant, chosen by grace"; he writes about *the salvation of those who had not been chosen,* of the "rest" that was "hardened" (11:7).

Note these words: "chosen by his grace." The mere existence of this remnant is the result of God's grace — not of the loyalty of these Jews, but of the God who elected them. "But if it is by grace, it is no longer on the basis of works" (v. 6). Thus, the future of Israel does not depend on Israel's obedience, but on the God who remains loyal to his disloyal people (3:3). Since all depends on grace, Israel's future is secure, however bleak it may appear.

God's Purpose with Hardened Israel

Earlier we referred to verses 8-10 (V, 2). God has hardened Israel. God gave them a spirit of deep sleep — eyes with which they could not see and ears with which they could not hear. These words of Isaiah were also quoted by Christ himself (Isa. 6:9, 10; Matt. 13:14-15). Paul adds the words of judgment from a psalm of revenge (Ps. 69:23-24), that appears to announce the end of God's mercy. But then we are told about God's purpose in his judgment: He will save them. He will achieve his purpose by making them jealous of "those who are not a nation" (Rom. 10:19).

> So I ask, have they stumbled so as to fall? By no means! But through their stumbling salvation has come to the Gentiles, so as to make Israel jealous. (11:11)

1. Calvin (*Romans,* comment on 11:2) discerns God's faithfulness to his covenant in the fact that he does not reject Abraham's posterity *in its entirety,* but elects some of them to be saved. He refers to "the hidden election" (*arcano electio*). This election has also been referred to as "representation." F. Dreyfus ("Le passé et le devant d'Israël," in W. G. Kümmel et al., *Die Israelfrage nach Röm. 9–11* [Rome, 1977], p. 142) remarks that the idea of representation is valid as long as the representative is regarded as the *pledge* of the totality that is to follow, and not as something that replaces that totality: "Le Reste *représente* la totalité du peuple; il est même . . . le gage du salut du peuple entier." Cf. also VI, 4.

These difficult words have been translated in many different ways. But the matter it is about is clear. First of all, it was not God's intention that the fall of hardened Israel would be irreversible. Second, as a result of the disobedience of hardened Israel, salvation has come to the Gentiles. And, third, the intent of salvation for the Gentiles was that Israel would become jealous and thus ultimately be saved.

Our real problem is with the second aspect: salvation comes to the Gentiles as a result of Israel's disobedience.[2] Israel is the people through which God wants to bless all nations. This requires that Israel keep the ways of the Lord (Gen. 18:18-19) — in a word: obedience! But has God's salvation now come to the nations as a result of their disobedience? Some scholars have argued that it has been a blessing for the church that most Jews did not become part of Christianity. Just remember how much trouble the Jewish Christians in Judea created for Paul. Those difficulties resulted in the main theme of his letter to the Galatians. What would have happened if all Jews had accepted the gospel! This way of thinking has long characterized the anti-Jewish tradition in the church.

That way of thinking does not make sense either.[3] For it is through the work of Jews who obeyed the gospel that the Gentiles were reached with the good news. Paul affirms this when he describes his calling: "I was not disobedient to the heavenly vision" (Acts 26:19). What would have happened if all Jews had been as obedient as Paul? That is the question that should be asked here! The answer to this question is in verse 12: When Israel obeys the Messiah, that will mean many more "riches" for the world!

Paul experiences the disobedience of Israel as great sorrow and unceasing anguish. Yet, this is God's way. God has allowed the majority of Israel to be hardened, and as a result salvation has come to the Gentiles. Why does God act like that? Once again we face the mystery of the

---

2. The Greek word *ethnos* has the dual meaning of "Gentiles" and "people." As a rule the word refers to non-Israelites. Thus "Gentiles" can always be understood as "peoples." If the members of these peoples are intended, the word "Gentiles" (i.e., non-Jews) is to be preferred.

3. Godet (*Aux Romains*, 2.373) argues that as a result of Israel's insistence upon the law as a means to salvation, God had no other option than to blind the eyes of Israel. Had he not done so, the gospel would have been judaized; the believing Gentiles would have become proselytes of Israel and salvation would not have reached all nations — as if God would not have been able to open Israel's eyes as he opened Paul's! Remarkably enough, a little later he views the absence of a converted Israel as the cause of the feebleness of the church (in his comments on 11:15; see IX, n. 3).

hardening of Israel — our total inability to understand God's dealings. But his dealings will eventually result in the "fullness" of Israel, which Paul refers to in verse 12.

But more needs to be said. Salvation has come to the Gentiles. But not to all Gentiles! It has reached those who had been chosen from among the nations: As many "as had been destined to eternal life," we read (Acts 13:49). So there is a limitation: the Gentiles of the church. God's purpose is that they will bring about the salvation of Israel! They are the people that will incite his disobedient people to jealousy (Rom. 10:19). He has in mind that their angry jealousy turn into a jealousy that desires to share in what these Gentiles have received from God. That is the mission to which God has called the believers from the Gentiles. Paul emphasizes this point: "I am speaking to you, Gentiles" (v. 13). God wants to open the eyes of disobedient Israel to its Messiah by what it sees in believers from the Gentiles. "It must learn to recognize the Savior of the world as its own Messiah. . . . It must discern its own God by seeing God's mercy for the ignorant and lost outside Israel, and what He wants to be, first and foremost, for Israel itself."[4]

The "Much More" of the Prophets: Riches for the Nations

> Now if their stumbling means riches for the world, and if their defeat means riches for the Gentiles, how much more will their full inclusion mean! (11:12)

The stumbling and defeat of Israel are contrasted with "riches for the Gentiles."[5] The important point here is riches for the Gentiles. It happens wherever the gospel is preached: Gentiles renounce their gods and praise the God of Israel for the salvation they have received. But these riches are restricted! These churches are only minorities "in the midst of a crooked and perverse generation" (Phil. 2:15). God has promised *much more!*

We are told about Jerusalem's future:

> Many peoples shall come and say, "Come, let us go up to the mountain of the LORD, to the house of the God of Jacob; that he may teach us his ways and that we may walk in his paths. . . . They shall beat their swords

4. Karl Barth, *CD*, II/2, p. 279.
5. The word Paul uses here is also found in 1 Corinthians 6:7, where it is also rendered "defeat."

into plowshares, and their spears into pruning hooks; nation shall not lift up sword against nation, neither shall they learn war any more." (Isa. 2:3-4; see also Isa. 45:22-23; 49:6; Jer. 3:17; 16:19; Zeph. 3:9; Zech. 9:10)

The Psalms echo the same theme: "All the ends of the earth shall remember and turn to the Lord; and all the families of the nations shall worship before him" (Ps. 22:27). It continues: "To you all flesh shall come" (65:2); and "All the nations you have made shall come and bow down before you, O Lord, and shall glorify your name" (86:9); the time will come when "the peoples gather together, and kingdoms, to worship the LORD" (102:22). The issue is nothing less than the promise to Abraham that through his posterity all nations of the earth would be blessed. Abraham will be the inheritor of the world (Rom. 4:13)! This blessing has no limits! — it goes far beyond the riches the church has received.

This is what Paul has in mind when he refers to the much greater glory of their inclusion. The greater riches that were promised by the prophets are not the salvation of *some* people, called by God from the nations, while the vast majority will remain doomed. No, the promise is for *all* humanity. Well, these greater riches will not come until "all Israel" is saved: All the people of the Messiah who serve him as their king. As long as only a fraction of Israel serves its Messiah, there can be no salvation for all the nations.

The "Much More" of the Prophets: Life from the Dead

But more needs to be said about this "much more" of the prophets. "For if their rejection is the reconciliation of the world, what will their acceptance be but life from the dead" (Rom. 11:15)! The word here rendered as "rejection" should in fact be translated as "loss." If we were to follow the usual rendering, we would here find the only place in the New Testament that speaks of the rejection of Israel. Those who hold this translation point to the contrast with their "acceptance" as proof that Paul indeed refers to their rejection. There are, however, two reasons why this view must be doubted. First of all, just before (11:2) he argued: God has not rejected his people.[6] Second, authoritative dictionaries indicate that the Greek word *apobolē*

---

6. In Romans 11:2 the word *apōtheō* has been translated "reject." Paul there quotes from Psalm 94:14 in the Septuagint. In this Greek translation it is frequently used for Hebrew words that mean "reject, cast away" (AV). But in Romans 11:15 "rejection" is the translation of *apobolē* — not the same word! This word does not occur in the Septuagint.

means "loss," not "rejection."[7] This isolated instance in the New Testament
that supposedly speaks of Israel's rejection in reality does not support that
idea at all! This is no small matter, even if it were assumed that this rejection
would be only temporary. For even a temporary rejection would contradict
what Paul says in v. 2. And this is, as many maintain, the present status of
Israel: temporarily rejected and replaced by the church! But Paul teaches
us that God has not rejected Israel, not even temporarily. That must be the
basis of our thinking about Israel.

The notion of "loss" agrees with that of "their stumbling" and "their
defeat" in verse 12; their stumbling is a loss to the world and their defeat
brings riches for the Gentiles; thus their loss brings reconciliation to the
world. Again Paul refers to the hardening of Israel as God's mysterious way
in having the gospel of reconciliation preached in the world. We note once
more that Paul, just as in 2 Cor. 5:19, speaks of the reconciliation of the
world and not just that of believers (cf. Col. 1:20; 1 John 2:2). True, the
preaching has not yet achieved its goal: that all people everywhere are
reconciled to God. The first phase, however, is visible in the church: We are
reconciled with God (Rom. 5:10-11). But the "much more," which, according to Paul, will far exceed this reconciliation, is as yet invisible; we hope
for it without seeing it (Rom. 8:25): life from the dead! But that is also

7. Liddell-Scott, *A Greek-English Lexicon* (ed. H. St. Jones, 1940), give as the meaning of this word *(apobolē):* "throwing away; dropping; loss." Its only occurrence in the
New Testament is in Acts 27:22: "For there will be no *loss* of life among you." W. Bauer
(*Wörterbuch zum Neuen Testament* [5th ed.; Berlin, 1958]) offers, in addition to "loss"
(Verlust): "rejection" *(Verwerfung),* when referring to God's rejection of the Jews. Bauer
points to Romans 11:15; in fact, he arrives at this meaning of the word from what he
understands as the *meaning of the text.* He also refers to Josephus's *Jewish Antiquities*
(4.314), but Josephus writes about the loss of cities and the temple for Israel; this
reference is, therefore, unjustified. We look in vain for the substantive *apobolē* in the
Septuagint, but this translation uses the verb *apoballein* twice (Isa. 1:30 and Prov. 28:24);
in both cases it does not translate a Hebrew word that has the meaning "reject." The
New Testament uses this verb twice: "throwing off his cloak" (Mark 10:50) and "Do
not, therefore, abandon that confidence of yours" (Heb. 10:35). Thus: "throwing off,"
"abandoning," but nowhere the active "rejecting," or "repelling." Only in the later Greek
usage of the church fathers would *apobolē* acquire that meaning (Lampe, *Patristic Greek
Lexicon*). In the Vulgate we find *amissio,* i.e., ("loss") in Rom. 11:15. Likewise, Luther
translates *apobolē* as "loss": "denn so ihrer verlust der welt versühnung were" (*Biblia. . . ,*
1534). In a 1741 edition we also read: "ihrer verlust." Remarkably enough, the modern
edition of 1912 reads: "ihre Verwerfung" ("their rejection"). Calvin translates: *reiectio,*
i.e., "rejection."

included in the prophetic promises. Earlier (IV, 2) we saw that, in his affirmation that God will destroy death forever, Paul tied 1 Corinthians 15:54 to Isaiah 25:8. This promise will be fulfilled with the acceptance of Israel, after its hardening has ended. Baarlink comments: "The end can be reached only when God has realized his salvific purpose with Israel and when they have accepted his salvation in Jesus as the Christ. Thus, the eyes of the Gentile-Christian reader, together with Paul, must look to the conversion and acceptance of Israel. Without Israel, the nations will not attain the resurrection of the dead."

The emphasis in this text, as we have said, is on salvation for the *world:* first the reconciliation of the world, and then life from the dead for the world. Paul wrote about this earlier in his epistle. The liberation of creation from corruptibility happens when God's children are revealed at Christ's coming (Rom. 8:19-21).[8] Hearing in this passage that the acceptance of all Israel means life from the dead for the world, we must conclude something about these children of God: The number of God's children is not complete, and they will not be revealed, until all Israel is accepted. After we have heard that "theirs is the adoption" (Rom. 9:4), this can hardly surprise us. And yet — therein lies a problem.

Cannot God Do without the Jews?

We asked ourselves: what would be the ground for the hope of the many? We have discovered that ground. In Romans 5:18-19 (and 1 Cor. 15:20-28) we read that all humanity, since Adam, will be saved through what God did for humankind in Christ. In Romans 8:19-21 we were informed about the role of God's children in this process of redemption. But now we hear that God will not do that without the Jews. The salvation of all peoples — full "riches for the Gentiles" and "life from the dead" — will not come about before the Jewish people have accepted Jesus as their Messiah. That is not what we were looking for! True, that all Israel must be saved — this was

8. Schlatter (*Gerechtigkeit*, p. 323) relates "life from the dead" in Romans 11:15 to Romans 8:21 and 1 Corinthians 15:23. "When from the multitude of the dead those are selected who receive life, they are resurrected. That is the new gift of grace, which is linked to the new revelation of Christ (8:21; 1 Cor. 15:23), and this will come when the rejection of Israel has come to an end through its reacceptance." Stuhlmacher likewise points to this link between Romans 8 and 1 Corinthians 15 (*Römer*, pp. 151-52). The rule of Christ begins with the resurrection of those "who are Christ's"; this will bring "life from the dead" within the reach of all (see IV, 2).

included in our hope that all people will be saved. But that the Jews are absolutely necessary for this makes no sense to us. Can God not accomplish his purpose without the Jews? The answer is: He does not do it without the Jews! And the Gentiles — the non-Jews — in the church must know this. The reason why they have been called is that God does not want to save the world without the Jews!

This brings us to the two verses we have so far ignored:

> Now I am speaking to you Gentiles. Inasmuch then as I am an apostle to the Gentiles, I glorify my ministry in order to make my own people jealous, and thus save a few of them. (11:13-14)

All Paul's efforts are aimed at winning Jews. As in his prayer for their salvation (10:1), he knows that God's Spirit is directing him in this desire. He knows therefore that his desire to make them jealous will not remain without fruit. As long as the hardening continues, only *some* will come, but there is no doubt that they will come. This is what God wants. And the Gentiles — the non-Jews — in the church must know this. They are called to follow the apostle in this. It is God's desire that the church he called to make all Israel jealous, not be without these few who have already been made jealous — as the firstfruits of the full harvest so that together with the church they will fulfill their calling toward all Israel. Paul must have had good reason to point this out precisely in his letter to the Romans.

2. The Olive Tree and Its Branches

It Must Have Started in Rome

Paul is worried about the church in Rome. He has heard what is happening there. A group of Gentile Christians were looking down upon the Jews of the synagogue. It was quite natural for Romans to look down upon Jews. By their peculiar religious customs, the Jews isolated themselves from society. Their refusal to work on the Sabbath, and their dietary laws, which prohibited them from eating with non-Jews, were causes of irritation and jest on the part of the Roman Gentiles.[9] Now there was a group within the

---

9. See J. N. Sevenster, *The Roots of Pagan Anti-Semitism in the Ancient World* (Leiden, 1975).

church with the same attitude toward the Jews of the synagogue that the Gentiles usually exhibited! To Paul this was an extremely serious matter. It may have been the reason why he wrote this section of his letter (chaps. 9–11), but it may even have been why he wrote the entire letter.

In the previous passage Paul has emphasized that God had not rejected his people (11:1); that he had called Gentiles to make Israel jealous (v. 11); and that God's plans for the world will not be accomplished without these Jews (vv. 12, 15). "I am speaking to you Gentiles," he had written (v. 13). Now we learn why he addressed these Gentile Christians so emphatically: They believed that God had indeed rejected Israel; they were no longer his people. The apostle now uses the image of the olive tree to clarify the relationship between the church and the Jews of the synagogue. The olive tree stands for Israel. The patriarchs are the roots, and the Jews who are their posterity are the branches. Some branches were broken off; they stand for those Jews who rejected the gospel. Some new branches have been grafted in; they are grafts from a wild olive tree or Gentiles who have accepted the gospel message. But the Gentiles who have become Christians must realize that the Jews who rejected the gospel continue to be the people of God! We hear this three times as Paul unfolds his argument. First, if the roots are holy, so are the branches (v. 16). We will see that the emphasis is here on the branches that have been broken off, the Jews of the synagogue. Second, the branches that have been broken off are to be grafted in, for it is contrary to God's will that they remain in their unbelief (vv. 23-24). Finally, at God's appointed time, this will indeed happen; they will recognize Jesus as their Messiah and Savior, and "all Israel will be saved" (v. 26); God will be "merciful to all" (vv. 31-32).

We live nineteen centuries later. The church does not know what to do with these Pauline words. First of all, the Jews of the synagogue have not accepted the gospel, and there is no indication that they ever will. Moreover, it is not necessary that they do! Christians believe that what Jesus did is all-sufficient. Nothing else is needed to save the world. However, here Paul tells us that the conversion of Israel to Jesus is a precondition for the liberation of creation. Why? Because without them the revelation of the children of God will not happen. The salvation of the nations was included in the promise given to Israel, and apart from Israel that promise will not be fulfilled. To make this promise come true, Jesus of Nazareth was sent by God as the Messiah of his people (Rom. 15:8, cf. VIII).

Israel is God's holy people. This holiness is not anchored in special qualities that people may have; Israel is not better or more obedient than other peoples. The entire Old Testament is very clear on this point. To be holy means

165

to be singled out by God from other peoples for a specific service. It began with the call to Abraham and the promise given to him. The Jewish people may refuse to heed this call, but this does not mean that God will give up on it. He will not rest before this people has fulfilled its calling. And that will happen only when Israel puts itself at the service of the Messiah. This is the point of the imagery of the olive tree, at which we will now look in greater detail.

Grafted as a Wild Olive Shoot

> If part of the dough offered as first fruits is holy, then the whole batch is holy; and if the root is holy, then the branches also are holy. (Rom. 11:16)

The "first fruits" were an offering brought to God from the first part of the harvest. By dedicating this to God, all the bread Israel used for its nourishment was holy (Num. 15:17-21). By using the image of the "first fruits," Paul refers to the patriarchs.[10] From this image, he immediately shifts to that of a "root." He will use the metaphor of an olive tree for what he is about to say. The root of the tree is holy: The patriarchs had been set apart by God in order that, through their posterity, they would be a blessing to all nations on earth. If the root is holy, then all the branches of the tree are also holy. *All* the branches — Paul wants to leave no doubt that God continues to regard the Jews of the synagogue as his holy people because they are the posterity of the patriarchs. The fact that, through their rejection of the divinely appointed Messiah, they have become broken-off branches does not alter the fact that, in God's eyes, they are still branches of the holy root; it remains "their own olive tree" (Rom. 11:24).

Through faith in Christ the Gentiles have now been grafted into the root of Israel. They are among the original branches of the olive tree — not "in their place" (NRSV), but "among them" (AV), as we shall see. This is how Paul pictures the tree: not as stripped of all its own branches and now provided only with new branches, taken from other trees. That is not

---

10. Some exegetes argue that "first fruits" refers to the first Jewish Christians. It is quite defensible to call them "first fruits"; we did so at the end of VI, 1. But in this parable they occupy another position: They are the original branches that were not broken off. Origen believes that the firstfruits and the root refer to Christ: "Ego autem radicem aliam quae sancta sit, et sanctas praemitias nescio nisi Dominum nostrum Jesum Christum" (*Ad Romanos*, p. 1193). Barth agrees with this view (*CD*, II/2, pp. 288ff.). In this passage, however, Paul does not write about the bond between the Gentile Christians and Christ, but about their bond with the Jews of the synagogue.

what the church of his time looked like. The core of the church consists of Jews who have come to believe in Jesus, along with others who have joined them. These others are now part of a community that is completely new to them. It is a family in which they must learn new patterns of behavior. The Jews around them are God's original children in the family into which they have been adopted. They are their brothers and sisters. And now, outside the church, they see the Jews of the synagogue. Are they also to be regarded as their brothers and sisters? To Jewish believers that was self-evident. But what will be the attitude of these Gentile Christians. This is Paul's great concern.

Are We Branches That Are Cut Off?

> Do not boast over the branches. If you do boast, remember that it is not you that support the root, but the root that supports you. You will say, "Branches were broken off so that I might be grafted in." That is true. They were broken off because of their unbelief, but you stand only through faith. So do not become proud, but stand in awe. For if God did not spare the natural branches, neither will he spare you. Note then the kindness and the severity of God: severity toward those who have fallen, but God's kindness toward you, provided you continue in his kindness; otherwise you also will be cut off. (11:18-22, RSV)[11]

Paul reminds the Christians of the danger in which they find themselves because of their contempt for the branches that have been broken off. He gives voice to their pride: They have been broken off in order that I — this "I" is emphasized in the word (ego) used by Paul — might be grafted in. Sure, Paul says, you have indeed become a branch of the olive tree. But then, think what might also happen to you! If God did break off even the natural branches, think what he might do with you! Remember what gave you your position: faith! To have faith is to live by the grace of God. To have faith is to be amazed over what God has done for you. Faith humbles a human being! That is how it had begun for these Gentile Christians. But now arrogance was rearing its head. God has broken off these branches and

---

11. Paul refers to the Jews as "broken-off" branches, while he uses the term "cut-off branches" in reference to the non-Jewish church members. I have respected that difference. Some interpreters have pointed out that the latter term seems to imply harsher measures. However, I am not sure. The emphasis is on the similarity. "Otherwise you also will be cut off" means: Otherwise you will face the same fate.

has accepted us in their place — we are a better species of branch! This is no longer living through faith in God's grace! Those who indulge in such pride must know what will happen: They also will be cut off. The example of the Jews is all too clear: They have been broken off precisely because they did not live from faith in God's grace alone.

Is it possible to keep on reading? For nineteen centuries the church has done precisely what Paul warned against. She has been arrogant toward the Jews. She has claimed to be the better people of God, which has replaced the Jews. Let us now look at the picture Paul paints of the church: the olive tree and its branches, with the wild shoots grafted among these; a church where the Gentile Christians live among the Jews who have come to believe. Where are *we* in this picture? We are not even mentioned! Paul says nothing here about an olive tree with only wild shoots. Are we then branches that have been cut off? It could be. A church that persists in her arrogance toward the Jews is a church threatened with being cut off. God is not only a God who warns, but also one who does what he says.

So, indeed, we are branches that have been cut off. Furthermore, we know this, for all is not well with the church. Paul repeatedly writes about the growth of the church; he prays that the church may be filled with the fruit of righteousness; that she may increase and abound in love; that Christ will live in their hearts, in order that all may come to the unity of faith and the full knowledge of the Son of God (Phil. 1:9ff.; 1 Thess. 3:12-13; Eph. 3:17; 4:13-16). The inability to arrive at this unity of faith will continue as long as we are cut-off branches. As long as this situation remains, the church will not be able to fulfil her calling to be a church that makes Israel jealous.

Yet, however terrible this may be, it is not the final word. This passage from the Bible is, even today, the Word of God to us. It is not there to tell us that God has written us off as cut-off branches. He does not abandon the work of his hands! He reminds us of our calling. This will require a *conversion,* a conversion from our centuries-old disobedience with regard to Israel. We will return to this. But one thing is already clear: God tells us in his Word that we must become what we ought to be: branches of Israel, the olive tree.

The Jews, Cut Off and Still Part of It

In order that the church may know what her task is, she must first listen closely to what Paul is impressing on her: God's plan for the branches that were cut off, for the Jews of the synagogue.

> And even those of Israel, if they do not persist in unbelief, will be grafted in, for God has the power to graft them in again. For if you have been cut from what is by nature a wild olive tree and grafted, contrary to nature, into a cultivated olive tree, how much more will these natural branches be grafted back into their own olive tree. (Rom. 11:23-24)

"If they do not persist in unbelief," Paul writes. Faith is a prerequisite: faith in the redemption offered "as a gift" by God in Christ (Rom. 3:23-26). But will that really happen? We are not told that there is a guarantee that they will come to believe. No, but these words do tell us that God does not want them to remain in their unbelief; that he looks forward to the moment when he can graft them in again. In other words, to be "cut off" is not the same as to be "rejected." God continues to be their God. The Gentile Christians in Rome must think along these lines with regard to the Jews of the synagogue: What God has done for us, the wild shoots, how much more will he do that for the native branches of the olive tree!

So their situation is: cut off but at the same time preserved with care. They remain holy branches, set apart to serve God in this world; set apart to fulfill his promises to Abraham for the peoples of the earth. Notice how God preserves them. Paul writes about them: "I can testify that they have a zeal for God" (10:2). The apostle is keen to mention one of their good points. It is zeal for the true God. Of course, that will, contrary to their own opinion, not save them, but that does not make this zeal worthless in God's sight. Paul also refers to their hardening in 2 Corinthians 3:14. There is a veil when they read the Old Covenant. But they continue to read the Old Covenant! Why? How is it to be explained that they have not relinquished their faith in the one God of whom the Scriptures testify? It is the work of God himself. He maintains their faith, day after day, century after century. Had he not done so, this people would not only have been scattered but would have totally disappeared among the Gentiles. But even now, nineteen centuries later, we are witnesses that throughout the centuries he has not stopped being their God. He keeps them, for he has a plan: He wants to graft them once again into their own olive tree.

Following Human Wisdom: In Rome and Later

> For I would not, brethren, that ye should be ignorant of this mystery, lest ye should be wise in your own conceits; that blindness in part is happened to Israel, until the fullness of the Gentiles be come in. And so all Israel shall be saved. (Rom. 11:25-26a, AV)

169

Paul refers to a mystery. He summarizes its content. First, there is the hardening of part of Israel. Then, there is the coming in of the "fullness" of the Gentiles. Finally, there is the salvation of all Israel. This fully agrees with the imagery of the olive tree. The hardening of part of Israel is the cutting off of part of the branches. The coming in of the fullness of the Gentiles is the grafting of the wild shoots. And the salvation of all Israel is the grafting in of the branches that had been cut off. Paul emphasizes this latter aspect. The believers in Rome were ignorant about it; literally Paul writes: "I would not . . . that ye should be ignorant of this mystery." Their own wisdom ("conceits") had prevented them from understanding the mystery of God's plan for Israel. They felt sure that the Jews were no longer God's people after they had rejected the Messiah. What else could one expect from people who had been Gentiles! How little in fact did they know about Israel's God!

They had not grown up with the prophets, who also speak of this cutting off, but never as the last act of God in relationship to his people: "And just as I have watched over them to pluck up and break down, to overthrow, destroy, and bring evil, so I will watch over them to build and plant, says the LORD" (Jer. 31:28). Reading on in Jeremiah, we find these remarkable words about the impossibility that God would reject Israel:

> Thus says the Lord, who gives the sun for light by day and the fixed order of the moon and the stars for light by night. . . . If this fixed order were ever to cease from my presence, says the LORD, then also the offspring of Israel would cease to be a nation before me forever. Thus says the LORD: If the heavens above can be measured, and the foundations of the earth below can be explored, then I will reject all the offspring of Israel because of all they have done, says the Lord. (Jer. 31:35-37)

As impossible, even ridiculous, as it is to think that we can measure the heavens, so impossible it is even to consider that God would reject Israel because of all they have done. *All* they have done! including the rejection of the Messiah. Was that worse than the rejection of God himself, something Israel had repeatedly been guilty of? And, says Jeremiah, this is true for all: all the offspring of Israel.

The Doctrine of Substitution, No More Hope for the World

"Note then the kindness and the severity of God: severity toward those who have fallen," Paul writes. He goes on: "Even those . . . will be grafted in";

and so "all Israel will be saved" (Rom. 11:22, 23, 26a). Those who were the objects of his wrath (Rom. 9:22) will become the objects of his mercy (11:31-32). God's judgment, however terrible it is, is not the end of his mercy. God's way of dealing with Israel makes that clear.

But there is more. It is not enough to know that God will save all Israel. Paul is writing to the Gentile Christians in Rome because they must know that they have been called by God to serve him in bringing Israel's salvation about: They are called to make them jealous. That is God's way of saving Israel. They have been grafted into the olive tree, into which God will also soon graft the branches that have been cut off. This means: they must look forward to the homecoming of their brothers and sisters. Together with them they will be the complete olive tree.

But what had happened in Rome? The new branches had said to God: Why do you need those branches that were cut off now that you have us? Be careful! Paul exclaims. "So do not become proud, but stand in awe." For he might also cut you off. As long as they stick to their opinion that they are the more excellent people of God, they will not be able to make the Jews of the synagogue jealous. And so this re-grafting of the branches and the fullness of the complete olive tree will not come about. Not only because the branches that were cut off are still missing, but also because they themselves are in danger of being cut off as useless branches.

But there is something even more important. For the fullness of the olive tree does not represent the salvation of Israel or the salvation of the church, but the salvation of the *world*. Romans 11:12 informs us that the riches that have been promised to the nations will not come about until the fullness of Israel has become a reality. In addition 11:15 tells us that creation will not be delivered from the power of death until hardened Israel has been accepted. Having said these things, Paul draws a picture of the olive tree. For the present, these Jews are still broken-off branches. As long as this situation continues, the riches for the world, of which the prophets have spoken, will not happen.

The teaching that Israel has been replaced by the church as the people of God has, from the beginning, dominated — and derailed — Christendom. For when the church no longer anticipated the salvation of all Israel, she changed her thinking about God. This was inevitable: The God who drops his own people because of its disobedience and chooses another people is not the kind of God who will save a disobedient world. He becomes a God who wants to save only a few from the mass of humanity.

THE ONE PURPOSE OF GOD

Thus the doctrine of election could find acceptance.[12] The wonderful expectation described by Paul that the coming of Christ and of God's children would set creation free, disappeared. This had been the theme of the hymns of praise of the early church. When there is hope that Israel — disobedient Israel — will be saved, there is hope that the world will be saved. That joy, however, has been smothered. The hope for the world had lost its foundation. The church, which had substituted herself for Israel, operated with a shortened expectation of the future (the "shortened eschatology"), which we know only too well: The revelation of the children of God was not to be the beginning of the saving kingly rule of Christ, but its end. He would come, so the church taught, not to save the lost world but to condemn the world. Ever since, the church has been perplexed about the prayer, *Thy kingdom come!*

We must return to this subject. These words of Paul about Gentile Christians and Jews are not the final words he says about it in this letter.

3. The Fullness of the Gentiles, a Mystery

The Promised Salvation of the Nations?

We must now take a closer look at the mystery to which Paul has referred. The word "so" at the beginning of verse 25 indicates that he is now ready to discuss further what he just said about the olive tree, in particular about the regrafting of the branches that were cut off: "all Israel will be saved." But prior to the saving of all Israel there is the coming in of the "fullness of the Gentiles" (AV).

Some translations are somewhat more vague about the coming in of the Gentiles. Instead of translating "until they have come in," they render: "until they come in." They connect this with the coming of the nations to

---

12. This does not imply that the doctrine of eternal damnation originated when the church no longer expected Israel's salvation. We noted that this doctrine has earlier roots, outside the church (I, 5, on 2 Esdras; cf. I, n. 15). But if the church had continued to expect Israel's salvation, the teaching of the lost majority of humankind could not have penetrated. On the relationship between the expectation of salvation for the world and the future of Israel, see H. Bietenhard, *Das Tausendjährige Reich* (Zurich, 1955), pp. 52-67, 90-126, 152-58. "God will end his plan for the world in such a way that Israel plays a decisive role. There is no Israel without eschatology, and no Christian eschatology without Israel" (p. 153).

Zion spoken of by the prophets and psalms (e.g., Ps. 102:22-23; Isa. 2:1-4).[13] Many exegetes take it like that. This view has also found favor with some scholars who, as in the translation of the NRSV, render the words as "has come in." They view the grafting of the Gentiles as the fulfillment of these prophecies, which has already begun and will continue until all the Gentiles, spoken of by the prophets, have come in. Some interpreters think here of the salvation of all humanity, but most exegetes refer to that part of humanity which God has destined for salvation. They say that this part "represents" all the Gentiles. It does not comprise all people, but God regards this part as the whole. We already rejected that interpretation when we discussed Romans 11:1. God does not view part of Israel as all Israel; nor does he regard a part of all people as all people.[14] Since we will return to "all Israel," we will not discuss it any further at this point. Here the question is: What does Paul mean when he speaks about the coming in of the "fullness" of the Gentiles?

The Fullness of Those Who Have Been Called from the Gentiles

The view that Paul here refers to the fulfillment of the promises for the nations cannot be correct. We mention two reasons:

1. This view is not in harmony with the promise to Abraham that God would bless all nations through his posterity. If God begins by saving the nations, and *subsequently* saves Israel, it cannot be said that He saves the nations *through* Israel. The "reversal of the order" has been defended by pointing to Jesus' word that many who were first would be last, and many of the last would be first. If that, however, was what Paul meant — first the nations and then Israel — this would have been not only a reversal of the order of the fulfillment of the promise, but a *negation* of God's promise to

13. Both translations are possible. Jeremias (*Sprachliche Beobachtungen,* p. 196): "something that happens at a precise future moment" ("will go in" or "enters"), as well as "the future completion of an event that occurs over a period of time" ("has come in"). He chooses the second option, since the coming in of the Gentiles is a process that has already begun; I agree with this view. We also find this translation in the NRSV.

14. See VI, n. 1. Jeremias (*Sprachliche Beobachtungen,* p. 197) says that the fullness of the Gentiles does not refer to "die Utopie einer All-Bekehrung" (the utopia of a universal conversion), but indicates rather that through the "Einzug der Representanten der Völker" (the coming of the representatives of the nations), the promise of the prophets (Isa. 2:2-4) is fullfiled. He does not consider that promise as "All-Bekehrung" (universal conversion), but fails to give arguments for his view.

Israel! Of course, one might say that the Gentiles were not saved without Israel, for the apostles were Jews. But nonetheless, this view implies that Israel as a whole is not the people through which God saves the world. That was the promise, and that promise remains unfulfilled.

2. This interpretation also disagrees with Paul's arguments about Israel in the same chapter. Israel's fall has brought salvation to the Gentiles. But these Gentiles, to whom salvation has come, are only a small part of the nations. All the nations will be saved once Israel has come to its fullness (Rom. 11:12). In other words: Paul there maintains that the salvation of the nations *follows* upon the salvation of all Israel. Therefore, he cannot mean here that the salvation of the nations precedes that of all Israel.

The order is thus as follows: First, there is the "coming in" of the "fullness" of the Gentiles; the church has obtained its fullness as far as it concerns the Gentiles: All the branches of the wild olive tree have been grafted into the olive tree that represents Israel. Second, all Israel will be saved: The branches that had been cut off are now regrafted into the original olive tree; the olive tree is complete. Third, then follows the salvation of the nations of the earth (Rom. 11:12), life from the dead (11:15), the deliverance of creation (Rom. 8:19-21; 1 Cor. 15:20-28).

"Fullness" — Emphasis on the Qualitative Aspect

The Gentiles to whom Paul refers in this passage are the same as in Romans 11:11: the Gentiles to whom salvation had come. He refers to the fullness of these Gentiles who have been called. Of course, this fullness implies completeness in number; but the emphasis is on the qualitative aspect: the fullness of growth and of fruit.[15] The branches draw directly from the roots and bear fruit. It is the church that has increased and abounds in love for one another and for all (1 Thess. 3:12-13); the church that has come to the unity of faith, to "the measure of the full stature of Christ" (Eph. 4:13).

The grafting of the new shoots does not result in failure; the fullness of the Gentiles will indeed come in. God has called them in order that they might, together with the Jews who confess his name, be the church that causes the other Jews to be jealous. However long that road may be, and

---

15. Therefore I prefer the term "fullness," as in the AV, to the rendering of the NRSV, "full number." Here I follow S. P. Tabaksblatt, *Bladen uit mijn levensboek* (Kampen, 1980), p. 25. Cf. IX.

however improbable that goal might seem, it will come about: There will eventually be the church that manifests this fullness of Christ; the church in which the mercy of the Father, made visible in Christ, will radiate as a light in the world (Matt. 5:14-16; Phil. 2:15).

The First and the Last

The saying of Jesus about the first and the last has been misused to defend the view that the nations will precede Israel in their salvation. Yet, these words have a significant bearing on Paul's argument. We already encountered them in Luke. After the severe statement that many will try to enter but will not be able to do so since the door was shut, we hear:

> There will be weeping and gnashing of teeth when you see Abraham and Isaac and Jacob and all the prophets in the kingdom of God, and you yourselves thrown out. Then people will come from east and west, from north and south, and will eat in the kingdom of God. Indeed, some are last who will be first, and some are first who will be last. (Luke 13:28-30)

And in Matthew we read about the coming in of the Gentiles:

> I tell you, many will come from east and west and will eat with Abraham, Isaac and Jacob in the kingdom of heaven, while the heirs of the kingdom will be thrown into the outer darkness, where there will be weeping and gnashing of teeth. (Matt. 8:11-12)

Matthew is even more emphatic than Luke in emphasizing that this refers to the Jews, the people of the patriarchs. Jesus calls them the children of the kingdom (AV). We already surmised that Jesus' statement is not intended as the final word about the judgment.[16] In the passages in Matthew and Luke, however, one could still raise the question whether those who are last will in fact enter the kingdom. Paul answers that question. First those who are called from among the Gentiles enter. Then the hardening of those who had been shut out is taken away, and they enter the kingdom. Then all Israel will be saved.

---

16. Cf. II, 3, "Did Jesus teach an eternal punishment?" Even the severe statement by Jesus to the Jewish leaders — "The kingdom of God will be taken away from you and given to a people that produces the fruits of the kingdom" (Matt. 21:43) — is not the final word; it has not been taken away irrevocably.

The Mystery: Gentiles Become Partners with Israel

Speaking about the first and the last, Jesus refers to the sequence in which they will enter the kingdom. As we discussed earlier (IV, 3), entering the kingdom — or, inheriting the kingdom (1 Cor. 6:9-10; Gal. 5:21) — is more than being saved. It is a partnership with Israel, the people of the Messiah, through which God will deliver the human race in its entirety. Paul speaks in this context of a *mystery.* Toward the end of his letter we see that word once more. He writes:

> . . . the revelation of the mystery that was kept secret for long ages [AV: since the world began] but is now disclosed, and through the prophetic writings is made known to all the Gentiles. . . . (Rom. 16:25-26)

"For long ages" this mystery was kept secret. This must have to do with what God did not reveal through the Old Testament prophets. It was, in other words, a new revelation. Does Paul identify this mystery with that of Romans 11:25? We believe he does: The metaphor of the olive tree is a new revelation. The prophets announced that all the Gentiles would come and praise the God of Israel as the God of their salvation. But they did not announce that many of those Gentiles would enter as children of Abraham, Isaac, and Jacob, while the original children of the kingdom are shut out and will enter only at a later time. This, however, is what Paul indicated with his image of the olive tree: Shoots of wild olive trees are grafted in, and afterward the original branches that had been broken off.

When Peter receives the vision of the clean and the unclean animals, followed by the instruction to go to the Roman centurion Cornelius — is that not a new revelation? He must explain it: "You yourself know that it is unlawful to associate with or to visit a Gentile; but God has shown me that I should not call anyone profane or unclean" (Acts 10:28). He then preaches the gospel, and the Holy Spirit falls on those who hear the word (v. 44). Gentiles enter into the kingdom, while the majority of the children of the kingdom are still outside.

Paul's eyes have been opened to the fact that this is the way through which God makes Israel into what he wants it to be. Through these Gentiles God will make his people jealous, as Moses had prophesied. This also belongs to the things that had been kept secret. For in the Song of Moses we hear that God will provoke Israel to jealousy and anger through another people (Deut. 32:21), but this passage does not tell us that this is God's way of bringing about his plan with Israel — the way by which Israel becomes the messenger of his mercy for all nations.

Ephesians 2 and Romans 11

The letter to the Ephesians speaks in the same way about the mystery as the parable of the olive tree does.

> So then, remember that at one time you Gentiles . . . were . . . without Christ, being aliens from the commonwealth of Israel, and strangers to the covenants of promise, having no hope and without God in the world. But now in Christ Jesus you who once were far off have been brought near by the blood of Christ. For he is our peace; in his flesh he has made both groups into one, that he might, . . . thus making peace, . . . reconcile both groups to God in one body through the cross, thus putting to death that hostility through it. (Eph. 2:11-16)

Here we also hear how it could happen that Gentiles have become partners with Israel: through the blood of Christ; the cross has taken away the separation (the hostility) between Jews and non-Jews. It is "the mystery of Christ" (literally: of *the* Christ, the Messiah) "which was not made known to earlier generations, as it has now been revealed to his holy apostles and prophets": that the Gentiles (the non-Jewish nations) share in the inheritance, and have part in the promise of Christ Jesus through the gospel (Eph. 3:4-6). At the beginning of that same letter, this promise is described as God's plan of salvation, to gather all creation under one "head," under Christ (1:10; here also: *the* Christ), and to bring them to the fullness of him who fills all in all (1:23; cf. Col. 1:20). That is the fulfillment of God's promise to Israel (Gen. 12:3). These Gentiles now share in that promise.[17]

---

17. This statement is very similar to that in Colossians 1:26-27; the content of the mystery mentioned in those texts must be identical. For the link between Ephesians 2 and Romans 11, see Markus Barth, "The People of God," *Journal for the Study of the New Testament,* (Supplement Series 5. Sheffield, 1983). For the exegesis of Ephesians 2:11-22 through the centuries, see W. H. Rader, *The Church and Racial Hostility: A History of the Interpretation of Ephesians 2:11-22* (Tübingen, 1978). This study gives surprising examples of voices deviating from the traditional doctrine of substitution from the history of the church.

The Israel of the Messiah

Let us now summarize what we have said so far. The fullness of the Gentiles that enters the kingdom before the hardening of Israel is taken away does not refer to the coming of all nations to the salvation announced by the prophets. The prophets did not know that this would precede the coming of the nations. God calls people from among the nations to be partners with his people Israel. This has been pictured for us in the metaphor of the olive tree: Shoots from the wild olive tree are grafted into the original olive tree, Israel. They were not to *replace* the branches that were temporarily cut off, but *added* to all Israel; inserted, would be another word for it. Note that Paul refers to "some of the branches" when he speaks of this cutting off (Rom. 11:17) — do not think that there is nothing left of the original tree![18] After the process of adding the new branches has been completed, the branches that were cut off are regrafted. Only when that has been done, has God's plan for Israel reached its goal.

This is not described as a sad state of affairs: If only Israel had been obedient, this would not have been necessary! No, this disobedience is what it was all about from the start. When God calls people to serve him in the carrying out of his plan to show mercy toward all people, he calls disobedient people. No others were available. Admittedly, there is a sequential order in his calling — first Israel, and then these Gentiles — but this sequence is not determined by a difference in degree of obedience between Israel and the Gentiles. Nor is their disobedience greater than he had foreseen; neither on the part of Israel, nor on the part of the Gentiles. And whatever he does for these Gentiles in no way diminishes his work on behalf of Israel; on the contrary, it surpasses all expectations. In the letter to the Ephesians, this is only cause for praise. The letter to the Romans also climaxes in exuberant praise (11:33-36). The olive tree in its fullness is greater and richer than before: It is the tree with all the original branches and the numerous new branches that have been grafted in.

This is the Israel of the Messiah. It is Israel that has reached its fullness, together with the fullness of the Gentiles. That God *in this way* — through Israel's hardening and by calling this "other people" from the Gentiles, thus causing Israel to be jealous — fulfills the promises to the fathers was hidden, and has now been revealed. The goal, however, has not yet been reached;

---

18. While in Romans 11:17 "some of the branches" have been broken off, Ephesians 2:11-22 remains silent about Jews who have rejected the Messiah. Evidently this in no way minimizes the bond between the Gentile Christians and the Jewish people.

the branches that were broken off must yet be regrafted. But once that has happened, the original branches of the olive tree, together with the newly grafted branches, will live in unity from that one root, the ancestors of Israel. Together they will be witnesses in this world of God's mercy for the disobedient.

4. All Israel

The Denial by the Church

Believing that the vast majority of humankind would not be saved, the church had to find another way of explaining Romans 11:26a: "And so all Israel will be saved." "All Israel" could not mean all the people, but only a part; if "all Israel" had to be taken literally, the doctrine of eternal punishment could not be maintained. For no one wanted to defend the proposition that the people of Israel would be saved in its entirety, but the other peoples only in part. This immediately makes clear how much is at stake. Let us review a few examples of this interpretation.

Calvin emphasizes the future conversion of the Jewish people. In the course of history, it seemed more and more as if "the church virtually consisted of Gentiles." But that is going to change.

> When the Gentiles have come in, the Jews will at the same time return from their defection to the obedience of faith. The salvation of the whole Israel of God, which must be drawn from both, will thus be completed; and yet in such a way that the Jews, as the first born in the family of God, may obtain the first place.

Here the preferential position of Israel is clearly taught! But this first place remains imprisoned in a restriction; it is *from* both groups. Calvin writes that a number of the Jews will remain (*residuum numerum*), "who, after having repented, will enjoy the grace of deliverance." For God wants the church that is to be saved to consist not only of Gentiles, but of Jews and Gentiles in equal measure. The church becomes "all Israel" only when the elect part of the Jews has been added. The root of this exegesis is found in Romans 9:6, "not all Israelites truly belong to Israel"; Calvin adds that the majority of the Jews are not included in "the true election of God."[19]

19. Calvin, *Romans*, comments on 11:26 and 9:6 (pp. 196ff., 255).

Bavinck agrees with this interpretation of Romans 9:6. He states that "God's promises have not become void, because they apply to Abraham's spiritual seed": God never intended anything else than the chosen part of Israel. However, for Bavinck, unlike for Calvin, "all Israel" in Romans 11:26a is not the church from the Jews and the Gentiles, but "the *plērōma,* which through the centuries has come from Israel." *Plērōma* is the word Paul uses in v. 12: fullness. Then, however, we hear these enigmatic words: "In this *plērōma* all Israel is saved, just as in the church as a whole all humanity is saved." Thus, we must not expect a future conversion of the Jews. According to him, Paul clearly states "that the hardening has come over part of the Jews, until the *plērōma* of the Gentiles has entered, and not that *subsequently,* but, rather, that *in this manner* all Israel will be saved." For, "just a little earlier, in vs. 24, Paul has declared that this hardening always affected only part of Israel . . . we always find among them a remnant, according to his merciful election." Thus it will continue: "Besides those who come from the Gentile world, there will always be some from Israel who come to faith in Christ" . . . "but however numerous that group may be, it will always be a remnant according to his merciful election."[20]

Herman Ridderbos follows Bavinck's exegesis: "'All Israel' in Romans 11:26 can apply only to all those from Israel who will convert as a result of hearing the proclamation of the gospel and will be brought to the Lord. They constitute the chosen ones of Romans 11:7, who are already identifiable, *together with* those who will convert from the hardening that has come over Israel and will come to faith in Christ."[21] Ridderbos believes that the hardening is permanent: "The words *and so* etc. imply that the partial hardening, which was according to God's purpose, has not been lifted, but that this fact does not prevent the salvation of 'all Israel.' The hardening of the majority of Israel is permanent, and yet 'all Israel' will be saved. How can that be? It just depends on how these words 'all Israel' are explained. This term is not simply an indication of a quantatively complete number, however large or small that might be — but of the kind of fullness and completeness, which qualitatively represents the totality or fullness of Israel."[22]

20. Bavinck, *Dogmatiek,* 4.649-52.
21. C. Aalders and H. Ridderbos, *Israël* (The Hague, 1955), pp. 58-62.
22. Ridderbos, *Romeinen,* p. 264. In *Israël,* p. 62, Ridderbos, like Bavinck, refers to Israel as a *remnant.* He corrects that view in *Romeinen:* It is much *more* than that (p. 265). But in his view a *part* still represents the whole. His criticism of the traditional exegesis of Romans 11 did not lead him to the conviction that disobedient Israel *in its entirety* would become the object of God's compassion.

All Israel Is Not Part of Israel

Our objection to this interpretation begins with Romans 9:6. Paul distinguishes between the Jews who through faith are children of Abraham and those who are so only by birth. He is in particular concerned with this latter category. They cause him "great sorrow and unceasing anguish" (9:1-3). God has hardened them (9:18; 11:7), they are the object of his wrath (9:22; 11:8-10), they have stumbled (11:11-12, 22), and they are branches that are cut off (11:17-20). But Paul also says that this group will again be accepted (11:15). God wants to regraft them (11:23-24), the hardening is taken away from them (11:25-26), and they become the objects of his mercy (11:31). All this is affirmed without further qualification — it is for some, not for others. Making such a qualification would be in total contrast with what motivates the apostle.

Then we come to the word *represent*. We encountered it in the comments on Romans 11:25: "The fullness of the Gentiles" supposedly represents all the nations.[23] Bavinck does not use the word, but means the same thing: In the part that is saved (the *plērōma*) all Israel is saved, in such a way that God is satisfied with this remnant. This view, however, has no basis in Scripture. The Bible does speak about representation, but in a totally different fashion. It is what Moses does on behalf of Israel. He "stands in the breach" for them — for all of his people. He indignantly rejects the thought that he himself would be saved, while the people he represents would be lost: "But if not, blot me out of the book that you have written" (Exod. 32:32). As we noted, that was what God was looking for. And that is what motivates Paul (Rom. 9:3)! The salvation of part of Israel, "representing" all Israel — that would not give him comfort in his anguish!

Finally, *the hardening*. It, we hear, is not to be removed. How is that view defended? Paul, it is argued, does not state: *After this*, but *so* — in this manner — all Israel will be saved. This, they say, does not indicate a time sequence. The idea is that God uses the hardening of Israel as an open door, as an opportunity to let those who have been chosen from among the Gentiles enter. As soon as the elect from the Gentiles have entered, the door is shut. At that moment the saving activity of God is complete; there is nothing more to follow. Those who are outside have

23. See VI, n. 14. Also VI, n. 1.

been shut out forever. But that is not true! There *is* a time sequence, and there *is* more to follow!

That the hardening continues *until* the full number of the Gentiles has come in, sets a limit; it implies that the hardening ceases as soon as these Gentiles have entered. And so all Israel will be saved: not a part, as before, but now in its entirety.

In Sight of the Harbor

In his argumentation that for Paul "all Israel" refers only to the part that has been chosen, Bavinck turns against another viewpoint that has been defended within his own tradition. We saw that Calvin expected a future conversion of Israel. This receives a surprising emphasis in the margin of the Dutch Authorized Version: Do not underestimate the future of the Jews! By this phrase *all Israel,* we read: "That is, not only a few, but a very large multitude, like the whole Jewish nation." That was taught in the churches that followed Calvin! We find this in Greijdanus's commentary on Romans. When the full number of the Gentiles has entered, he writes, God will end the hardening of Israel: "In this context 'all Israel' can hardly refer to anything but Israel in its entirety, and not to a small part. . . . Then Israel in its fullness, the Jewish people in its completeness, comes to conversion and to acceptance of God's gospel and Christ the Lord." The word *so* indicates the manner in which Israel will be saved. Of that it is said in 11:11, 14 "that Israel must be made jealous and will become jealous through the salvation of the Gentiles. . . ; thus, through and because of the inclusion of the Gentiles, Israel is brought to conversion and faith and redemption." It cannot be true, Greijdanus continues, that Paul intends this term "all Israel" simply to mean that Israel will experience what the other nations experience: that only a part is elected and saved. This is Bavinck's view, which is followed by Ridderbos. But why would Paul have written these chapters 9–11 if that were all he had to say? "That in the end the full number of God's elect from among the Jews would be saved, just as from among the Gentiles, would not have required such argumentation as the apostle has presented in this chapter and in all three chapters 9–11."[24] We are in complete agreement with this. Here we are in sight of the harbor!

24. Greijdanus, *Romeinen*, 2:515-16.

Also the Israelites Who Have Died?

Now we come to the core issue. There is a difficulty that caused Bavinck to reject this possibility. Even if in the future all Jews were to be saved, he writes, "such a massive conversion at the end would not do any good for the millions of Jews who, through the ages until the end-time, have died in unbelief and a hardened state."[25] So the difficulty lies with those Israelites who have died. Ridderbos agrees. He writes that initially he also thought that Paul intended a future conversion of all Jews. But he changed his mind. For, "what do we do with all those millions of Jews who lived before the time of the end? Are they not part of 'all Israel'? Can we maintain that all Israel as a nation is saved if that is to be understood as a fraction of that nation, the small part of it that reaches the end of history?" Even if Paul had counted on a conversion of the Jews of his time, the problem remains of "all the unbelieving and disobedient members of Israel, who lived before the coming of Christ, and who so often, even in divine pronouncements cited by Paul, have been threatened with punishment and perdition."[26]

Just as Greijdanus later did, G. Doekes in a fine study published in 1915, defended the view of the Dutch Authorized Version: Paul refers in Romans 11:26 to the future conversion and salvation of the entire Jewish people. Doekes's book makes for exciting reading. One wonders how he can do this within the familiar tradition. This exegesis cannot but lead to the denial of the doctrine of eternal punishment! But then, near the harbor, we are in for disillusionment. For Doekes also admits that the Israelites who died remain outside this salvation: "Paul does not deal with judgment to those who died in their disobedience. That judgment is irrevocable." The conclusion, therefore, is: all Israel, but without those who died in a state of sin and unbelief! The remarkable aspect of Doekes's study is that he does not ignore this point. He does not fail to recognize what this must mean for Paul: There is no comfort for his sorrow! His brothers and sisters cannot be saved, for when they were alive they did not come to faith in Jesus. Yet Paul ends the passage with exuberant praise. But "Those who feel that this spirited doxology removes or compensates for the sorrow of his wounded heart have misunderstood the apostle. He rather wants to let it be known that the unceasing anguish he experiences at the sight of his people's misery

25. Bavinck, *Dogmatiek*, 4:651.
26. Aalders and Ridderbos, *Israël*, p. 61. Ridderbos does not believe in the possibility of salvation after God's judgment.

(9:2) does not take away, or does not need to take away, from the joy of his hope. . . ." We note Doekes's hesitation: it does not need to take away from his joy. Here the apostle manifests, he continues, "a combination of anguish and joy: he sings and sighs simultaneously, with tears of grief in his eyes he lauds the blessed hope. . . . However dark the depths of God's judgments may be, he finds reason for praising the virtues of the Lord, be it with a wounded heart. . . ."[27] Doekes takes Paul's sorrow seriously! However, we find no trace of a wounded heart or secret tears in the praise at the end of Paul's statement! We only discover undiluted joy since all Israel receives mercy from God (Rom. 11:31). In what Doekes writes about this we meet the pessimism of our tradition rather than that of Paul.

Still the Harbor Paul Intends

So, the broad vista presented to us in the margin of the Dutch Authorized Version, which seems to do full justice to what Paul says, has a restriction: Those who died in the past are excluded. Bavinck and Ridderbos have argued that this restriction makes the vista misleading: In reality we do not dock in this harbor. In the interpretation of the seventeenth-century Dutch translation (margin) defended by Doekes and Greijdanus, we also find that only a remnant of Israel will be saved; with the exception of the final generation, it is always a remnant.

Nonetheless, this interpretation has led us to the harbor Paul had in mind. There is no doubt that Paul writes about the impending change in the fate of Israel; the hardening will be taken away and the people in its entirety will accept Jesus of Nazareth as its Messiah and be saved. The only argument adduced against this view is that the dead are excluded from this number. But this exclusion wreaks havoc with the interpretation of Romans 11:26a. Here the faulty exegesis in our tradition of Romans 5:12-21 takes its toll. It denies that God's redemption in Christ includes all generations since Adam, while this is precisely the point Paul wants to make. If we grasp that, then we know that if all Israel will be saved, this will include all Israelites who have died.[28] The presumed prohibition to enter the harbor is shown to be without foundation.

27. G. Doekes, *De betekenis van Israëls val.* (Nijkerk, 1915), pp. 317-19.

28. See III, 6. See also: J. C. Blumhardt: "If this were not the case, the compassion of God over *all* and over *all Israel* would not be real, when out of all of Abraham's people only the last generation would share in God's mercy, while all who died before would

Once again we discover that the doctrine that excludes the dead from conversion and redemption cannot be reconciled with Paul's statements. We can summarize it in the picture of the olive tree. We heard that it was always God's plan to regraft the branches that were broken off, and that He is perfectly able to do so (11:23). That these Jews may have died without accepting the Messiah does not change anything. Just as in the case of the living, God — "who gives life to the dead" (Rom. 4:17) — is able to regraft them. Paul's vision for the future is determined by what God did in the resurrection of Jesus.

Ezekiel's Vision

In Ezekiel's extensive prophecy of Israel's restoration (Ezek. 36 and 37), we hear that God leads the prophet to a valley filled with bones. "There were very many in the valley, and they were very dry." Ezekiel is told to prophesy to these bones. As a result they come to life. The Spirit enters them and they become alive, "a vast multitude" (37:10). Then God says:

> ". . . these bones are the whole house of Israel. . . ." Thus says the Lord GOD: "I am going to open your graves, and bring you up from your graves, O my people; and I will bring you back to the land of Israel. And you shall know that I am the LORD, when I open your graves, and bring you up from your graves, O my people. I will put my spirit within you, and you will live." (Ezek. 37:11-14)

It is usually said that this is a prophecy about the end of the exile and the return to the land of Israel. That may be true, but the return from Babylon is only the prelude. What is promised here trancends the boundaries of world history. It refers to all Israel: "These bones are the whole house of Israel" (v. 11). In addition we are dealing here with Israel after the judgment. The judgment brought the rule of death. The prophecy mentions

---

be eternally lost" (*Blätter aus Bad Bol* [1874], p. 159); see IX, n. 9. Cf. E. F. Ströter: Restricting salvation to the last generation "would be a purely arbitrary distinction between equally guilty generations of the same people." For that reason "this salvation must extend as far into the past as the judgment of the national hardening" (cf. also Rom. 3:22b, "there is no distinction!"); E. F. Ströter, *Die Judenfrage nach Römer 11* (1903); abbreviated in *Der Fürst des Lebens muss einst alles erben* (Stuttgart, 1966), p. 103. See also H. Schuhmacher, *Das biblische Zeugnis von der Versöhnung des Alls* (Stuttgart, 1959), pp. 202-4.

"these slain" (37:9), the many who were killed by God's judgments. The dominion of death is past now and will never come back because Israel will not turn anew to disobedience. God will "put his Spirit within them" and make them fulfill his commandments (36:26-27). Emphatically the resurrection of Israel's dead is tied to that promise of the Spirit: These dead come to life because God breathes his spirit into them. It is impossible to conclude that this prophecy met its final fulfillment in Israel's return from exile.

We will have to return to this prophecy; this matter of salvation after the judgment will require some further thought. But whatever one might think about the interpretation of this vision, we know that when Paul describes the salvation of Israel, this future resurrection of Israel's dead was the awesome reality which he expected. "What will their acceptance be but life from the dead" (Rom. 11:15)!

The Role of the Church in Israel's Salvation

Out of Zion will come the Deliverer; he will banish ungodliness from Jacob. And this is my covenant with them, when I take away [or: will have taken away] their sins. (vv. 26b, 27)[29]

Israel's salvation differs from that of the church. The believers from the Gentiles will be saved through the preaching of the gospel in the course of history; they have been called as a few among the many of the nations of which they were part. But Israel will be saved as a people in its entirety. Their salvation will not be the fruit of the church's proclamation of the gospel throughout the centuries. Anyhow, that is impossible as long as God continues to lay the hardening on his people. He alone can take this hardening away, and that will happen when he sends his Messiah.[30]

29. Jeremias, *Sprachliche Beobachtungen*, p. 201, points out that *hotan* together with the conjunctive aorist expresses "Vorzeitlichkeit": "wenn ich ihre Sünden von ihnen genommen haben werde" (when I will have taken their sins from them).

30. Paul writes, "Out of Zion." He quotes from Isaiah 59:20, which reads: "*to* Zion." But the Messiah has already come to Zion (cf. Rom. 9:33). He is there now (he acts "from Zion" [Ps. 110:2]). In whatever way this text is to be explained, Paul's use of "Zion" underlines the continuing bond between Jesus and the Jewish people. I agree with Schlatter: ". . . does Paul intend to say that Christ will never deny his bond with Israel, but that even in his heavenly glory he will be linked to her and belong to Zion?" (*Gerechtigkeit*, p. 328).

Even though this salvation is not the fruit of the preaching of the church, it does not occur without the church. When the Messiah comes to Israel, this will also involve Israel's encounter with the church! These two are meant for each other: the two which he, the Messiah, made into one (Eph. 2:14), the Israel of the Messiah, the one people of God's children, through which he will deliver all creation. Hence, the salvation of Israel cannot be a matter in which the church is not involved.[31]

Da Costa believed that the Jews would be converted "independently from the Christian church, in a separate, miraculous and marvelous way; and thus through an immediate act of God they will return to glory."[32] We would not be surprised if this view resulted from a pessimism regarding the church: God would do better not to involve the church. If Israel's salvation must wait for a church that makes the Jews jealous, it will never happen! If Da Costa did not think along those lines, we certainly have. But if God were to save Israel without the church's involvement, that salvation would no longer be our concern. In that case we could be the church of Christ without looking forward to Israel's salvation. We know that that has been the mind-set of the church, but with that it turned aside from the task Paul had charged it with.

We have no idea how, at the coming of the Messiah, the conversion of Israel and the resurrection of the dead will take place.[33] We know only our own role. The church has the task of bringing Israel to jealousy. That is the role God has entrusted to the church for the salvation of Israel, and nothing in the world can relieve her of that task.

31. Paul refers to the coming of the Messiah *together with* his church (1 Thess. 3:13; 2 Thess. 1:10; Col. 3:4). But see n. 33 below.

32. Isaac Da Costa, *Bijbellezingen, opgetekend door J. F. Schimsheimer* (Amsterdam, 1880), 4:282. Franz Mussner, a Roman Catholic theologian (*Traktat über die Juden* [Munich, 1979], pp. 57-61), points to the separate road (the "Sonderweg") along which God leads Israel. That is correct, but a separate road can also be understood to mean that each group is saved in its own specific way, without any linkage between the two; that would be a misconception.

33. "Paul never allowed for questions such as whether the people in its entirety will confess Christ prior to the Second Coming, or as the result of it, or whether this is one of the signs of his parousia, and what relationship there will be between this converted people and the church of the nations" (Schlatter, *Gerechtigkeit*, p. 327); commenting on verse 15 ("life from the dead") he writes: "Paul does not deal with the question of the causal and temporal relationship between the restoration of Israel and what will happen at the parousia" (*Gerechtigkeit*, p. 323).

187

5. God's Calling Is Irrevocable

What Are the Jews for Us?

> As regards the gospel they are enemies of God for your sake; but as regards election they are beloved, for the sake of their ancestors; for the gifts and the calling of God are irrevocable. (Rom. 11:28-29)

Paul has not finished his attempts to convince the Gentile Christians of God's purposes with the Jews. What do they see when they look at the Jews? Enmity against the gospel. It is *enmity for your sake:* It is caused by God's compassion on the Gentiles.[34] It is the resistance of the eldest son in Luke 15 against the behavior of his father, who throws a party for his lost brother — not on the basis of his works! Nevertheless, the older no less than the younger son remains his dear child! We observed how the parable ended: The hands of the father remain outstretched toward him (Rom. 10:21).

"Beloved, for the sake of their ancestors." God's beloved, his own children, and, therefore, our brothers and sisters! It is no easy relationship, for the love is one-sided. For them the gospel of Christ, which links us with them, is a cause of separation. That is inevitable. As long as God himself has not opened their eyes to the Messiah, following Jesus implies that the love comes from one side only.

The Jews, Messengers of the Gospel

"Enemies for your sake": the fact that God was willing to show compassion to the Gentiles made them angry. But that will not remain the case. The church has been called to look for the day when that will change. "For," Paul writes, "the gifts and the calling of God are irrevocable." God has called Israel to proclaim his deeds among the nations, and to tell of his miracles (Pss. 9:12; 96:3; 105:2). Therefore, if God's calling is irrevocable, this implies that Israel will eventually respond to that call!

34. Some interpreters maintain that "for your sake" means "enmity that will profit you," an assertion somewhat similar to 11:11: "through their stumbling salvation has come to the Gentiles." But that view would not fit the comparison with the anger of the eldest son (Luke 15). Verse 31 (if correctly translated), in particular, underlines what Paul refers to: resistance to God's compassion on the Gentiles, who have not kept the law.

In the following words Paul informs us about what will happen.

> Just as you were once disobedient to God but have now received mercy
> because of their disobedience, so they have now become disobedient in
> order that, by the mercy shown to you, they too may now receive mercy.
> (Rom. 11:30-31, altered version)

Israel will receive mercy. As the Gentile Christians were disobedient and
received mercy, so it will be for Israel. As disobedient people they will
receive mercy. Paul contrasts the two cases of disobedience: that of the
Gentiles in former times, and that of Israel at present. These two cases
appear to be very similar. The proud in Rome are put in their place. The
present disobedience of Israel is their rejection of the Messiah; that disobedience is no worse than that of the Gentiles when they found mercy
with God.

"You have received mercy because of their disobedience." Here Paul
refers back to Romans 11:11: "Through their stumbling salvation has come
to the Gentiles." The Gentiles owe their riches to Israel's disobedience. So
there is no reason for complaint! This introduces the next phase of his
argument: "They have now become disobedient . . . by the mercy shown
to you" (v. 31). This fits perfectly with verse 28: "As regards the gospel . . .
enemies of God for your sake."

Here we run into a problem in the translation that we must discuss
in some detail since it has a bearing on Paul's intention. In the NRSV we
read: "So they have now become disobedient in order that, by the mercy
shown to you, they too may now receive mercy."[35] That would reflect the
content of verse 11: by saving the Gentiles God makes the Jews jealous.
However true that may be, it is not a correct translation. Some interpreters
have argued that in verse 31 Paul cannot have intended that the Jews
became disobedient as a result of God's mercy to the Gentiles. In the
previous verse the salvation of the Gentiles is rather the result of the
disobedience of the Jews. How then is it possible that in the next statement
Paul says that the disobedience of the Jews has been caused by God's mercy
for the Gentiles? That seems contradictory. Several solutions have been
proposed to solve this contradiction, as is reflected in some of our ver-

---

35. One may also translate "disobedient to," or "against the compassion shown to
you." The translation makes no real difference: The issue is disobedience to God because
of his compassion for the Gentiles.

sions.[36] Yet we would miss Paul's intention if we read something other than the rendering quoted above.

In writing "So they have now become disobedient. . . ." what does Paul mean by "now"? It is their resistance against the saving righteousness of God, which has *now* been revealed in the coming of the Messiah, Jesus of Nazareth (Rom. 3:21). It is their resistance against the gospel, the message of salvation by faith alone, without the works of the law (3:28).

Now they are disobedient, but what will happen when Israel finds mercy with God? Then this disobedience to the gospel will be a thing of the past. Paul is an example of what will then happen with the Jews. No longer an enemy of the gospel, he became the messenger of the gospel as no other. People's amazement about this knows no bounds: "The one who formerly was persecuting us is now proclaiming the faith he once tried to destroy" (Gal. 1:23).

That is what will happen: The people who fiercely resisted the gospel of God's grace that is offered as a gift will — as no other people — become messengers of that same gospel! Even the elder brother in the parable of the lost son has come to himself. His eyes have been opened to his true condition: he, no less than his younger brother from the Gentiles, is a son who is disobedient to the Father's love. He has recognized him; it is indeed his brother. Now he likes nothing better than to tell others about that Father, *together with him.*

The Calling of the Church — Also Irrevocable

The time will come when there will be the "fullness of the Gentiles," the fullness in quantity and quality from among the Gentiles. These Gentiles in their fullness will make Israel jealous, "and so all Israel will be saved" (Rom. 11:25-26).

---

36. Romans 11:31. The word "in order that" (Gk. *hina*) is usually connected with the words that *follow* (as in English). So here ". . . *disobedient by the mercy shown to you, in order that* they too may now receive mercy." The AV, RSV, and NRSV assume that, in this exceptional case, "in order that" should be connected with the *preceding* words and translated: ". . . *disobedient in order that by the mercy shown to you,* they too may now receive mercy." Admittedly, this usage of *hina* does occur from time to time, but never in such a way that it gives another meaning to what is said — in this case, what is said about the relation between God's mercy to the Gentiles and Israel's disobedience. For that reason we should follow the normal Greek word order, as do the Vulgate, Luther, Calvin, and Schlatter. Schlatter writes: "so haben diese jetzt dem euch gewährten Erbarmen widerstrebt, damit auch sie jetzt Erbarmen erhalten" ("so these have now resisted the mercy shown to you, in order that they too may now receive mercy").

We have asked ourselves whether this would still apply to us — are we still branches in the olive tree after all that the church has done for many centuries, despite Paul's warning? Can we still hope to make Israel jealous after all the things the church has done to the Jews? Here is Paul's answer: God's calling is irrevocable. Paul writes this about the Jews, who have become enemies of the gospel. That their disobedience has now continued for many centuries changes nothing as far as the irrevocability of God's calling is concerned. But if that is true of God's calling, then it also applies to us. For the believers from among the Gentiles have also been called by God. Paul affirmed this at the beginning of this letter. He is a servant of Jesus Christ, ". . . to bring about the obedience of faith among all the Gentiles, including yourselves who are called to belong to Jesus Christ. . . . God's beloved in Rome, who are called to be saints" (Rom. 1:1, 5-7). And in the parable of the potter he writes about the objects of God's mercy: "Including us whom he has called, not only from the Jews, but also from the Gentiles" (9:24). Therefore, if it is also true that God's calling is irrevocable for those who have been called from among the Gentiles, this must imply that they continue to be in God's care in order to regraft them in the olive tree Israel, even though they have become cut-off branches.

Paul was not so sure that everything would go well with those who had been called from among the Gentiles. He does write: "Just as you were once disobedient to God . . ." (v. 30), but a little earlier he writes: ". . . provided you continue in his kindness; otherwise you also will be cut off" (11:22). The disobedience could return, and that is in fact what happened. We saw it in the parable of the prodigal son: There is nothing specifically Jewish in the behavior of the elder son. The church faces that danger just as much as Israel. It has just been converted from service to other gods, and, look, that same pride (11:20)!

But if God's calling is irrevocable, then there is hope; then it is in fact impossible for things to end in total failure for the church. Just as he knew what he began when he called the Jews, he knew what he did when he called the believers from among the Gentiles. He foreknew all the disobedience of the church through the ages, no less than he foreknew Israel's disobedience. It has become abundantly clear that in the church — just as in Israel — God was dealing with a stiff-necked people. Therefore — even though there is no indication as yet, and even though it seems totally improbable — just as he will not rest until Israel responds to her calling, he will not rest before the believers from the Gentiles fulfill their calling. It will come about: the church in which Israel recognizes its Messiah, the church which makes Israel jealous. He does not abandon the work of his hands — for the gifts of God and the calling of God are irrevocable!

The Gospel: Mercy for All Who Are Disobedient

> For God has imprisoned all in disobedience so that he may be merciful to all. (11:32)

Most interpreters explain this text as a summary of verses 30 and 31. "All" refers to both categories: first the believers from the Gentiles and then the Jews as disobedient people will find mercy with God. That supposedly is all there is to say about God's compassion. For once the believers from among the Gentiles and the Jews have received God's mercy there is nothing more to follow. But that is not true: There is much, much more to follow. Paul has written about the salvation of humanity: Condemnation has come to all people, and there will be justification and life for all (Rom. 5:18).

So in verse 32 Paul does not simply summarize verses 30 and 31, but he takes matters a step further. That becomes clear if we note the second *now* in v. 31: the now of God's mercy over Israel. This points to a sequential order. Now in God's plan the time for his mercy over Israel has come.[37] But at the same time this is not where everything ends for Paul. This "now" is not to be understood as "finally." God may have shown mercy toward Israel, but lost humanity is still locked into its disobedience. Having shown his mercy toward Israel, he proceeds with the next phase: the full riches of his mercy toward the nations. This we heard in Romans 11:12. Only then has his plan been fully accomplished.

Romans 11:32 is the finale of Paul's unfolding of the gospel, in which he summarizes his entire argument: All people have become disobedient, and all will find mercy with God. This is confirmed by the song of praise that immediately follows, and to which we will return below. This praise comprises all of creation, and ends with the words: "To him are all things" (v. 36). From the beginning of his letter the apostle emphasized that God

---

37. The "now" in verses 30-31 (*now* disobedient, *now* receive mercy) do not coincide, but are consecutive. Paul envisions the moment when God will take away the hardening of Israel in the near future. Even though it takes longer than Paul had expected, the church should not push it toward a distant future, for it is *now* part of the task of the church to serve God in this respect. The AV and the RSV have omitted the second "now."

wants to save all people without distinction (Rom. 3:23-24). Now he once more puts this message of joy before his readers in its absolute comprehensiveness.

What have we learned in verses 30-32 of chapter 11? First of all, in v. 30 Paul refers to those who have been called from the Gentiles: They were disobedient, but they have now found mercy with God. They are the wild shoots, grafted into the olive tree Israel. Second, in verse 31 he continues with Israel, which at present is disobedient in regard to the gospel, but will find mercy. The original branches that were broken off are regrafted in order that they may form, together with the other branches, that one olive tree: the Israel of the Messiah. Third, the story does not end with God's mercy toward Israel. For what God did for Israel is only the beginning of what he will do for all nations. Then the prophecies will be fulfilled: He will forever destroy death and he will wipe away the tears from all faces (Isa. 25:8). This is the mercy toward all who have been disobedient as described by Paul in Romans 11:32.[38]

The Road to Mercy Leads through the Judgment

But there is still more to be said about the all-inclusiveness of God's mercy as found in verse 32. That this mercy encompasses *all* people is further supported by the words "imprisoned in disobedience." That is to say: incarcerated together, prisoners of their disobedience. These words refer to the divine judgment. People cannot simply live on as if they do not have to worry about what they have done. They will never be delivered from this, except as God sets them free from the evil they have done. That does not apply only to a part of humanity. For there are no other people but disobedient people. And there are no disobedient people who have not been imprisoned by God in disobedience (cf. Gal. 3:22).

That includes the dead! Their death did not set them free from what they had done. We know the ominous words: "Whoever believes in the Son has eternal life; whoever disobeys the Son will not see life, but must endure God's wrath" (John 3:36). And: "I am going away, and you will search for me, but you will die in your sin" (John 8:21). The dead are truly imprisoned in their disobedience. But God has not imprisoned them — none of them — with the intention of leaving them in that state, but rather of leading them back to obedience and to be merciful to them.

---

38. We see thus in 11:30-32 the order that we pointed out at 11:25.

The Song of Praise and God's One Purpose

Paul began this section of his letter by writing about his great sorrow and unceasing anguish over Israel. He called upon God in his misery, and God answered him (Ps. 118:5). God led him to this song of praise that now concludes his exposition of the gospel:

> O the depth of the riches and wisdom and knowledge of God! How unsearchable are his judgments and how inscrutable his ways! "For who has known the mind of the Lord? Or who has been his counselor?" "Or who has given a gift to him, to receive a gift in return?" (Rom. 11:33-35)

God's riches! Paul wrote about these riches in this letter. He refers to the riches of his goodness, his patience, and his tolerance (2:4); the riches of his glory over the objects of his mercy (9:23). His riches are for all who call upon him (10:12); he gives his riches to the nations, now already even though Israel is not yet included; so how much greater the riches when Israel is fully included (11:12). God's riches are solely the riches of his mercy toward the disobedient (11:30-33). Therefore, the depth of his riches is not a depth that hides something unknown, a depth that might even contain disaster. This depth contains nothing but salvation, nothing but mercy. It is the depth of his wisdom and his knowledge. In his wisdom God created all things (Ps. 104:24). Things that have been made with wisdom cannot simply fail. The work of his mercy will conquer all powers that resist him. Nothing is unknown to him!

The following words, his judgments and his ways, speak of that. Paul wrote about God's judgments in Romans 9–11: the hardening of Israel and its disobedience; Israel as the object of God's wrath. God uses his judgments to lead the disobedient toward his mercy for them. "Unsearchable and inscrutable" are the words Paul uses in this connection. He quotes from Isaiah 40:13-14: Who would counsel God about the way that leads to the goal? "Who indeed are you, a human being. . . !" (Rom. 9:20). We will not arrive at the certainty, the joy, that God will reach his purpose if we rely on what we see and on our own attempts to make sense of what we see. His thoughts and his ways differ from ours (Isa. 55:8). The certainty that his ways will lead to the goal is the certainty of *faith,* which does not see, nor understand, but trusts that he who has spoken his Word will also be able to do what he has promised (Rom. 4:21). It is the certainty that can be found only in the encounter with that Word.

Then follow these tremendous words about the one goal of God: "For from him and through him and to him are all things. To him be the glory forever" (11:36; cf. 1 Cor. 8:6; Col. 1:16). All that exists is from him: He wanted it to exist. It is also through him; it exists even today only because he wants it to continue to exist. And he wants this because he has created everything. These two words "to him" exclude the possibility that there could be any creature created by God for the purpose of being and remaining far from him. There is a being "far from him." Paul wrote about it: Those who do not know God and do not obey the gospel will suffer the punishment of eternal destruction, separated from the presence of the Lord (2 Thess. 1:9). We may not detract from that. But eternal destruction is not the final word. For even those who are eternally far from him, are created "to him." That they remain. Therefore, their destiny is that eventually they come, from their eternal destruction, "to him."

CHAPTER VII

The Prophets Speak about Judgment and Hope (Romans 14:11 and the Prophets)

1. The Judgment and the Song of Praise

The Judgment of the Church

From our perspective there is a sharp contrast between God's future judgment and the salvation of all humanity. We saw that this is different with Paul. He knows of the day of wrath, the coming judgment in which God will do to each according to his deeds. For most people this means anguish and distress (Rom. 2:5, 6, 9). But, nonetheless, he is sure that all people will be justified through the redemption in Jesus Christ (3:24; 5:18-19). What Paul wrote about Israel, in particular, showed that God's wrath is not the final word: The objects of his wrath (9:22) become the objects of his mercy (11:31).

As he continues his letter, Paul returns to the judgment:

> For we will all stand before the judgment seat of God. For it is written: "As I live, says the Lord, every knee shall bow to me, and every tongue shall give praise to God." So then, each of us will be accountable to God. (Rom. 14:10b-12)

Disagreements in the church constitute the underlying reason for this statement. We will return to that topic later. The apostle warns believers: They will be accountable for their behavior toward one another in the coming judgment. Jesus spoke in similar terms about our giving account of what we have done in his service (Matt. 25:14-30). The church must also face the judgment, just as the Israel that rejected the Messiah.

Referring to death, Paul comments: "We do not live to ourselves, and we do not die to ourselves. If we live, we live to the Lord, and if we die, we die to the Lord" (Rom. 14:7-8). Likewise, in his second letter to the Corinthians Paul begins by writing about our death and then deals with the judgment upon what we have done during our life ("in the body"). "For all of us must appear before the judgment seat of Christ, so that each may receive recompense for what has been done in the body, whether good or evil" (2 Cor. 5:10). These words hardly put us at ease. "Recompense for what has been done" — that is the "repayment according to our deeds" mentioned in Romans 2:6. Even the believer may have to face the anguish and distress of Romans 2:9. We hear about this in Paul's first letter to the Corinthian church. Paul is writing about people who have built their faith on Jesus Christ as their foundation — the church. How have they built on that foundation? Will it pass the test? That will be revealed on the day of Christ's return:

> . . . the work of each builder will become visible, for the Day will disclose it, because it will be revealed with fire, and the fire will test what sort of work each has done. If what has been built on the foundation survives, the builder will receive a reward. If the work is burned up, the builder will suffer loss; the builder will be saved, but only as through fire. (1 Cor. 3:13-15)

Strange words: suffer loss and yet be saved.[1] That salvation must mean: not being condemned with the world (1 Cor. 11:32), and thus belonging to those who are Christ's at his coming (1 Cor. 15:23). We cannot say more about it. Here we face things which have not been revealed to us. Scripture speaks of the judgment of Israel, of the church, and of the world. We also

---

1. On 1 Corinthians 3:10-15, see Joachim Gnilka, *Ist 1 Kor. 3,10-15 ein Schriftzeugnis für das Fegfeuer, eine exegetisch-historische Untersuchung* (Düsseldorf, 1955). Gnilka offers a wealth of information about the exegesis of this passage throughout church history. The subject of the judgment is constantly referred to. Cf. also 1 Cor. 5:5 regarding the man who is handed over to Satan, "so that his spirit may be saved in the day of the Lord"; also in that passage: judgment followed by salvation. See Barth, *CD*, II/2, pp. 440-84.

know that somehow the judgment of Israel and of the church comes first — see the order of 1 Cor. 15:23 — before the judgment of the world. But how we must interpret that "before" and how it relates to our death (Rom. 14:7-8; 2 Cor. 5:1-10) remains hidden from us. Nor is it possible to link this passage to what is said about the day of wrath and the dual result of the judgment in Romans 2:5-11. But one thing is very clear: Paul gives full weight to the message of judgment; yet this never obscures the hope of salvation.

Judgment and Salvation in Isaiah 45

In Romans 14:10-12, in particular, this coexistence of judgment and salvation is very conspicuous. In the same breath, Paul writes about the judgment seat of God and that "every tongue shall give praise." In so doing he refers to a prophecy of Isaiah. We know that in Israel's prophets the proclamation of divine judgment was very prominent. We will now have a closer look at their message. We will find that they speak about judgment in such a way that hope for those who are being judged never fades; through the judgment they are led to praise God.

We read the prophecy of Isaiah, to which Paul refers, in its context:

> . . . There is no other God besides me, a righteous God and a Savior; there is no one besides me. Turn to me and be saved, all the ends of the earth! For I am God, and there is no other. By myself I have sworn, from my mouth has gone forth in righteousness a word that shall not return: "To me every knee shall bow, every tongue shall swear." Only in the Lord, it shall be said of me, are righteousness and strength; all who were incensed against him shall come to him and be ashamed. In the LORD all the offspring of Israel shall triumph and glory. (Isa. 45:21b-25)

Is this indeed a prophecy of judgment? Yes, it is. It is part of a series of statements about judgment, in which Israel's God calls upon the nations with their gods to enter into judgment with him. ". . . let the peoples renew their strength; let them approach, then let them speak; let us together draw near for judgment" (Isa. 41:1). "Set forth your case, says the LORD; bring your proofs, says the King of Jacob" (41:21). "Let all the nations gather together, and let the peoples assemble. . . . Let them bring their witnesses to justify them, and let them hear and say, 'It is true'" (43:9). "Accuse me, let us go to trial; set forth your case, so that you may be proved right" (43:26). "Assemble yourselves and come together, draw near, you survivors of the nations! . . . Declare and present your case" (45:20-21). We are informed about the verdict at the end of Isa. 45:21: "There is no other god besides me, a righteous God and a Savior; there is no one besides me'. That apparently is the main concern in the judgment.

In the ensuing words we learn that this judgment ends the anger and rebellion of the nations against God: Every knee shall bow before him. They submit and recognize that he is God and must be obeyed. They are ashamed of what they have done: They have raged against the only One who is worthy to be called God, the righteous, redeeming God. At the same time we notice that a way has been opened to him; they can *come* and be saved. And they do come. The judgment of Israel's God does not end in perdition but in songs of praise. For there is salvation after the judgment.

Again the Denial

Paul writes that every tongue will praise God. For this statement he appeals to Isaiah's prophecy. But the church has read this prophecy differently. First of all, we read in the Authorized Version: "Surely, shall one say, in the LORD have I righteousness and strength: even to him shall men come; and all that are incensed against him shall be ashamed." This is a faithful rendering of the original text. Our concern here is with the last few words. The question is whether those who are described as "ashamed" are identical with those who "come," kneel before him and exclaim: "Surely, in the LORD have I righteousness and strength." In the Revised Standard Version this no longer is a question: "All that were incensed against him shall come to him and be ashamed." But the Reformers held another view. Luther translates these words as: "Every knee shall bow before me, and every tongue will swear, saying: 'In the LORD I have righteousness and strength.' These will also come to him; but all who withstand him must be put to shame."[2] Luther sees a contrast: There

2. The AV ("are incensed and shall be ashamed") can be understood as saying: Those who are now incensed will not remain in that state; they will be ashamed and bow their knees. However, it can also be understood to say: They *remain* incensed and end in shame — they are the condemned in contrast to the others who kneel and are saved. The RSV says that they *were* incensed; but they are no longer so, for they are ashamed: In shame they bow their knees. (Luther: "Mir sollen sich alle knie beugen / und alle zungen schweren / und sagen / Im HERRN habe ich gerechtigkeit und stercke

is a group of people who come, bow their knees, and swear by the God of Israel; they are those who will be saved. But there is also another group. Those are the ones who are "incensed" against him, who are offering angry resistance against the God of Israel and his service. For them he is not the redeeming God but the condemning God, who makes them stand ashamed and sends them to the punishment they deserve. Thus, Luther envisions a separation into two categories. He underscores this contrast by translating the Hebrew for "and" by "but." Indeed, this word can sometimes be understood in this sense (just as our word "and"), but only when the context indicates that a contrast is intended. Luther was of the opinion that this was the case in this particular text.

Calvin held the same view. Referring to the bowing of every knee, he writes: "We are here dealing with genuine confession, which springs from the knowledge of God that is deeply rooted in the heart." But not all will come and bow their knees. "I believe," he continues, "that this passage simply refers to believers who submit themselves to God; there is some sort of contrast between this group and the rebels, who persist in their resistance against God. I therefore view what is said here as follows: 'Those who acknowledge that their righteousness is anchored in him will come to him.'" Calvin refers at this point to Psalm 65:2: "To you all flesh shall come." Nonetheless, there are also those who do not come: "All who are afraid of his majesty will try to flee away from him as far as possible. Of them it is said that they will be ashamed."[3]

But neither in Psalm 65 (cf. Pss. 22:7 and 86:9) nor in this prophecy do we hear of a contrast. The appeal to turn to God only has to do with redemption: "Turn to me and be saved, all the ends of the earth." And God vows that all will do this. If some were to come and something else would happen — a group of people would be condemned and face per-

---

/ Solche werden auch zu jm kommen / Aber all die im widerstehen / müssen zu schanden werden.")

3. Translated from W. A. de Groot and J. F. Wijnhoud, *Verklaring van de Bijbel door Johannes Calvijn, De Profeet Jesaja* (Goudriaan/Kampen, 1985), 3:396, 398. Delitzsch agrees that there will be a separation: ". . . whereas all his enemies are put to shame. They separate themselves irretrievably from the men who serve Him, the restoration of whom is his direct will, and the goal of the history of salvation" (C. F. Keil and F. Delitzsch, *Commentary on the Old Testament* [Grand Rapids: repr. 1976], 7:231). J. L. Koole (see n. 4) refers to E. J. Young, *The Book of Isaiah* (Grand Rapids, 1972), vol. 3, who thinks that this kneeling is partly a voluntary and partly a forced submission to God.

dition — this would be contrary to what God has sworn![4] It would imply that it was not the *truth* that came forth from his mouth! This is not to be construed as if there will be no judgment and no condemnation. But it does mean that God's purpose is not achieved in that condemnation. His purpose is that all will come to him, from the ends of the earth, and be saved.

All Idol Worshipers, without Distinction

Who are those "all" who are "incensed" toward God? In Isaiah 41:11 those who attack Israel are also described as "incensed" against them. But in the prophets and the psalms the enemies of Israel are simply the enemies of God (e.g., Ps. 83:3-5). Scripture makes no distinction between Gentiles who are bad and less bad: between Gentiles who are "incensed" against God and those whose behavior is such that they will be saved. All will be ashamed. This we read time and time again in the second part of Isaiah:

> They shall be turned back and utterly put to shame — those who trust in carved images, who say to cast images: "You are our gods." (Isa. 42:17)

> All who make idols are nothing, and the things they delight in do not profit; . . . And so they will be put to shame. . . . Look, all its devotees shall be put to shame; . . . Let them all assemble, let them stand up; they shall be terrified, they shall all be put to shame. (44:9-11)

> All of them are put to shame and confounded, the makers of idols go in confusion together. (45:16)

So, who are those in Isaiah 45:24 who are ashamed? All non-Israelites are idol worshipers. There are no others. They turn from their idols to God, and they cry out that there is salvation only with the God of Israel. What

---

4. Luther and Calvin point to a contrast between those who kneel and are saved, and those who are ashamed and will be condemned. The same contrast between the redeemed and the lost has also been argued from another angle: Those who kneel are saved; those who come are not the same as those who kneel; they come before the throne of God's judgment and are condemned (J. L. Koole, *Jesaja II* [Kampen, 1985], 1:368). We defend the view that this text does not intend to indicate any contrast: Those who kneel are the same as those who come; all are ashamed because of their resistance against God.

a discovery for them! Things are not as they had always thought! The idols that they have worshiped cannot provide redemption; only the God of Israel is able to do so. Those who kneel are *all* ashamed for what they did as they served their idols. What kind of Gentiles could they be, who would turn their backs on other gods and not be ashamed? All are ashamed and bow their knees before the God of Israel as the only true God. What they heard about him is true: There is no other righteous, redeeming God except him! *They are totally convinced.*[5]

The statement that every knee shall bow and every tongue shall swear to God must not be diluted in any way. Paul took this prophecy as it reads. He did not know of an interpretation of this prophecy that would allow for people who would not be willing to kneel. That interpretation is the result of doctrinal views of a later date and attempts to harmonize Isaiah's prophecy with those views. We will yet see to what peculiar statements this notion has led (VII, 4). When quoting this prophecy, Paul has nothing else in mind than what he wrote at the beginning of his epistle: "For there is no distinction, since all have sinned. . . ; they are now justified by grace as a gift, through the redemption that is in Christ Jesus" (Rom. 3:23-24). Therefore, the judgment will result in what Isaiah 45 proclaimed: Without distinction, every knee shall bow and every tongue shall praise God. There is absolutely no restriction or contrast! This is how Paul understood Isaiah's prophecy, and that is also how it was understood by the early church, which included this prophecy in its hymn of praise (Phil. 2:6-11).[6]

5. Claus Westermann (*Das Buch Jesaja/Kapitel 40–66* [Göttingen, 1976], p. 143) writes: "His victory in the lawsuit against the gods of the nations involves something entirely new. There is no longer overthrowing and destroying, but convincing!" This explains the emphasis (by the use of the singular) on the individual: "*every* knee" and "*every* tongue"; the choice for God is not made *en masse*, by all at the same time; each individual is convinced in his own heart.

6. Westermann (*Das Buch Jesaja*, 143) comments: "Those who once were his enemies and fought against him (v. 24b) arrive on the scene and together with Israel participate in his salvation (v. 25). This text is taken up into the New Testament (in Rom. 14:11 and Phil. 2:10-11). No violence is done to the subject-matter and both citations strictly adhere to the sense of the original" (Eng. trans., *OT Library*, p. 176).

2. The Judgment and the Shame

The Nations Are Ashamed

Isaiah 45:22-25 states the outcome of God's judgment. All will come, from the ends of the earth. But there is something special about their coming: They come in shame. Things have not gone well for them. Earlier the prophet said about those who worship idols: "They shall be terrified, they shall all be put to shame" (Isa. 44:11). Terrified and ashamed — these are the conditions for this coming to the God of righteousness and redemption.

Let us look in more detail at the word "ashamed." As such the term does not say anything about the mentality of the people involved. When we are told that Israel's enemies are put to shame (as, e.g., in Isa. 44:11), this means only that they have failed in their plans to destroy Israel. It does not say that they repent of what they have done. It may well mean that they grudgingly withdraw in order to lick their wounds, waiting for a new opportunity to settle their account with Israel. But that is not the case in Isaiah 45:24! There they bow their knees before God and swear that there is salvation only with God. They are ashamed about their rebellion against him. People who are ashamed like that do not look for opportunities to continue that rebellion.

Similar to the second part of Isaiah, Psalm 83 refers to the putting to shame of Israel's enemies, and in this instance too, more is implied than simply the nullification of their plans:

> They say, "Come, let us wipe them out as a nation; let the name of Israel be remembered no more." . . . "Let us take the pastures of God for our own possession." . . . Fill their faces with shame, so that they may seek your name, O LORD. Let them be put to shame and dismayed forever; let them perish in disgrace. Let them know that you alone, whose name is the LORD, are the Most High over all the earth. (Ps. 83:4, 12, 16-18)

We already pointed out that enmity against Israel inevitably implies enmity against Israel's God: "Even now your enemies are in tumult; those who hate you have raised their heads" (v. 2); "against you they make a covenant" (v. 5). "Let us take the pastures of God for our own possession" — for a hereditary possession, it reads literally. That would put a definite end to the worship of Israel's God. What this psalm requests is the permanent demise of those peoples that are intent upon removing Israel, with its worship of God, from the face of this earth. When Israel's enemies have been put to shame *forever*, every possibility of starting all over again has been excluded.

This may be the end of their enmity, but it is not the end of the enemies themselves! For immediately something else is added: "So that they may seek your name." When praying for the destruction — the destruction that will last *forever* — of her enemies, Israel does not pray that God may wipe them from the face of the earth. Her intention is that God's enemies will be put to shame and subsequently come and *seek* the Lord. Here again we find this "coming," of which we heard already in Isaiah 45:22, 24.

As soon as the enemies of Israel and of Israel's God are not only put to shame, but in their shame seek Israel's God, then the goal has been reached that is described in Isaiah 45:24. It is reached via the route of shame.

There are two words here that demand our attention since they belong inextricably together: retribution and shame.

Ezekiel's Description of God's Judgment of Israel: Retribution

That God punishes evil is an oft-repeated message in the Old Testament. God makes the evil return upon the head of the evildoer: "Their mischief returns upon their own heads, and on their own heads their violence descends" (Ps. 7:16; see also Judg. 9:57; 1 Sam. 25:39; Joel 3:4, 7; Obad. v. 15). This message receives special emphasis in the prophet Ezekiel. But now the issue is not God's judgment of the Gentiles, but rather his judgment of Israel. Just as is the case with the other nations, the only way for Israel to obtain salvation is the way of judgment. As we learned earlier, the God of the covenant is the God who *visits* the sins of his people (Exod. 34:7).

We will first look at Ezekiel 16, the chapter to which we referred in our discussion of Abraham's prayer on behalf of Sodom. There we read: God will judge Jerusalem (16:38) because Israel has been worse than Samaria and Sodom (see also Ezek. 5:5-7 — "more wicked than the nations and the countries all around"). He will return Jerusalem's deeds upon her head (16:43; see also 7:3-9; 9:10; 11:21; 22:31). Then we hear: "They shall bear their punishment" (14:10; 44:10, 12; cf. 23:35, 49).

Retribution! But the retribution does not have its purpose in itself. God's wrath is not a wrath that wants to continue endlessly. That is what we may have been told in the doctrine of eternal punishment, but it is not Ezekiel's message: "So I will satisfy my fury on you, and my jealousy shall turn away from you; I will be calm, and will be angry no longer" (16:42). God's wrath is a wrath that wants to stop! As soon as the purpose of his wrath has been achieved — and not earlier — his jealousy will turn away from Israel. Then he will no longer be angry with his people. We meet the same message in the extended discourse about judgment in Leviticus 26. If Israel does not obey God's commandments, then "I will bring terror on you" (v. 16). If they persist in their disobedience, then "I will continue to plague you sevenfold for your sins" (v. 21). Again and again we hear that God will punish sevenfold if they continue in their disobedience in spite of his judgment. Why? Because he does not give up on them. He wants to win them back! That is what we are told in verses 40 to 42: "But if they confess their iniquity, and the iniquity of their ancestors . . . then I will remember my covenant with Jacob; I will remember also my covenant with Isaac and also my covenant with Abraham, and I will remember the land." Then we hear about the attitude of the Father. They spurned and abhorred God's statutes (vv. 15, 43); they broke God's covenant (v. 15). That is what *they* did. And how did God respond? "Yet for all that, when they are in the land of their enemies, I will not spurn them, or abhor them so as to destroy them utterly and break my covenant with them; for I am the LORD their God" (v. 44). Whatever Israel may do, she will never lose her place in the heart of the Father. His judgment underlines the fact that he does not give her up, nor does he abandon her to other gods. He wants her to return. He wants the covenant with her ancestors to be restored. He wants to fulfill to Israel the promises he made to her (v. 45). That motivates him from the beginning of his wrath until its end.

Moreover, that goal will be achieved. We read it in Ezekiel 16: "Yet I will remember my covenant with you in the days of your youth, and I will establish with you an everlasting covenant" (v. 60). There we also learn how God will achieve his purpose.

Shame and Atonement in Ezekiel

What will be the result of the punishment? "Then you will remember your ways, and be ashamed . . ." (16:61). Similar to the way in which the message has been repeated over and over again, we hear the emphasis given to this shame:

> So be ashamed you also, and bear your disgrace (v. 52); in order that you may bear your disgrace and be ashamed of all that you have done (v. 54); you must bear the penalty of your lewdness and your abominations, says the LORD (v. 58), in order that you may remember and may be confounded, and never open your mouth again because of your shame. (v. 63; cf. 23:35, 49; 44:13)

205

God returns Israel's behavior upon her own head. And this confrontation with the deeds of the past brings shame and disgrace. Then comes the moment that had always been the purpose of all God's judgments: the restoration of the bond with him. Ezekiel 16 ends on that note: ". . . when I forgive you all that you have done, says the Lord GOD" (v. 63).

The prophet here uses the word that has often been translated "atonement."[7] It signifies the restoration of unity with God since all Israel's disloyalty toward God has been forgiven. In this "atonement" of all Israel's unfaithfulness lies the heart of the eternal covenant that God has established with her. Ezekiel 36 expresses that reconciliation:

> I will sprinkle clean water upon you, and you shall be clean from all your uncleanliness, and from all your idols I will cleanse you. A new heart I will give you, and a new spirit I will put within you. . . . I will put my spirit within you, and make you follow my statutes and be careful to observe my ordinances. (36:25-27)

The atonement is the cleansing of the past, the removal of the evil deeds that have been committed. That is the beginning of the new life with God. Then God will put his spirit in their hearts and will ensure that they will have no desire to return to what they once did. But there is more: They themselves do not want to fall back, not at any price! This we hear in the following words:

> Then you shall remember your evil ways, and your dealings that were not good; and you shall loathe yourself for your iniquities and your abominable deeds. . . . Be ashamed and dismayed for your ways, O house of Israel. (36:31-32)

This "remembering" is a thorough and permanent rejection of that past. Their way of life, their dealings with God and with one another, have come to light and been unmasked. Israel loathes herself because of her iniquities and abominations. Why? Because she sees what she should have done, and how *good* that is. And because she sees what she really did, and that nothing good can be said about it. The eyes of the prodigal son have been opened, and he comes to himself. The way that leads to the Father lies open!

---

7. This word is often used in Leviticus; see *The Englishman's Hebrew and Chaldee Concordance of the Old Testament* (London, n.d.), pp. 614-15, s.v. *kāphar;* the Day of Atonement (Lev. 23:27-28) is called Yom Kippur. It has the same root.

206

Shame and the New Covenant in Jeremiah

The prophet Jeremiah also writes about Israel's shame. Once again we note that the word "shame" as such does not indicate repentance or conversion. When the enemies of the prophet — almost all of Israel — stumble and are unable to prevail against him, they stand "greatly ashamed, because they do not succeed" (20:11). That does not automatically imply that they are ashamed of their evil purposes, and turn away from them. They remain a danger for the prophet. But elsewhere we hear about another kind of shame, the shame that touches the heart:

> A voice on the bare heights is heard, the plaintive weeping of Israel's children, because they have perverted their way, they have forgotten the LORD their God: "Return, O faithless children, I will heal your faithlessness." "Here we come to you, for you are the LORD our God. . . . Let us lie down in our shame, and let our dishonor cover us; for we have sinned against the LORD our God, we and our ancestors, from our youth even to this day; and we have not obeyed the voice of the LORD our God." (Jer. 3:21, 22, 25)

Here is a people that has truly repented and does not look for opportunities to continue their disobedience.

The great prophecy of Israel's restoration is of special interest to us:

> Indeed I heard Ephraim pleading: "You disciplined me, and I took the discipline; I was like a calf untrained. Bring me back, let me come back, for you are the LORD my God. For after I had turned away I repented, and after I was discovered, I struck my thigh; I was ashamed, and I was dismayed, because I bore the disgrace of my youth." (Jer. 31:18-19)

Israel's shame results in her return, and in the establishment of a new covenant. Here Jeremiah appears as the great precursor of Ezekiel:

> The days are surely coming, says the LORD, when I will make a new covenant with the house of Israel and the house of Judah. It will not be like the covenant that I made with their ancestors when I took them by the hand to bring them out of the land of Egypt — a covenant that they broke. . . . But this is the covenant that I will make with the house of Israel after those days, says the LORD: I will put my law within them, and I will write it on their hearts; and I will be their God, and they shall be my people. No longer shall they teach one another, or say to each other, "Know

the Lord," for they shall all know me, from the least of them to the greatest, says the LORD; for I will forgive their iniquity, and remember their sin no more. (Jer. 31:31-34)

When Jesus institutes the Lord's Supper, he says, "For this is my blood of the covenant, which is poured out for many for the forgiveness of sins" (Matt. 26:28). Luke renders this statement: "This cup that is poured out for you is the new covenant in my blood" (Luke 22:20). With these words "new covenant" and "for the forgiveness of sins" Jesus refers to the prophecy of Jeremiah. He faced death in order that he might fulfill the prophets. In Christ's death God himself acted and paid the price for his faithfulness toward the unfaithful.[8] Therein, and only therein, is the certitude that God will achieve the purpose of his covenant. This, and only this, guarantees that God's judgments over Israel are not in vain, but will lead to the return of his disobedient people. But more than that: They will lead to the return of all humanity. For that purpose God made his covenant with Israel.

The Content of the New Covenant

Jeremiah writes about the *new* covenant, which is not to be confused with the old covenant that Israel had broken. Ezekiel calls this covenant an *eternal* covenant (Ezek. 16:60; 37:26). What do these prophets tell us about the content of this covenant?

1. *Israel has become a people that lives by grace only.* Reflecting on its own conduct produces nothing but shame. What God now gives to his people is a free gift; it is exclusively his work. He forgives their sins (Jer. 31:34); he cleanses them from their uncleanliness and delivers them from their idols (Ezek. 36:25; 37:23). Ezekiel strongly emphasizes that this is only by grace: "It is not for your sake, O house of Israel, that I am about to act, but for the sake of my holy name, which you have profaned among the nations to which you came" (36:22, 32).

2. *God will give his spirit in the hearts of his people.* They had a "heart of stone," a heart without feeling. God will remove that from their bodies,

8. Before God returns the iniquity of sinners, upon the heads, he does something else: He lays all their iniquity on him, the Lamb of God (Isa. 53:6). This is the basis of Barth's soteriology: The Judge himself has allowed himself to be judged (Karl Barth, *CD*, IV/1, pp. 211-82: "The Judge Judged in Our Place'). "There does not fall on them anything that God has not decreed from all eternity to fall upon himself, and has actually caused to fall upon himself" (*CD*, II/2 p. 494).

and he will give them hearts of flesh, hearts with feeling, hearts that are willing to be led by God's Spirit — not partially, but completely; no trace will be left of the former disobedience. "A new heart I will give you, and a new spirit I will put within you . . ." (36:26-27; see also 11:19-20; cf. Deut. 29:4 and 30:6). Jeremiah speaks in similar terms: "I will write my law within them," and: "For they shall all know me, from the least of them to the greatest" (31:33, 34).

3. *In this covenant death is conquered.* The rule of death will end when Israel has become the people that allows itself to be fully led by the Spirit. We see this in Ezekiel 37:1-14, the vision about the resurrection of Israel's dead to which we referred earlier. Those who believe that this vision was fulfilled in the return from the Babylonian exile disregard the context of Ezekiel 36:24-32.[9] The return from this exile did not bring an end to Israel's disobedience. It was a liberating act of God, but subsequent to this return Israel rejected the Messiah, Jerusalem was destroyed, and Israel became dispersed among the nations. What is promised here is not something that is followed by new disasters. It cannot be anything but the acceptance of Israel that Paul describes as life from the dead (Rom. 11:15). This includes the dead from Israel, who will share in the salvation that God bestows upon his people.[10] Every exegesis that excludes them falls short of what God here reveals to his prophet.

The same is true of Jeremiah. Death is not mentioned in the context of the new covenant he describes. But we learn about the relationship between this new covenant and the victory over death when Jesus institutes the Last Supper: "This cup is the new covenant in my blood. . . ." His death validated this new covenant, and what that means becomes clear when God resurrects him from the dead, as "the first fruit of those who have died" (1 Cor. 15:20).

4. *In this covenant Israel's salvation will extend to all nations.* Ezekiel as

9. W. Zimmerli (*Ezechiel* [Neukirchen, 1969], 2:897-902) believes that the vision is intimately linked with the promise of Ezekiel 36:26-27, in order that "sich nicht die Alte Unheilsgeschichte im Lande erneut wiederholt" (the old story of disaster would not be repeated in the land). This puts the vision in eschatological perspective, as the prophet intended. C. F. Keil (*Biblischer Commentar über den Propheten Ezechiël* [Leipzig, 1882], pp. 360-64; reprinted) further clarifies the matter by referring to the return from exile as a pledge rather than a fulfillment.

10. It must include the dead, too, because Ezekiel here writes about the salvation following the final judgment over Israel. With regard to this vision and Israel's dead, cf. VI, 4.

well as Jeremiah puts all the emphasis on Jerusalem. When this has become the place of God's salvation, all nations will come. Ezekiel announces that precisely through this new covenant God will make Sodom the daughter of Jerusalem (16:60-61). Not *only* Sodom, but *even* Sodom! Here again is an indication that Ezekiel believed the covenant included the dead. And Jeremiah tells us:

> At that time Jerusalem shall be called the throne of the LORD, and all nations shall gather to it, and all nations shall gather to it, to the presence of the LORD in Jerusalem, and they shall no longer stubbornly follow their own evil will (3:17) . . . then nations shall be blessed by him, and by him they shall boast. (4:2; cf. 12:16)

They come with shame. We do not hear the word itself, but there is nonetheless an echo in a prophecy that is closely linked to Isa. 45:23-24:

> O LORD, my strength and my stronghold, my refuge in the day of trouble, to you the nations come from the ends of the earth and say: Our ancestors have inherited nothing but lies, worthless things in which there is no profit. (Jer. 16:19)

Salvation after the Judgment: All Israel

To whom then is this future promised? Not to the loyal remnant, but *to the people that has gone through the judgment.* Ezekiel writes about those whose deeds have returned upon their heads; people who loathe what they have done, who have been worse than the people of Sodom! These prophecies make no distinction between a loyal part and a disloyal part of the people. The house of Israel in its entirety had turned away from God, and without exception all will have to bear the consequences of their ungodliness (Ezek. 14:3-11). Ezekiel says further about Israel in its entirety after it has gone through this experience: God will cleanse them from their idols; he will remove their hearts of stone and give them new hearts (36:25-26). Jeremiah also refers to Israel as being ashamed of what it had done — the outcome of God's judgment (31:18-19). Then we hear that God will not reject "all the offspring of Israel" for what they have done (31:37; cf. v. 34).

This is not just *a* judgment; this is the *final judgment.* All Israel's deeds have returned on her head. Now, in the new covenant, Israel lets herself be led by the Spirit of God. This covenant will never be broken; it is, according to

Ezekiel, an eternal covenant. No further deeds will follow which God will have to return upon the head of the perpetrator. God's purpose in calling Israel has been achieved. After the judgment there is nothing but salvation!

3. What the Prophets Say about Eternal Punishment[11]

The Old Testament — Jesus' Bible

Usually advocates of the doctrine of eternal punishment appeal to three texts in Matthew in which Jesus refers to eternal fire (Matt. 18:8; 25:41) and eternal punishment (25:46), and to the words of Paul about "the punishment of eternal destruction" (2 Thess. 1:9).[12]

In present-day parlance the word "eternal" means "everlasting," that is, "endless." Is that correct? That is the question we must now face: Is *eternal* punishment *everlasting* punishment, without end? We already saw that Jesus' statements about the judgment cannot be harmonized with a punishment without end (II, 3). We now want to consider the word "eternal." We shall see that the prophets, too, used this word in connection with punishment. What did they mean to say? This must be of great importance for a correct interpretation of Jesus' words, for the Old Testament was his Bible. Whatever meaning this word may have carried for the prophets, it must have meant the same for him.[13]

11. For the word "eternity" I consulted the articles *'olām, 'ad,* and *nētsach* in the *Theological Dictionary of the New Testament* and the *Exegetical Dictionary of the New Testament;* and the articles *aiōn* and *aiōnios* in the *Theological Dictionary of the Old Testament* and the *Lexicon of the Old Testament.* E. Jenni, "Das Wort *'olām* im Alten Testament," *Zeitschrift für alttestamentliche Wissenschaft,* 64 (1952):197-249; 65 (1953):1-35; J. Barr, *Biblical Words for Time* (end ed.; Naperville, 1969), pp. 86-110; J. Schmidt, *Der Ewigkeitsbegriff im Alten Testament* (Münster, 1940); W. Michaelis, *Versöhnung des Alls* (Gümligen, Bern, 1950), pp. 44-67; J. H. Brown, *Eternity: Is It a Biblical Idea?* (London, 1926); H. Schumacher, *Das Biblische Zeugnis von der Versöhnung des Alls* (Stuttgart, 1959), pp. 133-44.

12. Another passage that mentions this word is in Jude, v. 7 (see II, 1); for Revelation, see VII, 5.

13. I used G. Lisowski, *Konkordanz zum Hebräischen Alten Testament* (Stuttgart, 1958), to check all the passages where the Hebrew Bible has the words "*'olām,*" "*ād,*" and "*nētsach.*" *'Olām* is by far the most frequently employed word for "eternity"; it is most often translated "forever" or "everlasting." A great help in this respect was the Dutch Authorized Version, better known as the States-General Bible (1637; comparable

There is a difficulty with which we have to come to grips. Since many English translations usually render the Hebrew words for "eternal" as "everlasting" or "forever" (except when referring to punishment), we have in the following paragraphs consistently added the word "eternal" or "eternity" to indicate that this translates this particular Hebrew word (*'olam*).

Jeremiah: Eternal Fire Followed by Restoration

Thirteen times Jeremiah uses the words "eternal" or "eternity" in the context of divine punishment.[14] We limit ourselves to five pronouncements on Israel. At the same time we notice another expression, which Jesus also used, as we just saw: fire that cannot be quenched (Mark 9:43).[15] We encounter both expressions in Jeremiah 17:

> For in my anger a fire is kindled that shall burn forever [eternally]; (v. 4). Then I will kindle a fire in its gates; it shall devour the palaces of Jerusalem and shall not be quenched. (v. 27)

---

to the English AV of 1611), which almost always translates this word with the Dutch equivalent of "eternity." I also consulted Trommius's *Concordantie ofte Woord-register* (Leeuwarden, 1750-54; 3 vols.) and George Wigram's *The Englishman's Hebrew and Chaldee Concordance of the Old Testament*. The comments in the margin of the Dutch "Statenvertaling" also offered significant information; they are evidence of the importance that was attached to this word. The meaning of this word (*'olām*) is rather extensively discussed in connection with Genesis 13:15: "That is, a long period, namely until the *Messiah*, the seed of the blessing, born from your [i.e. Abraham's] flesh, will have completed the work of redemption on earth. In other passages the Hebrew word may have another meaning: 'the whole period of the law . . . ,' or: 'a long time period,' or: 'until Christ' (in the context of the giving of the law); sometimes: 'during his life time' (e.g. when referring to the slave in Exod. 21:6 and Deut. 15:17)." Commenting on Isaiah 32:14, the note in the margin says: "that is: a long time"; and on Jeremiah 17:4: "With regard to the unrepentant, who will feel the fire of my wrath in all eternity; or: a long time, that is, 70 years, as the word *eternity* may sometimes indicate . . . ." Of special interest is the marginal reading on Jonah 2:6: "In such a way that there was no chance of escape, were it not that you had miraculously saved me."

14. Five times in the context of the judgment on Israel (17:4; 18:16; 20:11; 23:40; 25:9) as well as eight times in connection with the judgment on other nations: on Babel (25:12; 51:26, 39, 57, 62); on Edom (49:13); on Kedar (49:33); — all *'olām*; in 50:39 *netsach*.

15. Unquenchable fire: Jer. 4:4; 7:20; 17:27; 21:12; always: fire that does not stop burning until all has been destroyed.

As a punishment of Israel's disobedience, God will bring the king of Babylon over the land and its inhabitants and all the nations around:

> I will utterly destroy them, and make them an object of horror and of hissing, and an everlasting [eternal] disgrace. (25:9)[16]

The expression "hissing" is also found as "everlasting hissing," alongside such expressions as "eternal shame" or "everlasting disgrace." We will turn to those texts in a moment.

This is, however, the point we should note: The everlasting burning of God's wrath, the unquenchable fire, and the eternal destruction (like the eternal shame and disgrace) are not the final words about Jerusalem's fate. They are followed by Jerusalem's restoration under the new covenant that God is ready to establish:

> The days are surely coming, says the LORD, when the city shall be rebuilt for the LORD . . . The whole valley of the dead bodies and the ashes . . . shall be sacred to the LORD. It shall never again be uprooted or overthrown. (31:38-40)

Wrath, Until the Purpose Has Been Achieved

What does Jeremiah mean when he speaks of God's eternal punishment? We read in Psalm 78 how God punishes Israel again and again because of her continuing disobedience:

> When he killed them, they sought for him; they repented and sought God earnestly. They remembered that God was their rock, the Most High their redeemer. But they flattered him with their mouths; they lied to him with their tongues. Their heart was not steadfast toward him; they were not true to his covenant. Yet he, being compassionate, forgave their iniquity, and did not destroy them; often he restrained his anger, and did not stir up all his wrath. (Ps. 78:34-38)

---

16. NRSV, following the Greek translation: "an everlasting (eternal) disgrace." In this case we prefer the Hebrew text and the AV. Cf. the Vulgate: "in solitudines sempiternas." We note that the Hebrew *'olām* is here translated as "sempiternas" (everlasting eternity!), and not as, e.g., in Isaiah 32:14 as "aeternus." The Latin word *aeternus* was not considered strong enough to indicate endlessness. This suggests that the word "eternity" must be preferred.

Disobedience — punishment — repentance — redemption — renewed disobedience — renewed punishment — the process keeps going. "Often he restrained his anger." But whenever God did this, disobedience flared up again. Speaking about a fire that has been lighted by God's wrath, which will burn eternally (17:4), Jeremiah means that God will no more restrain his anger. The wrath keeps burning until the purpose has been achieved.[17] We hear this twice:

> The anger of the LORD will not turn back until he has executed and accomplished the intents of his heart. (Jer. 23:20; 30:24; the AV refers to heart rather than mind. For this last word the rendering of the AV — which more closely reflects the Hebrew text — has been followed)

Here we are told precisely what "eternal" means when the prophet speaks of fire that will burn in eternity. It does not mean that God's wrath will burn forever, that is, without end. His wrath will burn without ceasing *until* his purpose has been accomplished — "until the intents of his heart are accomplished." The punishment is not terrible because of its endlessness. The prophets never speak of such a punishment, since it would be purposeless! Its terrible nature is determined by what happens between God and human beings, who are the objects of his wrath, and *remain* the objects until God's purpose has been achieved.

But the moment will come when that purpose will have been achieved, once and for all. We hear of this in the next section of this prophecy. Then, at last, we hear what God had in his heart all along: "I have loved you with an everlasting love. . . . Again I will build you, and you shall be built, O virgin Israel!" (31:3-4). "The days are surely coming, says the LORD, when I will make a new covenant with the house of Israel and the house of Judah. . . . I will put my law within them, and I will write it upon their hearts; and I will be their God, and they shall be my people. . . . for I will forgive their

17. See K. Barth (*CD*, II/2, pp. 480-90): "It judges men absolutely. It utterly abandons them. It burns them right down to faith . . ." (p. 487); it is God's acting for the sake of humans, so that "the only possibility which it leaves to the one handed over" is . . . "that he *appeals* to God: . . . not to try to change his mind about that which must necessarily befall him in his powerlessness and beneath that overwhelming might, nor to move him to alter his sentence or to halt the execution of his judgment, . . . that the last word for him might still be *his* Word and the last work upon him *his* Work" (p. 486). It would be difficult to find a more profound description of the seriousness of the judgment than Barth's "The Determination of the Rejected" (II/2, pp. 410-506).

iniquity, and I will remember their sin no more" (31:31-34). *The eternal punishment is followed by the era of the Spirit.*

Eternal Destruction, Until the Spirit Is Poured Out (Isa. 32:14-15)

In the book of Isaiah we find a prophecy that, as in Jeremiah and Ezekiel, in one breath links the eternal punishment to the coming of the Spirit. It is a prophecy about Jerusalem:

> For the palace will be forsaken, the populous city deserted; the hill and the watchtower will become dens forever [in eternity], the joy of wild asses, a pasture for flocks; until the Spirit is poured upon us from on high, and the wilderness becomes a fruitful field. . . . (Isa. 32:14, 15, RSV)

Also here the time of judgment is followed by the coming of the Spirit. The forsakenness continues unabated until the Spirit from on high is poured upon Israel.[18]

Jeremiah: Eternal Shame

We heard about shame in Ezekiel and Jeremiah. Three times Jeremiah uses the word "forever" in connection with "shame" and the "hissing" of Israel:

> But my people have forgotten me . . . making their land a horror, a thing to be hissed at forever [in eternity]. All who pass by it are horrified and shake their heads. (Jer. 18:15-16)

> But the LORD is with me like a dread warrior; therefore my persecutors will stumble, and they will not prevail. . . . Their eternal dishonor will never be forgotten (20:11). . . . And I will bring upon you everlasting [eternal] disgrace and perpetual [eternal] shame which shall not be forgotten. (23:40)

The word "eternal" here highlights the radical nature of the shame. Their deeds will always remain a reason for deep shame. The punishment has achieved its purpose: conversion, not temporarily, but permanently. A return

---

18. Some scholars have viewed this outpouring of God's Spirit after the eternal desolation of Jerusalem as contradictory and, therefore, as a later addition. Even if the latter is admitted, this remains Scripture as it has been given to us and as it was read by Jesus (cf. Matt. 23:38-39!). See H. Wildberger, *Jesaja* (Neukirchen, 1982), 3:1276-78.

to disobedience is precluded by their intense disgust for what they did in the past — the loathing described in Ezekiel 36:31. Then for Israel the time has come that God had been waiting for, the time of the New Covenant.

Two Disturbing Texts: Isaiah 66:24; Daniel 12:2

In Jeremiah the prophecies of eternal punishment are followed by the promise of Jerusalem's eternal restoration: For all eternity there will be no more destruction. But there are other prophecies to consider. In the last chapter of Daniel we read:

> Many of those who sleep in the dust of the earth shall awake, some to everlasting [eternal] life, and some to shame and everlasting [eternal] contempt. (Dan. 12:2)

"Many *of* those who sleep in the dust of the earth." The text does not deal with a judgment over all the dead. We will leave that problem aside; our interest here is limited to the term "eternal": eternal life and eternal shame and contempt. Jeremiah mentioned redemption following eternal shame, but Daniel does not.

We find another example in the third part of Isaiah (Isa. 56–66). The prophet points to a contrast between a part of Israel that does listen to God and a part that refuses to do so. This second group hears the announcement of the judgment: God will repay their iniquities (65:6) and they shall "be put to shame" (65:13). Yes, the disobedient will leave their name to be used as a curse to God's elect, and he will "put them to death" (65:15). This leads us to the horrifying conclusion of this final section of Isaiah. Jerusalem is restored, and "all flesh" will come to worship God. But outside are the corpses of those who have been killed by God:

> And they shall go out and look at the dead bodies of the people who have rebelled against me; for their worm shall not die, their fire shall not be quenched, and they shall be an abhorrence to all flesh. (66:24)

The word here rendered "abhorrence" is the same as in Daniel 12:2, where it is rendered "contempt." The adjective "eternal" is not used, but the meaning is identical. That is clear from the description of the fire; as in Jeremiah 17, it is fire that is not quenched, fire that will burn in eternity (Jer. 17:27, 4; cf. Isa. 34:10). But what does this word mean in Isa. 66:24? Does this final passage of the book crush the hope for all people that is proclaimed in the book of Isaiah? The great feast for all nations, the annihilation of death and the wiping away of all tears (25:6-8); the joyful message that all flesh will see God's redemption (40:5); that every knee shall bow before God and praise him (45:23) — will all this be cancelled? If that were so, these words would not have been included in this book! We must not forget what we learned from Jeremiah about the unquenchable fire and the subsequent restoration of Jerusalem. Yet, there is a totally different answer to these disturbing texts. For we hear exactly the same words in Jesus' preaching of the judgment.

What Jesus Did with the Eternal Punishment (Matt. 25:46; 26:1-2)

Matthew records, just as Daniel 12:2 and, in particular, Isaiah 66:24, the message of a dual outcome of the judgment. Isaiah 66:24 is quoted verbatim in Mark 9:47-48 as a statement about hell (*gehenna*); and Daniel 12:2 shows affinity with Matthew 25:46.[19] This last text in particular plays a major role in the doctrine of eternal punishment. Jesus does not follow it up with a word of salvation after punishment, to put us at ease. But something else does follow. Here is the word in its immediate context (26:1-2):

> And these will go away into eternal punishment, but the righteous into eternal life. When Jesus had finished saying all these things, he said to his disciples: "You know that after two days the Passover is coming, and the Son of Man will be handed over to be crucified."

People have become accustomed to reading Jesus' words about eternal punishment and eternal life as a description of the dual finale of history. And that is what they are. They not only constitute a serious warning, but they also describe what actually happens in the judgment. Did Jesus see this as the *end* of all things? Did he say: That is how it will end; this is how God wanted it — and did he simply acquiesce in it? That is precisely what he did not do, as we are told in the subsequent verses. Jesus does not shift

19. For the preaching of the judgment in the synagogues in Jesus' days, see P. Volz, *Die Eschatologie der jüdischen Gemeinde im neutestamentlichen Zeitalter* (Tübingen, 1934), pp. 309-32. More detailed information is found in H. L. Strack and P. Billerbeck, *Kommentar zum Neuen Testament aus Talmud und Midrasch* (Munich, 1928), IV/2, pp. 1029-1118 ("Gehinnom"). Opinions differ widely regarding the duration of the punishment of Isaiah 66:24 — *gehinnom*, or *gehennah*, is often translated "hell."

the focus to something that differs from what he has been discussing. He seems to be totally taken aback by the terrible nature of this finale. But then he speaks about what he must do. He now approaches his death. Now his life will be given as a ransom for many (literally: in exchange for many; Matt. 20:28). His blood will be poured out for many (26:28). Twice we read: "for many." Who are these "many"? They are the many who have entered the wide gate and walk the easy road that leads to destruction (Matt. 7:13; cf. Matt. 22:14). These are the same people of whom he just said that they will end in "eternal punishment."

But did he not give his life for "the few" who found the narrow road that leads to life (Matt. 7:14)? Certainly, also for them. But when he speaks of these "many," he does not refer to these "few"! He is the Lamb of God who takes away "the sin of the world" (John 1:29) ". . . and he is the atoning sacrifice for our sins, and not for ours only but also for the sins of the whole world" (1 John 2:2). One who thinks that in Matthew 25:46 Jesus announces the end of the history of the world as an outcome we simply have to accept, acts as if the entire history of Jesus' suffering and death does not affect the many who go to eternal punishment. What is happening here? It is what Moses was after when he put himself in the breach on behalf of disobedient Israel: "If you will only forgive their sins — but if not, blot me out of the book that you have written" (Exod. 32:32). God did not blot Moses out of his book; but this is the way Christ must go — the way of being forsaken by God. "How then would the scriptures be fulfilled, which say it must happen in this way?" (Matt. 26:54).

Jesus goes the way of the cross in order to open for these many the way of escape from eternal punishment; to make sure that their "going away to eternal punishment" will be followed by their return. For that very reason He became obedient until death on the cross. Therefore, every knee shall bow, and every tongue shall at last confess: Jesus is Lord, to the glory of God the Father (Phil. 2:8-11).

The Term "Eternal" and God's Purpose

We now return to the term "eternal." In Scripture "eternity" does not refer to a situation God wants to see continued without end.[20] That the fire of

---

20. The use of the word "eternal" in the context of the giving of the Mosaic law also indicates that it does not mean endless. About 30 times we read about an "eternal" (NRSV: "perpetual") ordinance.

God's wrath on Israel will burn eternally (Jer. 17:4), that God puts eternal shame, eternal contempt on Israel (18:40), does not indicate that this achieves God's ultimate purpose. On the contrary, as long as this state continues, it merely means that Israel is not yet what she should be. His purpose is, and remains, the return of his disobedient people to him, the making of a new covenant. Then, until all eternity, Jerusalem shall never again be uprooted or overthrown (31:31-40). Contrary to the everlasting nature of the punishment, there will be no end to the eternity of God's salvation. Why not? Because then Israel will fully answer to God's intentions; it has become the people of God that does his will with all its heart. That is God's one and only purpose for Israel. That is also the answer to the argument put forward by the church fathers Augustine and Chrysostom (I, 3), that the eternal punishment of Matthew 25:46 has to be endless, since otherwise it must be assumed that eternal life will also have an end. Eternal life continues, since it is God's purpose for humanity. Eternal punishment, however, does not forever continue, since that punishment itself is not his goal. When God's purpose has been achieved, there is no need for further punishment — for sin no longer exists!

Let us review. The word "eternal" has played a major role in the doctrine of eternal punishment. But what Scripture tells us about God's purpose with this punishment remained a secondary concern. We have seen that this divine purpose must be our first interest in any biblical discourse about the eternity of the punishment. Never is there any other purpose than that the unbeliever return to obedience to God. Nowhere in Scripture do we find a statement that tells us that God wants those who are punished to suffer without end — that is not the purpose for which God created humans! If we keep this singular purpose of God in focus, we understand that eternal punishment is punishment that has as its only purpose an obedient return to the God of love; it is punishment that leaves no other escape than a radical break with the past, the total loathing of the evil of the past, that prohibits a return to the former disobedience. It is punishment that fully accomplishes God's purpose in punishing; no other punishment will follow or will be needed. *When Jesus refers to this punishment as eternal, he simply underlines, as the prophets had done, the total seriousness — the eternal seriousness — of God in pursuing his one and only purpose.*

4. Every Tongue Shall Praise God! Forced Worship?

The Hymn of Praise of Philippians 2

We now return to our starting point, where Paul quoted Isaiah 45:23. "For we will all stand before the judgment seat of God. For it is written: 'As I live, says the Lord, every knee shall bow to me, and every tongue shall give praise to God'" (Rom. 14:10b-11). In preaching the seriousness of the judgment, while not quenching the hope of salvation, the apostle is firmly rooted in the prophetic preaching of judgment.

Twice we find the prophecy of Isaiah 45 in Paul's letters: here, in Romans 14:11, and in the letter to the Philippians.[21] Let us take a closer look at this second passage. Scholars agree that Paul here quotes from a hymn that was sung by the early Christians.

> And being found in human form, he humbled himself and became obedient to the point of death — even death on a cross. Therefore God also highly exalted him and gave him the name that is above every name, so that at the name of Jesus every knee should bend, in heaven and on earth and under the earth, and every tongue should confess that Jesus Christ is Lord, to the glory of God the Father. (Phil. 2:8-11)

The question might be raised whether this hymn of praise has anything to do with the judgment, as was the case with Romans 14:11. Once again the occasion was the conduct of church members toward each other: "Let the same mind be within you that was in Christ Jesus . . ." (v. 5). In this instance Paul does not point to the account we must all give before God's judgment seat. Nonetheless, we should not fail to note the warning that follows, that we should work out our salvation with "fear and trembling" (v. 12). That certainly is a reference to the judgment: Their salvation is at stake. Reading on, we notice that this church also has members who live as enemies of the cross of Christ. Paul writes that: "Their end is destruction" (3:18-19).

We should also note what he writes about the world that surrounds the church: "a crooked and perverse generation, in which you shine like stars in the world" (2:15). Of that crooked and perverse generation the

---

21. See T. Baarda, "Jes. 45:23 in het Nieuwe Testament," *Gereformeerd Theologisch Tijdschrift*, August 1973, pp. 137-79.

church sings; each of them will finally bend the knee and will confess: "Jesus Christ is Lord, to the glory of God the Father." For this crooked generation is part of God's creation that is mentioned in this hymn of praise. But how does this generation come to the point where it will bend the knee and confess the lordship of Christ? This is hardly an easy transition! For they await the same fate as the disobedient in the church: destruction (1:28). This is nothing else than the anguish and distress of God's judgment, when he repays each person according to his deeds (Rom. 2:5-10). Yet the church sings: every knee and every tongue! The life of these people will not end with the destruction that awaits them. The time will come when they will be delivered from that destruction and will sing God's praises — a multitude that no one can number (Rev. 7:9-15; VII, 5).

In the meantime, we should not ignore the task and duty of the church: ". . . in which you shine like stars in the world . . . holding fast to the word of life . . ." (Rom. 2:15-16). For whom would they shine if not for this "crooked and perverse generation" in the midst of whom they live? Lights in this world, pointing the way to the house of the Father — they can only be such lights if they manifest the same mind that was in Christ Jesus (2:5; cf. Matt. 5:14-16).

Forced Recognition?

In our journey through Romans, we discovered two texts in particular that ran contrary to the tradition of our faith: All will receive justification and life as a result of what Christ did for them (Rom. 5:18); and "all Israel will be saved" (11:26). Regarding both texts it has been said that Paul has only believers in mind. Once again, when confronted with Romans 14:11 and Philippians 2:10-11, the supporters of this point of view will have to prove that Paul does not refer to salvation for all the world. But in these instances surely it cannot be maintained that it only applies to believers. For when Paul says that every tongue will praise God, there is no alternative: This includes everyone. For the apostle here deals with the judgment seat of God (Rom. 14:10). And no one will want to deny that all people, believers as well as unbelievers, will have to appear before his judgment seat. So, all who appear before the judgment seat will also bend their knees before God to praise him.

Now if it be true that all people will praise God, how can it be denied that God's salvation includes all people? Why else would they sing his praises if they are not redeemed by him? But we are faced with the fact that attempts

221

have been made to explain this "praise" in such a way that the doctrine of the damnation of the majority of humankind can be maintained. There must be something peculiar in this praise, it has been argued. On the part of most people this cannot be genuine praise, they contend, for no joy rises from their hearts. But where in the Bible do we read about people *praising* God who do not do this from the heart?

The word Paul uses in his description of this praise is taken from the Psalms. In fact the word "praise" is one of the key concepts in the Psalms.[22] Everywhere it refers to the song of praise for the salvation God has prepared for his people. In Philippians 2:11 the same word is translated "confess": confessing that Jesus Christ is Lord, to the glory of God the Father. This text expresses the content of this praise: It is joy because of the redemption that God has worked in Christ Jesus.[23]

The Bible does indeed at times refer to submission forced on someone. The evil spirits, which at Jesus' command must surrender their spoils, acknowledge with regret: Jesus is Conqueror! Indeed, this is a form of praise; it is forced praise! But this kind of submission has nothing to do with the genuine *praise* that we find in Scripture! Nevertheless, some have tried to maintain that with this song of praise of all creation Paul thought also, and even in particular — in connection with the bulk of the voices — of the forced praise of God's enemies. We will not deal with the question when this view was first suggested. For our purpose it will suffice to offer a few examples from the Reformed tradition, which in this respect is undoubtedly representative of what is called "the church of the ages."

22. The word here used is the usual LXX rendering for the Hebrew word for "praise" and "give thanks" in the Psalms (*"yādah"*; hiphil: *"hodah"*; cf. George W. Wigram, *The Englishman's Hebrew and Chaldee Concordance of the Old Testament*, pp. 499-500, s.v. *"yādah"*).

23. O. Michel (*TDNT*, 5:199-200) believes that in Romans 14:11 the word means "das eschatologische Sündenbekenntnis" (the eschatological confession of sins). O. Hofius (*EDNT*, 2:8-9) agrees with him. Matthew 3:6, Acts 19:18, and James 5:15 do indeed use this word in the context of confession of guilt, but the latter is explicitly mentioned. Since this particular passage refers to what happens before the judgment seat of God, there is reason to think that this meaning also applies here. But even in that case, there is no indication of a forced act. Rather, this confession goes together with prayer and praise, says Michel. Together with most exegetes, I prefer the meaning "praise" in Romans 14:11. I believe the psalms leave no other option; see the same word in Romans 15:9.

The Annotations in the Dutch States-General Bible and Calvin

In the annotation of the so-called Dutch Authorized Version of Philippians 2:10 ("so that . . . every knee should bend") we read: "That is: that all rational creatures submit themselves, even his enemies against their will." It comments also on those who "are under the earth": "That is: all who have died and are in the graves, or all evil spirits and all who are doomed in hell. . . . For, although the devils and the godless and doomed people do not show Christ genuine submission and honor, they must, against their own will, submit to him as the Lord and the Judge over all." And about "every tongue" the annotation says: "That is: of all nations and peoples, and of all rational creatures, not only of the good, but also of the bad, who, although against their will, have often had no alternative but to confess him (Mark 5:7; Acts 16:17); in the final judgment they will have to acknowledge him as the Judge of the living and the dead, and as Lord." Three times it uses the words "against their will," that is to say, *forced*. The reference to Mark 5:7 concerns the exclamation of the evil spirit cast out by Christ: "What have you to do with me, Jesus, son of the Most High God?" Acts 16:17 relates the incident of the fortune-telling spirit of the woman who follows Paul. We will hear more about these spirits later in this chapter.

Calvin wrote before the Dutch AV was published. In his *Institutes*, he says regarding Philippians 2:10 that the apostle does not present "the bowing of the knee" as "true and godly worship. But since he is simply teaching that dominion has been given to Christ with which to subject all creatures, what hinders us from understanding by the expression 'nether regions' the devils, who will obviously be brought before God's judgment seat and who will recognize their Judge with fear and trembling." In his commentary on Philippians he translates the phrase "those who are under the earth" as "those who are in hell." He points to James, who writes that the demons also believe in God, but they "shudder" (2:19). Even they will bend their knees and confess the name of Jesus. Calvin argues that they do not submit themselves voluntarily.[24] Though unwillingly, they must acknowledge defeat, but for all eternity they will in their hearts oppose Christ's rule.

---

24. *Institutes*, 2.5.8 (pp. 344-45); *Uitlegging op de zendbrieven van Paulus aan de Efeziërs, Filippenzen en Colossenzen*, Dutch trans. A. M. Donner (Goudriaan, 1972), p. 129. In his commentary on Isaiah 45:23, Calvin gave another explanation of the bending of every knee.

Herman Bavinck: Brought to the Threshold

Bavinck follows this tradition in his *Gereformeerde Dogmatiek* (Reformed Dogmatics). Christ himself, "who is the gentlest of all people, will be the judge of humankind, a judge so just, that all will acknowledge his justice and every knee will bow before Him and every tongue will confess that Christ is Lord, to the glory of God the Father. In the end, God will be recognized as God by all creatures, if not willingly, then unwillingly." " 'Confessing' thus includes the *unwilling recognition* of the many who are definitively excluded from salvation. It is also a wanting to continue in sin. For: Whosoever sins is a servant of sin, and cannot and will not stop sinning." It is no longer possible for the sinner to put that will into practice, but "his inner compulsion is toward sin, and he would prefer to live eternally, so that he might sin eternally." Bavinck here relies on Augustine. This is how it will continue, forever: "Nowhere does Scripture indicate with even a single word, or even leave room for the possibility, that this situation, which then begins, could ever end. . . . Honest exegesis can find nothing else here but an eternal, never ending punishment."

Bavinck accepted this doctrine only with difficulty. This is evident from the words at the end of his discourse about eternal punishment: "Eternal punishment always manifests God's justice in such a manner that his goodness and love remain inviolate and can never be justly faulted. *Even in hell the statement is true, that he does 'not willingly afflict'* (Lam. 3:33); the anguish that he sends does not bring joy to him or to the blessed in heaven, but serves as a means to glorify his virtues, and its weight and measure is therefore determined by this final goal."[25]

We cannot but wonder whether this is what Scripture means when it says that God has no delight in punishments, but nevertheless never stops punishing. "Not willingly": In his heart he really wants to treat those who are punished differently. But why then does he not do so? The necessity that his virtues (i.e. his justice, which is viewed as punishing justice) are extolled prevents him from doing what he in fact wants to do! This leads us to the threshold: *the threshold of this tradition*. Here Bavinck stops. But Scripture does not know of this threshold. For even in this context, just before the words quoted by Bavinck, we read: "For the Lord will not reject forever. Although he causes grief, he will have compassion according to the abundance of his steadfast love" (3:31-32).

25. *Dogmatiek*, 4:696, 694-95, 697.

A Few Later Examples

S. Greijdanus, like Bavinck, is rather reticent on this matter. In his commentary on Philippans 2:11 we read: "The whole world, all creatures, and certainly all rational creatures, lost and rejected, angels and demons, will acknowledge the Lord in his power and majesty, each in his own way, the one with joyful thanksgiving and praise and worship, the other because he is forced to do so. The word 'confess' . . . does not exclude this latter aspect, *openly acknowledge,* though with a heart of enmity, and does not only refer to a recognition by the heart that rejoices in salvation."[26]

K. Schilder is less restrained in his study *Wat is de hel?* (What is hell?). For him, Dante's *Hell* is required reading. He speaks of the "groaning of the giants," that is more horrible than the "lamentations of the dwarfs," and of the "fuga of hell," which is a forced rendering of the same theme that is heard in the spontaneous burst of praise of heaven, extolling the riches of the Creator of the universe; and of an abyss that proclaims God's honor just as the heavens do, though not with a "joyful voice." Schilder has great difficulty with the words of Lamentations quoted by Bavinck (God does not willingly afflict); page after page he tries to find an acceptable explanation. It is obvious that he does not want to be led to this threshold.[27]

In his three-volume work *Over de laatste dingen* (On the Last Things), K. Dijk writes: "As far as Phil. 2:10 is concerned, it is clear that *every* tongue and *every* knee no doubt applies to all people. But not in all cases does this acknowledgment and worship arise from faith; on the day of judgment, Christ's glory will be so overwhelming that all, even those who have rejected him, *cannot but* acknowledge that he is the Lord, even though this confession is too late to lead to conversion."[28]

William Hendriksen, an American theologian of Dutch descent, contends in his exegesis of Philippians 2:10-11 that "those who are under the

26. S. Greijdanus, *De brief van Paulus aan de gemeente te Philippi* (Amsterdam, 1937), pp. 204ff.

27. K. Schilder, *Wat is de hel?* (Kampen, 1932), pp. 119-22; 142-51. It is the most depressing book that I have read in the last fifty years.

28. K. Dijk, *Over de laatste dingen* (Kampen, 1953), 3:157. Discussing the word "eternal," he notes that in Scripture this word certainly does not always mean "endless." But it does have this meaning when it is used in connection with the fires of hell, for "otherwise it would eliminate our hope for the endlessness of salvation"; ". . . hope would lose . . . its comfort and power; a denial of the eternal nature of punishment implies a denial of the eternity of salvation" (p. 158).

earth" are: *"all the damned in hell,* both *human beings* and the *evil angels* or *demons."* That is where they will remain. And there they will all acknowledge Jesus as Lord (Phil. 2:10-11). But what does this acknowledgment consist of? This we learn in his comments on Colossians 1:20: "There is, of course, a difference in the *manner* in which the various creatures submit to Christ's rule and are 'reconciled to God.' Those who are and remain evil, whether men or angels, submit ruefully, unwillingly. In their cases, *peace, harmony is imposed, not welcomed."*[29] With this "ruefully" Hendriksen seems to be heading toward "final remorse."

Final Remorse?

Bavinck is not the only one who has defended the view that the doomed continue to exist in unceasing rebellion against God. T. L. Haitjema also supports this view in his *Dogmatiek als Apologie* (Dogmatics as Apology). About those who are not redeemed he writes: "Their misery in the eternal pain is nothing but this, that they live in incessant hatred against God and against all saints, and cannot come to repentance. Their agony is that in their eternal dying they are so left to themselves that they will never be changed and never be renewed unto eternal life."[30] The condemned are punished for what they have done and their unceasing hatred justifies their unending punishment. In his lecture "Everlasting Punishment and the Problem of Evil," Henri Blocher pointed to support for this position by other conservative systematic theologians, such as W. G. T. Shedd and Charles Hodge.[31] Blocher disagrees with them. Rightly so! He argues that "the thesis of sin continuing is found nowhere in Scripture." The gospel flatly contradicts that notion: "The theory of sin forever flourishing ignores the message of Christ's perfect victory over sin and all evil. '*Every* knee shall bow and *every* tongue confess . . .' (Phil. 2:10-11), those of the lost included." The lost will remain lost. And one cannot consider their praise as forced.

29. W. Hendriksen, *Philippians* (Grand Rapids, 1962), pp. 115-18. In the same *New Testament Commentary* series, *Colossians and Philemon* (Grand Rapids, 1964), p. 82. The frequent reprints of these commentaries indicate that this tradition is still fully alive.

30. T. L. Haitjema, *Dogmatiek als Apologie* (Haarlem, 1948), p. 347.

31. Henri Blocher, Dean and Professor of Systematic Theology in the Faculté de Théologie Evangélique, Vaux-sur-Seine, Paris, in *Universalism and the Doctrine of Hell* — *Papers Presented at the Fourth Edinburgh Conference on Christian Dogmatics,* ed. N. M. de S. Cameron (Carlisle [UK] and Grand Rapids, 1992), pp. 298, 303, 307, 310ff.

It is true that "Sinners are forced to confess the truth, but they are forced by truth itself, by its overwhelming evidence and spiritual authority; they cannot longer refuse to see, they cannot *think* otherwise." They are convinced and cease their resistance. What brings them to this point? *Reconciliation!* "Through Christ, it has pleased God to reconcile (*apokatallaxai*), the whole universe, including all rebellious spirits (Col. 1:20). 'Reconciliation' does not imply *salvation,* here, . . . it means the restoration of order, of all within God's order, 'pacification,' as all are brought back to the divinely ruled harmony." They are filled with shame for what they have done, and "theirs will be the ultimate 'confusion of face,' as they shall be unable to escape the truth of their past actions." It will be ". . . final remorse, remorse-in-agreement with God." They agree with God; their condemnation to outer darkness is justified. That is the content of their praise. "If sinners ultimately glorify God, they do reach in a paradoxical way the *telos* [the end] of all creatures as such. And they *know* it, since they now see the truth of their lives; they see their evil works — which they now abhor — as included in God's plan, by his permissive will, and used for his purposes. . . . They are excluded from the fellowship of God; they cannot 'enjoy Him forever'; here is the tragedy and the meaning of 'outer darkness' (they have no share in the banquet-feast of salvation). Yet their thought is fixed in the knowledge that, through their very deprivation, they glorify God and agree with Him." Repeatedly Blocher uses the word "tragedy." Earlier he wrote: "The Biblical horror of sin . . . that tragedy that pervades the whole Scripture." And then: "That impenitent sinners should be 'reconciled' to God through the perfection of remorse, through condemnation embraced, in 'outer darkness' and death and not in the life-giving fellowship of God, remains a tragedy."

How can the message that all people will praise God be explained in such a way that those who are forever lost will share in it? That was the question these scholars had to face. Blocher provides a carefully constructed answer. All are there where God wants them, and all are at peace with their destination. But is this the message of the Bible? We just want to put three questions:

1. Where does Scripture refer in this way to the atonement through Christ's blood? In 2 Corinthians 5:18 Paul writes that in Christ God was reconciling the world to himself, "not counting their trespasses." But here we are told about a never-ending "counting." Following Colossians 1:20 ("through him to reconcile to himself all things"), the church is told about the ultimate goal of this reconciliation: "reconciled . . . in order to present you holy and blameless and irreproachable before him" (v. 22). Reconcil-

iation is the restoration of peace with God through the forgiveness of sins — never exclusion from fellowship with God.

2. Where does Scripture speak about the divine judgment in this way: God who punishes people, and *continues* to punish people who have repented and have ceased to sin? What must one think, with regard to this "final remorse," of the law that God gave to humankind: to love him with all our heart, and our neighbors as ourselves? Do these people keep this law, and does God nonetheless continue to punish them? Or do these people not keep this law, and does God want this situation to continue? Once more we see how the doctrine of eternal punishment contradicts the one law God gave (see III, 1 and 5).

3. Where does Scripture speak in this fashion about the song of praise of all that lives: not thanksgiving for the salvation he provides, but for the fact that he did not redeem them, but assigned them a place in outer darkness?

The Gospel — No Tragedy!

What we heard so far about forced praise and final remorse has only made things clearer for us; the Bible does not speak in such terms about the future song of praise of all creatures. There is no trace in the Bible of such a tragedy (the word used by Blocher; in reading Bavinck we felt the same sadness). When the church sings: "Every knee shall bow and every tongue confess," we hear the gospel, the message of good news! Not a superficial, easy gospel! Let us not forget what we have been told about the future condemnation of the enemies of the gospel. Nor let us forget that every member of the church must work out his salvation in fear and trembling (Phil. 1:28; 2:12). But at the basis of everything is not fear but joy, the perspective that has been opened by the death and resurrection of Christ! "He humbled himself, and became obedient to the point of death, even death on the cross" — not to lead the lost to acquiescence in their damnation, but to save them from it!

That was the hope that filled the early church. We referred to it earlier: The judgment of the godless will not be the end. All who are lost will one day come to conversion and return to the Father, the God of love; *together with* the church they will kneel and join in their hymn of praise for the salvation he extends to all in the name of Jesus. Thus it was announced by the prophets, and thus it was expressed in the psalms. To that hope they testified, "as lights in the world, holding fast the word of life" (Phil. 2:15).

Unfortunately, a change came about — the teaching of forced praise and final remorse is proof of this.

5. Does Scripture Also Teach Another End?

Praise in the Book of Revelation

One might have become convinced that Paul indeed taught that God wants all people to be saved, and that his teaching leaves no room for a doctrine of eternal punishment. But questions remain: "But the Bible also says . . . ," and then a series of texts is quoted that allegedly refer to eternal punishment. Since these questions are invariably asked, we must give some indication of the direction in which the answer can be sought.

We already pointed out that the Old Testament never refers to an unending punishment after death (II, 3). So for this type of eschatology we have to go to New Testament writers other than Paul. We already saw that Jesus' words about the two roads and about eternal punishment (Matt. 7:13-14; 25:46) are often taken as proof that the Gospel of Matthew teaches a punishment without end. We responded to this charge in II, 3 and VII, 3. In addition to these passages from Matthew, the book of Revelation also presents a picture of the last things that undeniably differs from what we find in Paul. "The lake of fire that burns with sulfur. . . . This is the second death" (Rev. 19:20; 20:10, 14, 15; 21:8) — that is quite different from all creation praising God! — Well, it may appear that way, but that is not what we are told. For the book of Revelation offers the same all-encompassing hymn of praise as Paul:

> Then I heard every creature in heaven and on earth and under the earth and in the sea, and all that is in them, singing: "To the one seated on the throne and to the Lamb be blessing and honor and glory and might forever and ever." (5:13)

This hymn is heard when the book of God's sovereign designs is placed in the hands of the Lamb. The Lamb that was "slaughtered" will execute God's plan for creation. As soon as this book is opened, one judgment follows another. But before the seals are broken, we hear praise. This expresses what will be the final result of the execution of God's plan. The outcome is secure, because of the victory of the Lamb (5:5-6). All creation will be subject to the divine judgment, but it will all end in this hymn of praise. The relationship between these judgments and this praise is not explained. In contrast to Paul, this book of the Bible was not written to provide insight into this matter.

The most difficult statement about the judgment is found in Revelation 14:10-11.

> And the smoke of their torment goes up forever and ever. There is no rest day or night for those who worship the beast and its image and for anyone who receives the mark of its name.

Earlier we heard: "And all the inhabitants of the earth will worship it [the beast]" (13:8). Satan has successfully seduced humankind. This is the fate awaiting the many. Nothing can be further removed from the hymn of praise in 5:13 than this! But the next vision informs us that all nations will come and will worship God (not the beast!), because his judgments have been revealed (15:4). These judgments are followed by praise! Calvin believed that beings endowed with reason do not join in this praise of 5:13 (*Institutes*, 3.5.8), but this cannot be true since every creature is included, and since 15:4 refers to "all nations." In other words, the "forever and ever" of 14:11 was not the final word! Just as the prophecy about Edom in Isaiah 34:10 — from which this imagery of the eternally ascending smoke is borrowed — was not the final word. Isaiah's prophecy and this vision are both related to the destruction of Sodom (Gen. 19:24, 28). We saw that God's judgment over this city did not imply the end of his compassion for it (II, 1). We may conclude that the book of Revelation uses the same language as the prophets used in referring to the "eternity" of the divine judgment.

The New Jerusalem, the Inviting City (Rev. 21 and 22)

We should also note the vision of the New Jerusalem.[32] It descends from heaven, and a voice says what is about to happen: God will dwell among human beings, and they will be his peoples. He will wipe all tears from their eyes . . . and death will be no more (21:3, 4). Note: It is not yet like that, but it is now about to happen! Outside the city the lake of sulfur still burns,

---

32. For the final chapters of the book of Revelation I concur with Mathias Rissi, *Was ist und was geschehen soll danach* (Zurich, 1965), and idem, *Die Zukunft der Welt* (Basle, 1965). See also the short commentary by Rissi, *Alpha und Omega, eine Deutung der Johannesoffenbarung* (Basle, 1966), and the meticulous commentary by Charles Brütsch, *Die Offenbarung Jesu Christi* (2nd ed.; Zurich, 1970, 3 vols.)

as we are told immediately after the previous statements (v. 8). There the old order has not yet passed; there all tears have not yet been wiped away; there death — the second death — still rules (20:14b).

Then follows a description of the New Jerusalem. It is the bride of the Lamb (21:9). Is this a reference to the church? We would do better to say: the people of the Messiah. Everything is placed in the context of Israel — the Israel of Ephesians 2:11-22, which now includes Gentile believers; or the Israel of the olive tree, which comprises both the fullness of Israel and the fullness of those who have been called from the Gentiles (Rom. 11). The gates of the city remain open day and night (Rev. 21:25), waiting for people to arrive! The kings of the earth bring their glory into it, not temporarily, but they have come to live there. And not without their subjects; what glory does a king have apart from his people? "The glory of a king is a multitude of people" (Prov. 14:28). This city is the place God has destined for humankind — all mankind — the place where he dwells among them and where they will be *his* peoples (Rev. 21:3). It is the place where he gives life to humankind, the place of which the first pages of Scripture tell us: There is the river of the water of life. There also is the tree of life, which is "for the healing of the nations" (22:2). This healing process is not completed; now it begins!

There lies the city, *inviting:* "Let anyone who is thirsty come. Let anyone who wishes take the water of life as a gift" (22:17). And "Blessed are those who wash their robes" (present tense); not "those who have washed their robes"; it is not a completed but an ongoing process (22:14). This statement does not apply to the church or to Israel, for they themselves are the holy city. They are the bride of the Lamb, already "clothed with fine linen" (Rev. 19:8). But there is still so much that is dirty and must be washed, the multitude outside the city: "the dogs and sorcerers and fornicators and murderers and idolaters, and everyone who loves and practices falsehood" (22:11). They are urged to *come* ("Let everyone who is thirsty come") and to wash their robes so that they may acquire the right to eat from the tree of life and to enter the city (22:14). When we bear in mind that all who are shut out of the city are the same as those of whom it is said: "Their place will be in the lake that burns with fire and sulfur, which is the second death" (21:8), we once again see that the second death is not the final word.[33]

Therefore, the last two chapters of the Bible do not describe the end, but what precedes the end: the beginning of Christ's rule. That is what the

33. For the "second death," see IV, n. 11.

church must keep its eyes on. She is called to reign with him as King, serving him as he rules as King (20:6; 22:5). Revelation 5 presents the finale, the hymn of praise. The kingly rule of Christ, described in 1 Corinthians 15:23-28, will climax in that praise.

The Multitude That No One Could Count (Rev. 7)[34]

There is a connection between Revelation 22:14 ("blessed are those who wash their robes") and 7:9-17, where we are told about the great multitude that no one could count. These are they who have come out of the great tribulation; they have washed their robes and made them white in the blood of the Lamb (7:14, RSV).[35] The 144,000 (7:1-8) must refer to the Israel of the Messiah, which Revelation 21 identifies as the holy city itself; even the measurements of the city remind us of this number. The church, to which John addressed these words, must have recognized herself in these 144,000. She was the church of Jews and Gentiles, the people of the Messiah — not the church as it later developed, the church without the Jews!

Then this multitude that no one could number is described. Most commentators view this multitude as identical with the 144,000. For they come out of the great tribulation and have washed their robes and made them white in the blood of the Lamb. This, it is argued, must refer to the church that has survived persecution — the great tribulation.

There is reason to question this exegesis. For it is the contrast, rather than the similarity, that strikes us. The multitude that no one could number comes from all peoples, tribes, nations, and tongues. This contrasts with the 144,000 who were sealed, mentioned just before: They come from one people, and they have been counted, a fixed number. In addition, the 144,000 are called "the servants of our God." This points to a service to be rendered. In a subsequent vision they are presented as those who have

34. The commentaries that I was able to consult all view the great multitude as the redeemed church; most identify this multitude with the 144,000; some argue that the 144,000 are Jewish Christians, while the great multitude are Gentile Christians. Brütsch rejects this view, and rightly so (*Die Offenbarung*, I, 326-30): Scripture does not substantiate such a distinction.

35. In this instance we must quote the RVS because it uses the word "tribulation" as the rendering of the Greek word *thlipsis:* "the great tribulation." Like the AV, the RVS consistently translates this word as "tribulation." The NRSV, however, employs a variety of words: "suffering" (Matt. 24:9); "anguish" (Rom. 2:8); "affliction" (Rev. 2:10); "distress" (Rev. 2:22); and "ordeal" (Rev. 7:14).

conquered the beast (15:2; cf. 14:1-5). We learned about this service: the service of "those who belong to Christ" (1 Cor. 15:23), of the "children of God" for the deliverance of lost humanity (Rom. 8:19-21). This lost humanity is presented as the multitude that no one could number. They have gone through "the great tribulation" (v. 14). We are often reminded that the church will have to suffer tribulation through persecutions (Matt. 24:21; Rev. 2:10). But we also hear of tribulation in the context of God's judgment of the disobedient. We find an example in Revelation 2:22: Those who refuse to be converted will "be thrown into great tribulation." Another example is found in Romans 2:9, where Paul writes about the "tribulation and distress" resulting from God's judgment over all who do evil. The scene of Revelation 7:9-17 follows the judgment! Those who have been freed from the rule of death can truly be said to have passed through the great tribulation and be led toward the springs of the water of life (7:17).[36]

Here we are given a glimpse of the future, following the redemption of the church, or, rather, following the redemption of the Israel of the Messiah (VI, 3). The great multitude is the great number of the dead, of whom Paul has written that all, from Adam onward, will be made righteous (Rom. 5:19). They will be restored to life in Christ, when death as the final enemy has been destroyed (1 Cor. 15:20-28). It is the deliverance of creation from death by the children of God already referred to in Romans 8:19-21. In this context no mention is made of the service rendered by God's children. This is simply presupposed: All these people have in one way or another been reached with the message of the Lamb that was slain (Rev. 5:12). They accepted that message: They have washed their robes in the blood of the Lamb. They have all passed through the great tribulation (the great ordeal, NRSV) of God's judgment of their deeds, and have been delivered from it. It is clear: Jesus is the atoning sacrifice for the sins of the whole world (1 John 2:2).

36. Blumhardt did not regard this as the redemption of the church, but of unredeemed humanity. Regarding the "great ordeal" he says: "Es ist der Stand der Unseligkeit der ohne Kenntniss Jesu Gestorbenen" (It is the state of lostness of those who died without a knowledge of Christ) (F. Zündel, *Blumhardt* [1887], p. 532). The same explanation is found in *Blätter aus Bad Boll* [1874], pp. 317-20): It is not the tribulation Jesus referred to in Matthew 24:21, but the judgment over the deeds of all who have died since Adam (Rom. 2:12-16, "in peinlichen Höllenzuständen" [in a painful state of hell]). At that time Blumhardt still believed that many would persist in their refusal to come. But this thought left him no peace. We read that in the final days of his life his great passion and his constant prayer were that not a single person would be lost (Zündel, *Blumhardt*, p. 223). For bibliographical details, see IX, n. 7.

But one thing still troubles us: Does this comprise all of lost humanity? We are told that they come *from* all nations. That seems to imply that some remain behind. This would point to a limitation. Yet there is nothing to substantiate the thought of a limitation. For this "coming" has not yet been completed; literally the text says: They are those who are coming. This is not a fixed number, as in the case of the 144,000; no line is drawn behind them to separate them from those who have not yet come. That they come from the great ordeal does not necessarily imply that this ordeal has now come to an end. That is where they come from, where they keep coming from, one after the other — so many that no one can count them! This process continues until the last ones have come. That is evident when they are tallied. In Revelation 5:13 we see that of all creatures none is left behind. All praise him who is seated on the throne and the Lamb — the hymn of praise of this multitude (7:10) is none other than the one of 5:13. Together with all created beings they praise God and the Lamb.[37]

The last words — "and God will wipe away every tear from their eyes" (7:17b) — further indicate that this passage concerns the redemption of all humanity. These words are taken from the prophecy of Isaiah (25:8); they are the fulfillment of that prophecy. There, too, the prophet does not limit himself to the redemption of Israel but refers to the banquet that God has prepared in Jerusalem for all non-Israelite nations, for those who have lived without God. Reading the text in its entirety leaves no doubt that it refers to the redemption of the dead: "He will swallow up death forever. Then the Lord will wipe away the tears from all faces." "All tears," John writes, from all faces — no sorrow is forgotten, nobody is overlooked. For all, death is something of the past; all find comfort, once and for all.

It is difficult to understand how, on the basis of what this last book of the Bible says about the redemption of humankind, one could construct a message about the final events that differs from what Paul has written.

37. On the difficult problem whether there will be any people who will ultimately respond to God with a final No, see IX, 1, "The Purpose of God's Punishment."

CHAPTER VIII

The Hope and the Jews
(Romans 14 and 15)

1. Steadfast in Hope — Difficulties in Rome

The Hope: All Peoples together with His People

When Paul concludes his message, all over the world the bells start ringing. All nations glorify the God of Israel for his mercy, "as it is written" (Rom. 15:9-12, RSV):

> Therefore I will praise thee among the Gentiles, and sing to thy name (Ps. 18:49);

> and again it is said, "Rejoice, O Gentiles, with his people" (Deut. 32:43);

> and again, "Praise the Lord, all Gentiles, and let all the peoples praise him" (Ps. 117:1);

> and further Isaiah says, "The root of Jesse shall come, he who rises to rule the Gentiles; in him shall the Gentiles hope." (Isa. 11:10, altered translations)

"I will praise thee among the Gentiles." That is how it begins. With this word "praise" Paul resumes the theme of Romans 14:11 (RSV): "Every tongue shall give praise to God." The prophecy, "The root of Jesse shall come, he who rises to rule the Gentiles," echoes the words of the same text:

235

"As I live, says the Lord, every knee shall bow to me." Both the clause "As I live" and the words "he who rises" immediately remind us of the resurrection to which Paul referred in 14:9. It is a message of joy: "Praise the Lord, all Gentiles." And it is a message of hope: "In him shall the Gentiles hope." Not a word about nations that shudder because of his coming, or about forced worship by the damned. Everything speaks of salvation — salvation for all nations.

In verses 9-12 Paul quoted from all three sections of the Old Testament Scriptures: the Torah (Deut. 32:43), the Prophets (Isa. 11:10), and the Psalms (Ps. 18:49; 117:1). This perspective of nations singing praise is the message of the entire Old Testament. These words give evidence of an ever-widening circle: From Israel salvation spreads to all nations. First, "I will praise thee among the Gentiles." Israel is still on its own among the nations that do not acknowledge Israel's God. But it is God's intention that the nations will join Israel. That is the next stage: "Rejoice, O Gentiles, with his people." At last, not just some of them but all "Praise the Lord." To be sure, together with his people. Israel and all peoples, together, praise God for the salvation he gives. That was the hope of the early church — the church of Jews and Gentiles.

Endangered Hope, Jews and Gentiles

But this hope is in jeopardy; the church is in danger of losing it. We are told: ". . . so that by steadfastness and by the encouragement of the scriptures we might have hope" (Rom. 15:4). The Revised English Bible more correctly translates the last phrase as: "Maintain our hope with perseverance." For that the church needs the Scriptures; they show her how to be steadfast in that hope. That is done by perseverance: We are going to be tempted to think that our hope is in vain. The Bible talks about Abraham's perseverance: He believed in God, "fully convinced that God was able to do what he had promised" (4:21). It is also done through comfort: Again and again God will use the Scriptures to encourage us. The Psalms, in particular, are full of it: "Those who wait for the LORD will not be put to shame" (Ps. 25:2).

What was the problem? Things went wrong between the Jews and the Gentiles in the church. They found it difficult to accept each other. Paul writes: "Welcome one another, therefore, just as Christ has welcomed you." The ensuing verses make it clear that Paul refers to the mutual acceptance of Jews and Gentiles:

> For I tell you that Christ has become a servant of the circumcised on behalf
> of the truth of God in order that he might confirm the promises given to
> the patriarchs, and in order that the Gentiles might glorify God for his
> mercy. (Rom. 15:8-9)

Paul makes two points. First of all, that Christ became a servant of the
circumcised. He was sent by God to fulfill the promises given to the fathers
of the Jewish people. The promise is: "By your offspring shall all nations
of the earth gain blessing" (Gen. 22:18 to Abraham; Gen. 26:4 to Isaac; and
Gen. 28:14 to Jacob). It must be shown that Israel is the people through
which God will lead all nations to his salvation. By becoming their servant,
Jesus accepted the circumcised as his people; he accepted them permanently,
for this service will not end until the promises to the patriarchs have been
completely fulfilled.[1]

Paul's second point has to do with the Gentiles. It follows from the
first: Israel is the channel through which God's salvation reaches all nations.
Having raised his Messiah from the dead, God sends his messengers into
the world with the words: "On behalf of Christ, be reconciled to God"
(2 Cor. 5:20). When the Gentiles accept the gospel and begin to glorify God
for his mercy, these Gentiles are likewise accepted by Christ.

Paul writes: "Welcome one another, just as Christ has welcomed you"
(Rom. 15:7). Christ has welcomed, has fully accepted, the Gentiles. Not
because they kept or began to keep the law of Moses, but on the basis of
their faith, without the works of the law (3:28-30). For that reason the Jews
in the church must welcome the Gentiles, without demanding that they
first keep the law. The Gentiles, likewise, must accept the Jews in the same
manner that Christ accepted them: He also accepted them on the basis of
their faith. He did not require that they first renounce the law and its
ordinances! This latter aspect is here emphasized, as we shall see.

By using the term "circumcision" Paul brought the Jewishness of the
Jewish members, with their observance of the law, into sharp focus. The
Gentiles must be willing to accept the Jewishness of the Jewish members.
We remember the words of Paul in his parable of the olive tree. He warned
the Gentile believers, the newly grafted branches: "So do not become proud,
but stand in awe . . . otherwise you will also be cut off" (11:20, 22). There
was an attitude of pride toward the Jews outside the church, the Jews of

---

1. Wilckens (*Römer*, 3:105) comments: "Christ became and remained the servant
of the circumcised."

the synagogue. This pride was the beginning of the pernicious idea that the Jews were no longer needed as God's people, since God had now called a new people from among the Gentiles. Here we see how this anti-Jewish attitude of the Gentile believers not only directed itself toward the Jews of the synagogue but also led to difficulties in the church between the non-Jewish and the Jewish members.

The Strong and the Weak

Some exegetes believe that Paul's previous statement about mutual acceptance of the "weak" and the "strong" (14:1 to 15:6) is entirely separate from the mutual acceptance of Jews and Gentiles in the church (15:7-9). No one disputes that this latter point is Paul's great concern. Ridderbos comments: "Paul here writes about the bringing together of Jews and Gentiles through Christ as the great example and the abiding mandate of unity in the Christian church. The realization of that unity between Jews and Gentiles is the main theme of the letter, and what Paul's lifework was about." And Lekkerkerker writes: "To this we might add that the first big step toward the unity of the churches is the unity of Jews and Gentiles brought about by Christ. That is the 'breakthrough' between Jewish and Gentile Christians that the apostle advocates in his epistles to the Galatians and the Romans."[2]

It is, however, important to recognize that when Paul talks about the weak and the strong he deals with the same issue.[3] For so we get a clear picture of

2. Ridderbos, *Romeinen*, p. 325. Lekkerkerker, *Romeinen*, 2:175. Both authors believe that the conflict between the weak and the strong was about something else, but that 15:7-12 is indeed about the mutual acceptance of Jews and Gentiles in the church.

3. This view was current in the first few centuries. R. Roukema (*The Diversity of Laws in Origen's Commentary on Romans* [Amsterdam, 1988], pp. 75-76) points out that Origen referred to 'the believers from the Jews, who still distinguish between the different kinds of food according to the tradition of the law." For Origen this is not a matter of the past. He knows such Jewish Christians and defends them. He himself believes in the spiritual significance of the law, but he feels that this view should not be promoted in such a way that a Jew "gets the impression that Christians believe that one can be saved only if one eats pork or other common food." John Chrysostom, likewise, identifies the weak as Jews (*Homilies on . . . the Epistle to the Romans*, Nicene and Post-Nicene Father [Grand Rapids, 1976 ed.], 12:521; see also Godet [*Romains*, 2:489-90] and O. Michel [*Der Brief an die Römer* (1963 ed.)], pp. 334, 358). Wilckens regards verses 7-9 as definite proof that the issue was a conflict between Jews and Gentiles in the church (*Römer*, 3:107); see, in particular, the excursus "Die Starken und die Schwachen in Rom" (The

what was the problem in the church in Rome and what was at stake. That the verses from 15:7 on deal with the same problem as the passage from 14:1 to 15:6 is already apparent from the repetition of the word "welcome" used in 14:1. There is no indication whatsoever that Paul now begins to deal with another problem that caused difficulties in the church. Let us take a closer look at what Paul writes about those weak and strong.

First, the weak. They refrained from certain kinds of food. They ate vegetables (14:2) rather than meat, and they possibly refrained from drinking wine (14:21). They also observed certain days (14:5). Why? To honor the Lord (14:6)! They were convinced that their service to the Lord required this. Moreover, they believed that others ought to do the same, condemning their conduct as taking liberties that were in conflict with faithful service of the Lord (14:3, 10).

The only possible explanation is that Paul is here referring to Jewish customs. Those exegetes who deny this link point to the fact that at that time there were groups of pagans who promoted vegetarianism for religious reasons and regarded certain days as taboo. In this view the weak are those who had not yet been able to free themselves from these customs. We list a few arguments against this position.

1. Paul speaks about clean and unclean foods (14:14, 20). These are familiar terms from the law of Moses. There is nothing that points to pagan dietary practices; they would not even employ these terms.[4]

2. It would be difficult to maintain that the weak would follow these pagan practices "in honor of the Lord" (14:6).

3. Therefore they would have no reason either to accuse those members of the church who did not follow the same practices of disobedience to the Lord.

4. Paul admonishes the strong to follow the weak (14:13-23). It is hard to believe that he would do so if this had to do with pagan influences concerning a refusal to eat certain kinds of food and an observance of certain days. How Paul approached such problems can be seen in Colossians 2:16-23 and 1 Timothy 4:1-5.

Strong and the Weak in Rome), 3:109-15. J. J. Meuzelaar (*Der Leib des Messias* [Assen, 1961], pp. 2-58) explains how in the first letter to the Corinthians Paul defends the weak, since the tie with the Jewish church in Jerusalem was in danger because of the behavior of the strong; for Romans 14 and 15, see pp. 27, 41-42.

4. Wilckens points out that the words "clean" and "unclean" are found only in Jewish and early Christian literature; they are not used in connection with pagan (Greek) ascetic movements (*Römer*, 3:112-113). Cf. Daniel 1:8-16.

5. Giving up these customs at the instigation of the strong could result in a loss of one's faith in God (14:15); relinquishing one's ties with some other religion would not have such consequences.

Was the observance of these customs limited to the Jews in the church? No, the core of the early church consisted of Jews and converts to Judaism (Acts 14:43; 16:14) who had accepted the gospel. These former converts to Judaism were just as strict in their observance of the law; other sympathizers with Judaism, the "God-fearers," were less stringent in their observance of the law.

Now let us move to the strong. They ate everything without any restrictions, and did not differentiate between one day and another. That first aspect in particular was for them a matter of their faith in Christ (Rom. 14:2, 22). It was only through faith in him that they were saved, and not through observance of the law. Those with a strong faith would follow their example, live as they lived. They regarded the faith of the others as weak; they even despised those who were weak (14:3, 10).

Who were the strong? They were Gentiles who had come to believe the gospel; they must be identical with those whom Paul admonished regarding their pride toward the Jews of the synagogue. Their contempt for Jewish customs points in that direction. But there were also Jews who felt no longer bound by the law, friends of Paul, such as Prisca and Aquila (16:3). Only we would not expect them to despise Jewish customs. Paul does, admittedly, say: "We who are strong" (15:1), but he emphatically distances himself from their attitude of contempt. The strong in Rome, who were predominant and threatened to overrun the weak, were of Gentile background; Paul addresses this disturbing situation.

Kosher Food and the Sabbath

What value did the weak attach to these Jewish customs? We should first of all note that God himself had given the Jewish dietary laws ("kosher" food) and the Jewish festivals to Israel to keep them focussed on his service. The weekly Sabbath was the most prominent among these festivals.[5] These

---

5. Regarding the Sabbath and the disparaging reaction of the Romans, see J. N. Sevenster, *The Roots of Pagan Anti-semitism in the Ancient World* (Leiden, 1975), pp. 124-32. Many proselytes did not let mockery, rejection by society, or even persecution intervene in their choice for Judaism (pp. 195-201). This mockery, of course, was also directed toward those church members who persisted in their Jewish customs.

customs kept them separate from the nations and prevented them from falling back into paganism. Jesus himself had observed these commandments, and so had the early Jerusalem church. But they were not obligatory for the Gentiles who accepted the gospel. For one was not saved by keeping those commandments but through faith in Jesus (Acts 13:39; 15:6-11; 21:25). But the Jews who believed in Jesus saw no reason to break with these customs.

The situation was similar with regard to the proselytes, worshipers of God from the Gentiles who had accepted Judaism. They had become attached to these Jewish customs, and often these had become vital to them in their worship of the God of Israel. These customs had helped them to break away from paganism and protected them against falling back. They continued to have that value; abandoning these customs under pressure from the strong might carry the danger of relapsing into paganism. Paul warns against this: "Do not let what you eat cause the ruin of one for whom Christ died." And: "Do not, for the sake of food, destroy the work of God" (Rom. 14:15, 20).

Paul thus defends members who continue to value these Jewish customs. But is it not strange that in his letter to the Galatians he fiercely resists the propaganda for observing the law of Moses, while here he supports church members who keep the law? We should note how the conflict in Rome differs from that in the Galatian churches. In Galatia, Judaizers from Judea had come and maintained that Gentiles could not be saved unless they were circumcised and observed the Mosaic law (Gal. 5:1-12; Acts 15:1-2). It was a prerequisite for one's salvation! This was not at all what drove the weak in Rome. There is not a word about circumcision, nor a word about the keeping of the Sabbath or days of fasting as a condition for salvation. This allows us to see the other side of Paul: He now speaks on behalf of those who defend the observance of Jewish customs.

What about Paul himself? He felt free to abandon these customs. But in other circumstances he was at liberty to observe them! For him the decisive question was what the Lord demanded of him in his contacts with both Jews and non-Jews (1 Cor. 9:19-23).[6] But whatever, he was a Jew and wanted to remain a Jew. He would not do anything that might be detri-

6. Opinions differ as to whether Paul used his freedom not to observe the law; see W. D. Davies, *Paul and Rabbinic Judaism* (London, 1970 ed.), pp. 69-74. The freedom must, however, mean that it was not forbidden for a Jewish Christian to use that liberty; it would not interfere with his Jewishness. The guideline is 1 Corinthians 9:19-23; cf. Mark 7:19b and Acts 10:15.

mental to his ties with the Jewish people. Those ties were essential for the gospel he served. And that precisely is the difference between him and the party of the strong in Rome. Their behavior showed that they cared little about this tie with the Jewish people. We saw it in the parable of the olive tree: the pride of the Gentiles toward the Jews. Nothing could be more at variance with what drove Paul than this!

What Does Paul Advocate?

Those exegetes who want to detach this passage about the strong and the weak from what Paul writes about Jews and Gentiles believe that the weak and the strong were arguing about minor details that did not amount to much: minutiae of eating and drinking.[7] But these were certainly no small matters to them! Was this really feasible? Just imagine: a church in which some observe the Sabbath in honor of the Lord, while some feel that this day has no special significance; a church in which some refrain from eating certain things in honor of the Lord, while others do not refrain from eating these kinds of food, also in honor of the Lord! That was the situation (Rom. 14:6). One group does in honor of the Lord what the other group refuses to do in honor of the same Lord. How can the members there "live in harmony with one another," and "with one voice glorify" God, as Paul writes in 15:5-6?

The apostle specifically addresses the strong. What are they to do? Nothing less than avoid everything that might be offensive to the weak. "It is good not to eat meat or drink wine or do anything that makes your brother or sister stumble" (14:21). In other words, when they have their meals together with fellow believers, they are to follow the customs of those who are weak! They are not to do so because it is a prerequisite for salvation, but because they ought "to walk in love" (14:15); that is to say, they are "to live according to the Spirit" (8:4).

Paul, however, pleads for *mutual* acceptance. The weak will also have to accept something, namely that some church members are convinced that

---

7. Lekkerkerker (*Romeinen,* 2:176) writes that Paul in Romans 15:7-13 had long forgotten this unimportant matter of the weak and the strong and their eating or not eating. P. Stuhlmacher disagrees: "The reason for the conflict seems only from our present perspective to be unimportant" (*Römer,* p. 195). Lekkerkerker remarks in passing: "But I do wonder how two groups can eat together when they differ so much in their use of meat and wine" (p. 156).

obedience to the law is no longer a divine requirement. This may mean that when they are invited to the homes of unbelieving Gentiles, they will agree to eat with such persons. Paul gave guidelines for that kind of situation (1 Cor. 10:25-30). The weak are to accept such guidelines because Christ has accepted the Gentiles without the requirement of keeping the law of Moses (Rom. 15:7).

Only if they interact in such a manner can the church be what God wants it to be: a church in which Jews and Gentiles who believe in the Messiah worship God with one voice (15:5-6). But it is obvious that the strong are expected to make the greatest contribution. Not in their interaction with the Gentiles, but regarding their behavior within the church. That would determine whether the church would continue to exist as a church of both Jews and Gentiles.

The two groups would go separate ways if they would no longer accept one another! Those who wanted to retain the Jewish customs would go their own way. But what could their future possibly be? Their own people would view them as apostates because of their faith in Jesus as the Messiah, while the Gentile Christians would no longer welcome them unless they forsook their Jewish customs. Would they be able to survive? The nonobservers of the law would continue without the Jews. Breaking with the Jewish customs would be a condition for membership. No longer would it be a church from both the Jews and the Gentiles (Rom. 9:24).

The Beachhead to God's Future

Paul viewed the church of Jews and Gentiles as the beachhead to God's future. That future was: "Rejoice, O Gentiles, with his people," and: "Let all the peoples praise him" (15:10-11). The church was a beginning of this future: There, already, the Gentiles rejoiced *together with his people*. If this venture were to end in failure, if in the church the non-Jewish members could not praise him together with the Jewish members, then this praise of God by all nations together with his people Israel would never come about.

This is Paul's motive when he writes: "Welcome one another, therefore, just as Christ has welcomed you, for the glory of God." The behavior of the strong threatened to destroy the work of God in the church of Rome.[8]

8. The destruction of God's work in 14:20 refers to the church member who loses his faith as a result of the stubbornness of the strong. There can be no true fellowship in a church where people lose their faith because of the behavior of others.

But there was another danger. In writing this letter Paul was extremely concerned about the link with the Jerusalem church. In the next passage (15:25-32) we read about the collection in the churches of Macedonia and Achaia for the church in Jerusalem. It was intended to undergird the ties between the newly established churches of Gentile Christians and the Jewish church in Jerusalem. Paul is on his way to Jerusalem to deliver the offering, and he urgently requests the church of Rome to join him in fervent prayer that he may be well received upon his arrival. For many in Jerusalem had grave misgivings with regard to Paul's work among the Gentiles. The story of what happened when he arrived illustrates this: Thousands of Jews have come to believe, and "all are zealous for the law." They feared that Paul's work would result in churches that would relinquish the tie with the Jewish people and its service to God (Acts 21:20-21). Precisely the behavior of the strong in Rome was apt to strengthen those doubts. As a result the Jerusalem church might refuse to accept the tangible proof of fellowship (Rom. 15:31). Thus these Gentile churches — God's beachhead to the nations — would be detached from Israel, the people through which God seeks to bring about his saving plan for all humanity. The church in Rome had to be aware of what was at stake![9]

2. The Hope and the Church without Jews

Not Accepted

"Welcome one another, therefore, just as Christ has welcomed you," Paul had written (Rom. 15:7). Emphatically he had demanded that the weak be allowed to keep their Jewish customs. He had even urged the strong to adapt themselves to these things. But that did not happen.

It has been argued that the Jewish Christians in Rome were simply absorbed by the majority of Gentile believers, and were no longer recognizable as a distinct group. But that was not the case. We do not know what happened immediately after they received Paul's letter, but we do know

9. For the "beachhead" of God's future salvation for the world, see J. C. Beker, *Paul the Apostle* (Edinburgh, 1980), p. 92; for Paul's motives in writing this letter, see pp. 59-93. Cf. also U. Wilckens, "Über Abfassungszweck und Aufbau des Römerbriefes," in his collection of essays *Rechtfertigung als Freiheit* (Neukirchen, 1974), pp. 110-39. See also Meuzelaar (n. 3 above).

how things turned out. After two centuries the church in Rome had become a church which fiercely opposed the Jews of the synagogue.

The replacement doctrine, the teaching of the substitution of the church for Israel, had taken hold. The vast majority of Jews had rejected their Messiah, and that had sealed the fate of the Jewish people. Jerusalem was destroyed, and its temple was no more. God no longer needed them. A new people replaced the former people. The church grew, and Christianity became the official religion of the empire. The victory of the Christian faith was ample proof that the God of Israel was now the God of the church and no longer the God of the Jews.

The pride of the Gentiles had persisted and done its work. The Gentile Christians wanted distance: Christians had nothing to do with Jews! That did not fail to have consequences for the Jews of the church. For keeping distance from Judaism could not be combined with a continued observance of Jewish customs. As early as the second century we hear of the preaching of Justin Martyr in Rome; Justin viewed the Jewish customs enshrined in the law as a punishment God had put on the Jews after their sin with the golden calf.[10] Pope Sylvester (314-35) declared: "If every Sunday is to be observed by the Christians on account of the resurrection, then every Sabbath on account of the burial is to be regarded in execration of the Jews *(exsecratione Judaeorum)*. . . . In fact it is not proper to observe, because of Jewish customs, the consumption of food *(destructiones ciborum)* and the ceremonies of the Jews." Pope Innocent I (402-17) adds: "As the tradition of the church maintains, in these two days [Friday and Saturday] one should absolutely not *(penitus)* celebrate the sacraments".[11]

10. S. Bacchiocchi, *From Sabbath to Sunday.* (Rome, 1977 ed.), pp. 186-87, 223-33. The statements by Justin in "Dialogue with Trypho," 18 and 21, in Ante-Nicene Fathers, (Grand Rapids, repr. 1981), 1:203-4. Justin was born in Palestine; he founded a school in Rome, where he was martyred ca. 165.

11. Bacchiocchi, *From Sabbath to Sunday,* pp. 194, 196. Bacchiocchi points to four factors that help explain the anti-Jewish sentiments in the church of Rome: 1. The relationship between Jews and Romans became extremely tense after the Jewish uprising in 135. 2. Jews had often been hostile toward Christians and at times even collaborated in their persecution. 3. At that particular time the Christians were enjoying a measure of protection from the emperor; therefore, it seemed prudent to keep some distance from the Jews. 4. Judeo-Christians, who insisted on the literal observance of Mosaic regulations by Gentile Christians, encouraged dissociation and resentment (pp. 182-83). "The adoption of a new day of worship appears to be motivated by the necessity to evidence a clear dissociation from the Jews" (pp. 233-34). The authority of the church

We note that the debate now became concentrated on the Sabbath. That these papal measures were deemed necessary indicates that special regard for the Sabbath had not yet disappeared, except perhaps among the Christians in Rome. In the East, in particular, the Sabbath long retained a special place, possibly because of the large percentage of Jewish Christians. The Sabbath was observed side by side with Sunday. Gregory of Nyssa says: "Do you perhaps ignore the fact that the two days are brothers and that if you hurt one you strike at the other?"[12]

I Do Here and Now Renounce . . .

After the first two centuries the church found itself on a track away from Israel. As a result, those Jewish Christians who wanted to remain Jewish disappeared from the church.[13] The church had become not only a church without Jews, but also a church *against* the Jews. "It is no exaggeration to

---

of Rome was steadily growing. "The Church of Rome, whose members, mostly of pagan extraction . . . and where the unpopularity of the Jews was particularly great, appears to have played a leading role in inducing the adoption of Sunday observance" (p. 212). Bacchiocchi convincingly shows the invalidity of the view that Sunday was observed by the early church from the very beginning. There is no doubt that the Jerusalem church kept the Sabbath, and that one should not look toward Jerusalem when trying to find the origin of Sunday as the day of remembrance of the resurrection (pp. 135-64).

12. Cf. Bacciocchi, pp. 217, 218, 298 for further details about a synod in Laodicea (ca. 360) that condemned the observance of the Sabbath and prescribed that Christians were to work on that day in honor of Sunday. See also M. Simon, "Les Judaisants dans l'Eglise" and the section about the Sabbath in *Verus Israel, Etude sur les relations entre Chretiens et Juifs dans l'Empire Romain* (Paris, 1983 ed.), pp. 356-93, and 274ff. The Ethiopian Church continues to observe the Sabbath alongside Sunday; see F. Heiler, *Die Ostkirchen* (Munich, 1971), p. 374; K. H. Rengstorf and S. von Kortzfleisch, eds., *Kirche und Synagoge. Handbuch zur Geschichte von Christen und Juden. Darstellung mit Quellen* (Stuttgart, 1968; repr. Munich, 1988), 1:199, 202.

13. Well into the fourth century there were Jewish-Christian churches in the East; initially these were regarded as part of the church universal, but increasingly they came to be viewed as sectarian, not as a result of their doctrines, but because of their continued practice of circumcision and their observance of the Sabbath. R. A. Pritz (in *Nazarene Jewish Christianity from the End of the New Testament Period until Its Disappearance in the Fourth Century* [Leiden, 1988]) observes: "These were direct descendants of the first Jewish believers in Jesus. . . . The fathers of the fourth century who wrote against them could find nothing in their belief to condemn; their objections were a matter of praxis" (pp. 108-9). See also G. Strecker, "Judenchristentum," *Theologische Realenzyklopädie* (Berlin and New York, 1988), pp. 310-25.

say that the empirical church, i.e. the church of history, has shown herself to be the greatest enemy of the Jewish people. The church has, therefore, been the first and foremost stumbling block in Jewish appreciation of Jesus." These are the words of Jacob Jocz, a Jewish-Christian scholar.[14] The oaths that were required of Jews who wanted to be baptized further illustrate the truth of his statements:

> I do here and now renounce every rite and observance of the Jewish religion, detesting all its most solemn ceremonies and tenets that in former days I kept and held. . . . I promise that I will never return to the vomit of Jewish superstition. . . . [I will] shun all intercourse with other Jews and have the circle of my friends only among honest Christians. With or apart from them I must always eat Christian food. . . .
>
> We will not on any pretext, either ourselves, our children or our descendants, choose wives from our own race; but in the case of both sexes we will always link ourselves in matrimony with Christians. We will not practice carnal circumcision, or celebrate Passover, the Sabbath or the other feasts connected with Jewish religion. We will not keep to our old habit of discrimination in the matter of food. . . . We swear . . . that whoever of us is found to transgress shall either perish by the hand of our fellows by burning or stoning, or if your splendid piety shall have spared our lives, we shall at once lose our liberty. . . .[15]

That surely sounds different from the kind of language Paul has been using! When baptized Jews were found to be observing Jewish customs, such as keeping the Sabbath, they were to be executed as heretics. What a terrible history of persecutions, murders, and forced baptisms, which though frowned upon, nevertheless remained valid once they had taken place. Thus

---

14. J. Jocz, *The Jewish People and Jesus Christ: The Relationship between Church and Synagogue* (Grand Rapids, 1979 ed.), p. 92. On the Jewish Christians in later times (inside and outside the church), see pp. 228-61. See, e.g., pp. 232 and 401 regarding Rabbi J. Lichtenstein (1831-1912), who refused to be baptized, continued to come to the synagogue, but openly professed his faith. See also "Judenchristentum," in *Die Religion in Geschichte und Gegenwart. Handwörterbuch für Theologie und Religionswissenschaft* (Tübingen, 1959), 3:967-76.

15. For the laws of the Spanish kings Recceswith (654) and Erwig (681), see James Parkes, *The Conflict of the Church and the Synagogue: A Study in the Origins of Antisemitism* (New York, 1981 ed.), pp. 394ff. See also Jocz, *The Jewish People and Jesus Christ*, pp. 66-96; K. H. Rengstorf and S. von Kortzfleisch, ed., *Kirche und Synagoge*, 1:210-90.

THE ONE PURPOSE OF GOD

what the apostle had warned against in the parable of the olive tree came about: The church developed into "branches that were cut off." And the Jews were en route to the holocaust.

Does God Still Want a Church of Jews and Gentiles?

Anyone who has studied this matter to some degree will hesitate even to ask the question here at issue. Yet the question must be asked, since the Bible itself confronts us with it: Does God, even today, still want us to be a church consisting of Jews and Gentiles? Or has he changed his mind after what has happened? The question in fact boils down to: Are we today the church that God has in mind?

For eighteen centuries the church has stubbornly refused to be true to her calling with regard to the Jews. We say: It is no longer possible. There are no Jewish Christians among us except for a few rare exceptions, whom we cannot locate. What does this objection imply? If we simply continue to disobey God long enough, with the result that the Jews have almost disappeared from our midst, God will no longer insist that they are essential; thus we can simply continue to exist as a church without Jews!

We have, however, noted that, for the church, too, God's calling is irrevocable (Rom. 11:29). So, if it is true that nineteen centuries ago it was God's intention to have a church consisting of Jews and Gentiles, it is still his intention today. If, as a result of the church's disobedience, the Jews are absent from the church, then it is his intention that as yet they will come!

Let us once more note Paul's remarks about "the glory of his ministry." His desire is to make his own people "jealous, and thus save some of them" (11:13-14). Paul was prompted in this desire by the Holy Spirit. The church has also been called to follow the apostle in this respect: not only in praying for their salvation (10:1) but also in making them jealous. If this, then, is God's will, and if we are to follow Paul, we will also be given "some." Then even today it is possible to become what God wanted us to be: a church of Jews and Gentiles.

What Does This Mean: A Church of Jews and Gentiles?

The letter to the Ephesians pictures for us the church of Jews and Gentiles. The cross of Christ has removed the wall of separation between Israel as the people of God and the Gentiles with their gods (2:13-17). By faith in him these non-Jews have also become Israel: The two are now one. They

are now citizens with the saints and members of the household of God";
they are "fellow heirs, members of the same body, and sharers in the promise
in Christ" that God had given Israel (Eph. 2:19; 3:6). Moffat, in 3:6, approaches the meaning of the original Greek term even more closely when
he introduces the terms "co-heirs" and "co-partners in the Promise."

One with Israel — note that this means not simply one with the Jewish
members of the church. By virtue of their bond with them, they are, just
as the Jewish church members themselves, united with the Jewish people.
For even though the majority of this people has rejected the Messiah, it
remains the people of God. "To them belong the promises" (Rom. 9:4). The
time will come when God will open their eyes to him. Then they also will
welcome Him as Israel's Messiah. Together with the Jewish brothers and
sisters, the non-Jewish church members look forward to that moment.

There is no question: We are not that kind of church. When a Jew
accepts the faith and is baptized, he is expected to renounce all that reminds
him of his Jewishness. He no longer belongs to the Jewish people: He now
is part of the church. That is the opposite of what we just read. If we were
to find that he still values his Jewish customs, we would tend to see that as
proof that his faith in Jesus is less than perfect. We would regard that as
the kind of superstition a Christian ought to overcome. A Jew cannot
maintain his Jewish identity in the church. He is welcome, but there is no
place for him as a *Jew.* That is totally at variance with what Paul wrote in
Romans 14 and 15! There must be a place for him as a Jew. Jewish members
must definitely be recognizable as Jews. The church needs that. They are
living evidence that God has not abandoned his plans for Israel. They are
the promised firstfruits, the pledge that all Israel will eventually embrace
the Messiah.[16]

One remark must be added. We do not intend to say that every local
congregation must have some Jews if it is to qualify as a church of Jews and
Gentiles. Even in Paul's day, that was not a condition for establishing a
church. But there was the condition that the bond with the Jerusalem
church was to be maintained. We find Paul untiringly nurturing that bond.

---

16. Heinz David Leuner, himself a Jewish pastor: "The Jewish Christian . . . is a
sign, a 'pledge' of the eschatological hope that all Israel will confess Jesus as their
Messiah . . . , a testimony of the unity of Jews and Gentiles in the church; this unity is
obliterated if after his baptism he is no longer recognizable as a Jew." See "Judenchristen
als Zeichen für die Treue Gottes," in *Peter von der Osten-Sacken — Treue zur Thora,
Festschrift für Gunther Harder zum 75. Geburtstag* (Berlin, 1979 ed.), p. 138.

A manifest example is his zeal for the offering for "the poor among the saints in Jerusalem" (Rom. 15:25-27; see also 1 Cor. 16:1-4; 2 Cor. 9). Everywhere Gentile believers must realize that they are called to unity with Jerusalem. Could it be that this matter still has significance for us today?

The Lonely Ones — Da Costa

Through the centuries they have always been there — the Jews who were called by God to faith in Jesus Christ and joined the Gentile church as it developed in history. There have always been some who, as was expected of them, adapted themselves to a church without Jews. But there also have always been some who did so without giving up their Jewishness. An example from a not so distant past is the Dutch poet Isaäc da Costa (1798-1860). "Yet, I remained (no, I truly became) an Israelite, when through the grace of the God and Savior of my fathers, I confessed Christ."[17] Da Costa did not want to hear of a rejection of the Jewish people because they had rejected their Messiah. We quote a few short passages from his *Bijbellezingen* (Bible Readings) about the prophets.[18]

"We, converted Jews, still consider ourselves as one body together with the Jewish nation, and do not see ourselves as part of the nations" (p. 414). "Israel may have rejected the Messiah, but the Messiah has not rejected Israel; on the contrary, he promised to return to his people with forgiveness in one hand, and honor and glory in the other" (p. 452). "For the end of all prophetic writing is: the restoration of Israel under the rule of its legitimate King. . . . Then we will rejoice in the future national restoration of Israel, for the salvation of the whole world is closely linked with that event" (p. 543). "Christ rules over them, without their realizing it . . ." (p. 544). "For Israel is not like the nations, which received from God something they never possessed. No, the Jews will receive what they possessed all along without knowing it. . . . O, when the covering will be taken away from the eyes and the hearts of Israel, then we will be able to say: How is it possible, you people of Israel! You have had your own Messiah in your midst . . . and yet you did not know him" (p. 547).

17. I. da Costa, *Israel en de volken* (Israel and the Nations) (Haarlem, 1848), p. iv. In *Isaac da Costa's weg naar het Christendom* (Amsterdam, 1946 ed.), p. 98, and *Martelgang of Cirkelgang* (Paramaribo, 1954), the Jewish author Jaap Meijer emphasizes da Costa's loyalty toward the Jewish people.
18. From *Bijbellezingen van wijlen Mr. Is. da Costa*, compiled by J. F. Schimsheimer (Amsterdam, n.d.), vol. 2.

Da Costa unceasingly protested against the doctrine of the substitution of the church for Israel — "the spiritualizing of Israel," as he called it. When speaking about God's promises to Israel, the prophets meant Israel, and not the church as a substitute for Israel. "Many want to recognize only spiritual Israel, the church from among the Gentiles, but did the church ever apply the judgments pronounced on Israel to herself? If not, they should also allow Israel to have its crown. The promises of the gospel given to Israel have not been taken away from Israel so that these might be given exclusively to the Gentiles; no, the promise to Israel is the unchanging basis for the acceptance of the Gentiles" (p. 330).

Da Costa and those other Jewish Christians who wanted to remain recognizable as Jews saw it as their calling to remind the church that had lost her Jewish roots of her bond with Israel. But they remained the lone voices. They were not at home in the church, and their own people could see them only as apostates who had joined the enemy. In the church they did have an impact on a small circle. When they died, their voice fell silent; there was no younger generation of Jews in the church to continue their work. The church could manage without them! Their message had not resulted in a constant presence and a distinct voice of Jewish Christians in the church of Christ as a whole. Nonetheless, these few individuals have prepared the way, and we must begin to understand how much we need them in order that we may be the church that God wants: the church of Jews and Gentiles that will make Israel jealous.

Messianic Congregations

In his monograph *Christelijke presentie in de Joodse Staat* (Christian Presence in the Jewish State), Simon Schoon describes the position of the Jewish Christians in Israel. A number of messianic congregations have been established, groups of Jewish Christians who want to keep their identity as Jews and their bond with their land and people. Their position is far from enviable. The Jewish community regards them as traitors to their people. Furthermore, the historic churches do not know how to deal with them: They are a roadblock to the dialogue with Israel. Schoon warns that it is because of the Gentile Christian churches that these messianic congregation are distrusted by their own people. This should lead those churches to display a large measure of solidarity towards them. "The Jewish Christians should not become the victims of the widespread desire for dialogue with Judaism. Christians should leave no doubt that Jewish Christians have the

fullest right to formulate their own identity, in and outside the church. . . .
There is room for a 'Jewish entity within the one body of Christ.'"[19]

What difficulty do these messianic Jews present for the dialogue? Nowhere does the confession that Jesus is the Messiah occupy a more prominent place than with these Jews; and nowhere does the promise that all
Israel will eventually accept the Messiah have greater force than with
them.[20] But Judaism inevitably views a conversion to Jesus as the demise
of the Jewish people. Even though these Jews have had nothing to do with
it, and even though they themselves bear the wounds, their fellow Jews
cannot detach them from what in that Name has been done to the Jews. It
is not easy to make them understand that these messianic Jews do not
regard Israel's conversion to Jesus as a wholesale incorporation into the
church. With regard to the churches, we understand that, in view of the
past, the discussion cannot begin with the promise that all Israel will accept
the Messiah; other things will first have to be said by the churches, and,
more particularly, be seen within the churches. Something visible must
incite the Jews who do not accept him to jealousy — something of Christ.
In no way can this be: keeping a distance from these messianic Jews, regarding them as an undesirable element in the important dialogue that has
been initiated between Christians and Jews of the synagogue.

These Messianic congregations are found not only in Israel. A growing
number of Jews in the United States are confessing Christ as the Messiah and
have formed independent congregations.[21] Characteristically, these congre-

19. S. Schoon, *Christelijke presentie in de joodse staat* (Kampen, 1983), pp. 232-33.
On the Jewish Christians, see also pp. 13-17, 84-102.

20. The "two-ways theory" plays a major role in the dialogue between Jews and
Christians. "Thus Rosenzweig says: 'As regards the significance of Christ and his Church
we are agreed: Nobody comes to the Father but through Him. Nobody *comes* to the
Father — it is different, however, for the one who needs no more to come to the Father
because he *is* already with Him.' And this is the case with Israel" (Jocz, *The Jewish People
and Jesus Christ*, p. 317). Rosenzweig regards faith in Christ as the sole road to salvation
for non-Jews; but not for the Jews. Some Christians follow Rosenzweig and maintain
that a Jew does not need to be converted to Jesus as his Savior. This idea is fiercely
rejected by any Jew who confesses Jesus as Israel's Messiah.

21. J. Gutwirth, *Les Judéo-chrétiens d'aujourdhui* (Paris, 1987), offers a fascinating
review of the rise and development of messianic congregations in the United States.
The *Messianic Times* (summer 1995) lists about 200 such congregations in the United
States. Isaac C. Rottenberg, *The Turbulent Triangle* (Hawley, PA, 1989), pp. 172-87:
"Messianic Jews — Conspiracy or Tragedy?" writes: "My observations lead me to believe
that we are witnessing a persistent albeit gradual growth of the Messianic Jewish move-

gations leave room for Jewish customs. They do so not because they are required for salvation, but because these messianic Christians want to maintain their bond with the Jewish people. Non-Jews are welcome; often they are even in the majority. But all members are united in their determination that Jews who come to believe in Jesus and want to follow him while remaining Jewish will find a place where they can do so. They also try to reach other Jews with the gospel of Jesus; it is: "to the Jews first" (Rom. 1:15-16).

These congregations face enormous difficulties. This is clear from an interview with one of the founding fathers of the Messianic Alliance of Israel. "We flutter around like a bird which hasn't yet learned to fly. We haven't developed strong wings with which we can rise like an eagle. The problem is that we're still such a mixture. . . . Our congregations still maintain many of the characteristics of the churches with which they have been in contact in the diaspora, or through which they came to faith, including the way in which they conduct their worship. We have charismatic and non-charismatic [congregations] . . . liturgical and others."[22] We might add: also including the different theologies these currents represent. In a draft-confession of faith we find the essentials of the Christian faith, completely in line with the churches. The last article, however, states: As Jewish followers of Yeshua, we are called to maintain our Jewish biblical heritage and remain a part of our people Israel and the universal body of believers. This is part of our identity and a witness to the faithfulness of G'd ("Yeshua," Jesus; G'd, God). This perspective and outlook does not go so far that they are unanimous in their rejection of the doctrine of eternal punishment as being unbiblical since all Israel will be saved. Usually, in line with historic Christian teaching, they expect eternal separation and eternal punishment.[23]

---

ment, both in Israel and in other parts of the world" (p. 185). He wonders what the mainline churches with all their criticism of these messianic Jews would say about Paul and the early Jewish Christians: "After all, their message and behavior were by and large rather similar to that of Messianic Jews today" (p. 183). Rottenberg is of Jewish descent; he is a minister in the Reformed Church in America. See also his article "Messianic Jews: A Troubling Presence," *First Things* December, 1992, pp. 26-32.

22. B. Hoekendijk, *Twelve Jews Discover Messiah* (Eastbourne, 1992), p. 99.

23. The Union of Messianic Jewish Congregations (UMJC, Menorah Ministries, Palm Harbor, Florida), kindly sent me the "Standards for Messianic Jewish Congregations." It says about eternal punishment: "We believe in the resurrection of both the saved and the lost, they that are saved unto the resurrection of life, and they that are lost unto the resurrection of damnation." Admittedly, the word "eternal" is not mentioned in this context, but this article is quite in line with church tradition.

This is also true of Da Costa, the author of the statements about Israel's future which we quoted above. He also held to the teaching of eternal separation as taught by the church through the centuries. That all Israel will be saved (Rom. 11:26) did not lead him to extend this salvation to Israelites of former generations.[24] We are aware that this new emphasis on the Jewish identity and the founding of messianic congregations does not bring an immediate correction of an ancient doctrinal tradition. It requires intensive study of the Bible to determine what Israel's enduring election implies for the confession of the Christian faith. Century after century the church ignored this. How does our expectation change when we express our belief in that election? All of us ought to reflect on that question.

Having listened to what Paul wrote to the church in Rome, we cannot but rejoice about this unexpected development. Unexpected indeed, for this is not the result of a longing of the churches for a Messiah-confessing Judaism! This development must be taken seriously. We face the immense danger that what has emerged outside the established churches will remain outside, and that they will not get their rightful place within the churches. That depends largely upon the answer of the churches to these Jewish believers in Jesus. Will they give that answer? Will they show gratitude for this development, and also realize their responsibility? Once, when the church was still young, the Gentile Christians refused to welcome them. Now, after many centuries, they again face the mandate: "Welcome one another." There is something to accept, something to welcome! Will this happen, or will the churches continue to act as they have done in the past, treating messianic Judaism as being superfluous?

Rejoice, O Gentiles, with His People

What does all of this have to do with hope? Let us return once more to Romans 15:8. Christ has become a servant of the circumcised in order to fulfill the promises given to the fathers. As long as Israel is not the people

24. Da Costa (in *Bijbellezingen,* vol. 2 [3rd ed.; Amsterdam, n.d.] comments on Genesis 3:15 with regard to the seed of the woman and that of the serpent (the elect and the damned): "The temporal distinction between these two will end in the eternal separation of the one from the other" (p. 59; see also pp. 35, 89). In vol. 9 (Amsterdam, 1880), he notes with regard to Romans 11:26, "'And so all Israel will be saved,' because at that time this people will consist only of the remnant that God in the sovereignty of his grace has promised to save" (p. 227).

that allows itself to be led by the Messiah, it cannot be the people through which God fulfills his promises and through which he brings all nations back to him (Gen. 12:3). And as long as that has not been achieved, the ministry of Israel's Messiah to his people has not been completed. The church he has called from both Jews and Gentiles has been called to serve him in the execution of his work on Israel's behalf. This can never happen as long as we fail to restore the bond with this people that has been given by God through the presence of Jewish believers in the church.

It seems unrealistic to expect that the historic churches will return from the path they have followed for so many centuries. We are told that the clock cannot be turned back to the first century. But if we have become convinced that Israel's election is still valid, we have no choice but to act upon that conviction. This is not a matter of returning to the early centuries, but of returning to obedience to the Word of God within the context of our own time.

"Welcome one another, therefore, just as Christ has welcomed you" — Jews and Gentiles. These are Paul's words to the church at Rome. We know that these words are repeated to us, in our time. If we listen and act upon these words, we will share in the blessing Paul pronounced over the church: "May the God of hope fill you with all joy and peace in believing, so that you may abound in hope by the power of the Holy Spirit" (Rom. 15:13).

This blessing involves a mandate: "Welcome one another." Jews and non-Jews in the church must accept each other as Christ has accepted them: the Jews as Jewish and the Gentiles as Gentile. As long as the church refuses to do this, she will not be filled with this hope for the world of which Paul speaks. But if the church begins to do what Paul says, "Welcome one another, just as Christ has welcomed you," she will become what God has in store for her: being filled with joy and peace, overflowing with hope by the power of the Holy Spirit! So the road is paved toward the future of God's redemption for the world: a church that provokes Israel to jealousy; Israel that puts itself at the service of its Messiah; and *all the nations rejoicing in the God of Israel, together with his people.*

CHAPTER IX

Looking Back and Looking Forward

1. Looking Back

Called Not to Acquiesce

From the beginning of this book we have been wrestling with a single question: What is God like? Since Augustine our tradition has taught us that God has two separate goals. He has predestined a small percentage of humankind to salvation, to eternal life. The rest of humanity has been predestined to eternal damnation. Since it is his will that many will be lost, we have no option but to acquiesce.

Our starting point was the question: Is it God's will that we passively accept the perdition of our fellow human beings? There can be no denial: The Bible teaches us that this is not his will. Being called by God means being called not to acquiesce in the perdition of our fellow human beings. This we discovered in the story of Abraham and his intercession for Sodom, in the story of Moses and his intercession for Israel, and in Jesus' parable of the prodigal son. We noticed this, in particular, in Jesus' ministry. He heals every sickness and disease, and when he sees the crowds, he is moved with compassion for them. He regards them as sheep without a shepherd, as a harvest that is at risk of being lost. And the calling of his disciples is to be workers in that harvest.

This calling, this refusal to acquiesce, became our starting point in our quest for an answer to the doctrine of eternal punishment. Everything the Bible says about judgment, from Sodom onward, is said to people who were called by God not to accept passively the perdition of their fellow human beings. We may argue about the exegesis of certain texts and can point to other passages, but there can be no difference of opinion regarding this calling, for there simply is no other calling.

God's One Purpose and the Power of the Cross

Having established this fundamental truth, we continued our quest. What does Scripture teach regarding God's purpose for humanity? What is the meaning of the preaching of God's judgment; how does it relate to this purpose? Does it agree with our calling to refuse to acquiesce? We searched for that answer as we journeyed through Romans. What we found confirmed our initial premise.

In the letter to the Romans Paul preaches the gospel as the message of salvation for all people. God brought about this salvation in the cross of Jesus Christ. Through his death, all humanity, from Adam onward — including all past generations — will receive "justification and life"; "the many will be made righteous" (Rom. 5:18-19). That is God's one and only purpose. This was further confirmed when we discovered how that purpose is the bottom line of the one law that God gave humanity: that all of them, without exception, shall love him and their neighbors with all their heart. This eliminates the possibility that he might have another purpose for part of humanity.

Paul leaves no doubt, also in his other letters, that this redemption includes humanity in its entirety. Yet we are faced with the fact that through the centuries the church, though founded on this message, has insisted that only a small portion of humanity will be saved. We then discovered a number of things in the writings of Paul and in those of Israel's prophets that have been ignored in the teaching of the church.

A Kingdom of Salvation

Christ called his apostles, and the church that resulted from their preaching, to serve him in his saving ministry. That ministry will not be completed until all humanity has been saved. We realize that at present only few accept the gospel that is preached to them. How can all humanity ever be saved as long as the history of humankind continues as it has until now? The Bible tells us that history will not always go on like that. God's kingdom comes!

At this point we had to deal with the first major difference with church tradition. In the church's teaching concerning "the last things," the coming of the kingdom coincides with the final judgment. Those who are saved at that moment will be saved forever; and those who are condemned will be condemned forever. That prospect paralyzed the prayer for the coming of the kingdom. For who can long for such a future? Paul also writes about this judgment — the day of God's wrath, when "he will repay according to each one's deeds" (Rom. 2:5-6). The judgment is the beginning of the great deliverance. Under Christ's kingly rule God's children — those who are Christ's — will lead lost humanity back to God. All who ever died will be made alive in Christ, and at last God will be all in all (Rom. 8:14-21; 1 Cor. 15:20-28). So there will be salvation for those who died in a state of unbelief; salvation after the judgment. There will also be salvation for those who rejected the gospel. The majority of the Jewish people did that, but all Israel will be saved. This is how Paul explains the kingdom of God.

This view differs radically from what we have been taught. Does this have anything to do with the millennium of Revelation 20? We did not explore this question. The passages are certainly related, but we cannot build our hope for the kingdom on this vision. Much remains mysterious, and it has led to strange speculations. In order to arrive at some understanding of Revelation 20, we would have to begin with what earlier parts of the Bible say about the kingdom, in particular with Paul's statements in Romans 8 and 1 Corinthians 15. We base our expectation of the kingdom on these Pauline words. In addition, these words prove to be solidly anchored in the prophets of Israel.

The Purpose of God's Punishment

We received a clearer understanding of the significance of the prophets for Paul when we established what the prophets said about the purpose of divine judgment. They tell us what the horror of the judgment consists of: God makes evil fall back on the heads of evildoers. He does not have in mind their destruction, however, but their redemption and healing; they will be ashamed and loathe what they did, and return to God. Eventually all will, with their whole heart, choose for the good for which God initially created them. Israel will do so first. Then all nations will join redeemed Israel. This is the second major difference with traditional church teaching about the last things.

One question remains: Will there be people who persist in their refusal to make that choice? We have also left this aside. God has given each human being the free choice to say No to him. But even if someone would persist in this refusal, this would not mean endless punishment. God's *punishment* is always directed toward God's single purpose: salvation. As long as the punishment is being administered, there is hope. Could this No result in nothingness — annihilation?[1] Surely, that is *possible*. God is free to accept this "No" of that particular person as his final choice. Scripture does not allow us to affirm that this will not happen. We do not know everything! Nor does Scripture, however, allow us to affirm that this will indeed happen, namely, that part of humanity will wind up in nothingness. Rather, it focuses our attention on our task as laborers in God's harvest. God wants to save the harvest in its entirety since Christ died for all people. This calls us *to hope for the salvation of all people.*[2]

1. Those who defend the possibility of annihilation reject Universalism, the view that all, without exception, will be saved. But they object in particular to the doctrine of eternal punishment. The passionate statement of John Wenham, during the Edinburgh Conference of 1991, is quite touching: "I have thought about this subject for more than fifty years. . . . Now I feel the time has come when I must declare my mind honestly. I believe that endless torment is a hideous and unscriptural doctrine which has been a terrible burden on the mind of the church for many centuries and a terrible blot on her presentation of the gospel. I should indeed be happy if, before I die, I could help sweep it away" ("The Case for Conditional Immortality," in *Universalism and the Doctrine of Hell,* p. 190; see I, n. 46). Such thinkers vary greatly with regard to the hope: from the hope that *many* will be saved, to the denial of that hope. Fudge (*The Fire That Consumes — The Biblical Case for Conditional Immortality* [2nd ed.; Carlisle, 1994]) rejects the possibility of salvation after death and believes that only the few will escape destruction (pp. 100-101, 116). On the opposite side we find J. C. Blumhardt. He strongly emphasized free will and did not deny the threat of annihilation ("the abyss," as he called it), but he prayed fervently that in the end no one would be lost (VII, n. 36).

2. John Stott, the well-known evangelical leader and clergyman of the Church of England, defends the view (in D. L. Edwards and John Stott, *Essentials: A Liberal-Evangelical Dialogue* [London, 1988]) that "the ultimate annihilation of the wicked should be at least accepted as a legitimate, biblically founded alternative to their eternal conscious torment" (p. 320). But Stott hopes that the *many* will be saved: "I have never been able to conjure up . . . the appalling vision of the millions who are not only perishing but will inevitably perish. On the other hand . . . I am not and cannot be a universalist. Between these extremes I cherish the hope that the majority of the human race will be saved" (p. 327). I prefer to follow Blumhardt (see VII, n. 36 and above, n. 1). Karl Barth writes in the line of Blumhardt (above, n. 1): "There is no good reason why we should forbid ourselves, or be forbidden, openness to the possibility that in the reality of God and man in Jesus Christ there is contained much more than we might

Not without Israel

The prophets of Israel did not discuss the salvation of the nations apart from Israel's salvation. That confronted us with another aspect that the church has failed to teach. This third difference, we felt, was the most far-reaching. Israel was given the promises that it would be the channel through which all nations would come to God. Even though the majority of the Jewish people has rejected him as their Messiah, the promise remains valid. That is Israel's election. Christ's ministry, in all its aspects, is the fulfillment of that promise (Rom. 15:8). He came for that reason, he died for that reason, and he was resurrected for that reason: to make them the people through which God would save the world. We, Gentile believers, have been called to serve him in that ministry. Our assignment is to make these Jews who do not recognize Christ as their Savior jealous, so that their eyes will be opened and they will acknowledge him as Israel's Messiah. Not until this happens will the promised redemption of the lost human race be accomplished (Rom. 11:11-15). Like it or not, God has anchored the hope of the world in this particular people!

We had not foreseen this complication, and, quite honestly, it was unwelcome. Who is willing to believe that the world will not be saved without the conversion of all Israel to Jesus as their Messiah, and that this conversion must be achieved through our labor for him? Can our hope not be grounded in Scripture without the connection with this people? It would have simplified our study considerably and would have made our conclusions more readily acceptable. But whatever way we turned, we saw no possibility of excluding Israel — unless we were to reject the Bible itself. *The only promises God gave to this world are the promises of the Bible. And these are the promises he gave to this specific people.* Detaching the promises for the world from Israel means abandoning the basis of Scripture for the hope for the world. This happened when the church accepted the view that

---

expect and therefore the supremely unexpected withdrawal of that final threat, i.e. that in the truth of that reality there might be contained that super-abundant promise of the final deliverance of all men, . . . If we are certainly 'forbidden' to count on this as though we had a claim to it, we are surely commanded the more definitively to hope and pray . . . that in spite of everything which may seem quite conclusively to proclaim the opposite, his compassion should not fail, and that in accordance with his mercy, which is 'new every morning' he 'will not cast off forever' " (*CD*, IV/3, 477-78). Not a doctrine (universalism), but obeying this command to hope and pray leads us to the joy of the psalms and prophets (see III, n. 10).

Israel had been replaced by the church. As a result, believers changed their thinking about God: No longer did they see him as the God of Israel's prophets, the God who would save the world.

This is no minor matter. For we cannot admit that the replacement theory is contrary to the Bible, and at the same time continue to be the church we have become and have grown accustomed to. In fact, the church wanted Jesus without the Jews. The holocaust, the attempt to eradicate Israel, makes it imperative that we search the Bible and find out what it says about Israel's election, and about the significance of this election for our faith in Jesus. If it is true that Israel continues to be the people through which God wants to save the world, we cannot serve him without his people.

2. Looking Forward

The Elder Brother Comes Home

There appears to be a strange inability to believe in Jesus' second coming and the arrival of God's kingdom *on earth* — the kingdom that will bring the resurrection of the dead of all generations from the beginning of humankind. We cannot imagine what this would be like, and we fail to get excited about it. That was not so for the apostles, nor for the early church. What separates us from them? We miss the bond with Israel that the apostles and the early church had — "to them belong the promises" (Rom. 9:4). Looking at the metaphor of Israel as the olive tree, we realize that we are branches that are cut off; we still belong to the olive tree, but we are no longer attached to it (Rom. 11:21-22). This statement does not apply to every believer. There have always been believers who continued to view the Jewish people as God's chosen people and acted accordingly. But they were the exceptions. The church throughout the ages has denied the enduring validity of that election and has broken the bond of unity with this people.

The following statement by the great Bible scholar Godet is a marvelous expression of the crux of the matter. "Do we not realize in our present situation that we are missing something — in fact, much — that prevents us from realizing the gospel promises in their fullness; that there is an inherent weakness in our spiritual life, a mysterious hindrance in the efficacy of the gospel proclamation, a lack of joy and power that strangely contrasts with the joyous outbursts of the prophets; that, in fact, the cele-

261

bration in the paternal home is not complete . . . why? Because this can only happen when the elder son has returned home."3

These are prophetic words, written over a century ago. Godet points to our deficiency. We are lacking what the early church possessed. He points to the empty seat, the seat of our elder brother, Israel. But these words demand a follow-up. When Paul says in Romans 15:7 that Jews and Gentiles in the church must welcome one another, this does not mean that we must patiently wait for Israel's return, but it refers to something that must be actively pursued. We must be converted. Conversion is not simply a matter of confessing our wrongdoing. The bond that has been broken, Israel's rightful place within the church, must be restored.4

This applies not only to the messianic movement of our time with its separate congregations, but also to the much greater number of Jews who have joined the church. Or do we feel that they already have their rightful place? They do not have this place as long as we fail to recognize the elder brother in them and rejoice in their presence among us. The welcome for our elder brother begins with these "first fruits," the advance party of all Israel that is to follow. Together with them we will learn to look forward to the promised homecoming of our elder brother Israel. This homecoming will not only be a feast for us, the believers from the nations. Paul tells us that it will also be the final fulfillment of all prophecy, life from the dead for the lost world in its entirety (Rom. 11:15). Only if we look forward to Israel's homecoming to the Messiah will we be a church that truly expects the coming of her Lord and the resurrection of the dead.5

3. F. Godet (1812-1900), *Romans,* (Paris, 1880), 2:383f. The three points are from Godet.

4. Concerning this conversion, see Michael L. Brown, *Our Hands Are Stained with Blood* (Shippensburg, PA, 1992). Brown also cites the oaths that were quoted in VIII, 2.

5. In his exegesis of Romans 11:11-15, Barth connects the role of Israel's conversion to the faith of the church with the expectation of Jesus' second coming. If the assignment given to the church to incite the Jews of the synagogue to jealousy would be for her "an alien, half forgotten or wholly forgotten concern, no more to be considered by it, if it no longer reckons with this divine wonder," this would be "a fatal but sure sign that it is also not really looking forward to the second coming of the Lord, to his judgment of the quick and the dead. But that will mean that its faith has been stripped of hope and that therefore . . . it has become vain. . . . Hope in the revelation of Jesus Christ, which is the life of faith, stands or falls with the hope for Israel" (*CD,* II/4, p. 284).

The Church, a Sparkling Gem

I now want to refer to my discussions with the friend to whom I have dedicated this book: Israël Tabaksblat, a Messiah-confessing Jew. These discussions stemmed from a series of talks with an elderly orthodox Jew. I wanted to find out what the Jews believe about the doctrine of hell (for the Jews: Gehinnom). I was utterly amazed about what he told me. He began by saying: "Who is worthy to enter Gehinnom?" Gehinnom was like purgatory, the front porch of Paradise. The stay in Gehinnom could not exceed twelve months. For eleven months they said their daily "kaddish," the praise to God for the deceased. Those who thought that their parents would need twelve months did not think much of them. Having heard this, I wanted to know what a Jewish Christian thought about the doctrine of hell as taught by the churches. Was this dark doctrine not difficult to swallow for someone who had been reared as a Jew? Who would be in a better position to inform me than a Jewish pastor? So I looked him up. My expectation that he would be troubled by this doctrine was not correct. He had never felt obliged to worry about the traditional view of the church on this topic. There were other "Gentile Christian doctrines" as well to which he did not subscribe. He had never been asked whether he agreed with this doctrine when he entered the ministry in the Dutch Reformed Church. But once we embarked on this topic, he insisted on further discussions. We had a series of meetings, spread over five years, until his death (early 1992). Since he still felt intimately connected with the Jewish tradition in which he had been reared, this became my first in-depth encounter with Judaism.

These discussions centered on the alienation of the church from the Jewish people. In his ministry he had done all he could to make the church realize what she was lacking: the presence of Israel in her midst, as emphasized by the apostles — Paul in particular. But it remained a church that thought it only natural that she did not need the Jews in order to be the church of Christ. He no longer felt at home in such a church without Jews. Our talks focused on the letter to the Romans. These meetings helped me to realize that Israel continued to be the people through which God wanted to save the world, and that, as a result, the church will never live up to God's purposes as long as the bond with Israel has not been restored. In our encounters I experienced a measure of this bond.

In his brochure *Bladen uit mijn levensboek* (Pages from My Life's Story) I read the following passage about the parable of the olive tree (Rom. 11): "The entire church of the Messiah, the Christian church, must realize that she has been grafted into the pure olive tree, Israel, and that, therefore, she is entrusted with the task of inciting her elder brother, the people of Israel, to jealousy by living out of the riches she has received from Israel's Messiah."[6] To make Israel jealous — that was the topic we discussed. I had always thought that the church should have done this; but she did not do it, and has behaved in such a way that she will never be able to do this anymore. How could he speak about the church as he did? For the church did not manifest the richness she had received in Israel's Messiah! Remember, I said, that this has been a failure for nineteen centuries. How can you expect the church ever to change its course? If God wants to save Israel, he will have to look at some other means than the Christian church! *"Nineteen centuries?"* he exclaimed, *"even if it takes another nineteen centuries, or even one hundred centuries, it will happen!"* Here I was in the presence of a Jew like Paul, who vowed that nineteen centuries of distortion and disloyalty would not in any way change God's resolve to incite Israel to jealousy through the "church of the Gentiles." "He does not abandon the work of his hands," he assured me. It was an ever-recurring theme in our conversations. Then, one day, it struck me how *real* his expectation was! It was nothing less than a revelation for me, the answer to a paralyzing question about the future of the church that had puzzled me for years! "It may take another hundred centuries, but it will happen!" That was Paul's answer to my question. That is what, today, the apostle wants us to understand. God's calling is irrevocable (Rom. 11:29). He is still looking for that church that will make Israel jealous!

From the beginning of my ministry J. C. Blumhardt had been a source of inspiration for me.[7] He had taught me not to acquiesce in the division

---

6. S. P. Tabaksblatt, *Bladen uit mijn levensboek* (Kampen, 1980), p. 25 (in the series Verkenning en Bezinning). Israel Paulus Tabaksblat (for his publications he used a double *t* at the end of his name), was born in 1902 in Kock, at that time a part of Russia. The *S* stands for "Srul," the Yiddish abbreviation for "Israel" (in the synagogue he was called "Israel"). And "Paul"? "I asked for that name at my baptism, as a token of honor to my great brother Paul"; emphatically and reverently he spoke these words. In the context of the hostility messianic Jews experience from other Jews, I should add that he was a welcome guest in the home of Prof. David Fluesser (for a discussion with him about this topic, *Bladen,* p. 36).

7. J. C. Blumhardt (1805-80 was a pastor in the Lutheran *Evangelical Church,* first in Möttlingen (Black Forest) and later in Bad Boll, where he was able to accommodate the crowds that came to hear him. To get acquainted with him, I suggest that you read *Ausgewählte Schriften* (abbreviated as *A.S.*) (Zurich, 1947-49), 3 vols.; repr. Giessen,

and powerlessness that marked the church. God still wants to give us what he gave the early church. God wants all people to be saved, and he calls us to serve him in the pursuit of his plan. That was Blumhardt's message. Jesus is Conqueror ("Jesus ist Sieger!") over the powers of evil. He had experienced this.[8] His church in Möttlingen to some extent reflected the time of the apostles. It encouraged Blumhardt: It would not be long until the promises of the Bible would be fulfilled for the whole church, and so all people would be reached with God's salvation. But that did not happen. I do not want to enter into Blumhardt's views on the end times; here I am interested in his longing for a new manifestation of the Spirit. He remained a lonely man in this respect. After his death his work was continued by his son; his labors, too, were blessed by remarkable answers to prayer for healing. But then it stopped. And that was the pattern in many of the revivals I had read about. Thus it would always be, I feared. It began and then it stopped.

Blumhardt wondered why after the first centuries the power of the Spirit gradually disappeared from the church. Everything he said about this (about how wrong it is to acquiesce) is true. God called us back to a life based upon his promises. If we were to claim these promises, if we persevered, as Jesus had taught in the parable of the unjust judge and the widow (Luke 18:18; Blumhardt returned to this time and again), those promises would be fulfilled. So it was promised in Joel's prophecy (2:28-29). But Blumhardt never suspected that the gradual disappearance of the work of the Spirit from the church might be related to the expulsion of the Jews from the church. Terrible things had to happen before any serious discussion of this issue could begin.

1991); F. Zündel, *Johann Christoph Blumhardt* (18th ed.; Giessen, 1969); a condensed version of F. Zündel, *Pfarrer Johann Christoph Blumhardt, ein Lebensbild* (5th ed.; Zurich, 1887), referred to as Zündel, 1887; and Blumhardt's autobiography, *Blätter aus Bad Boll* (1873-77), republished in 5 vols. in J. C. Blumhardt, *Gesammelte Werke* (Göttingen, 1968-75). Blumhardt was of great significance for Karl Barth, who wrote about him in *Die protestantische Theologie im 19. Jahrhundert* (Zurich, 1946), pp. 588-97; *CD*, IV/3, pp. 168-71; and *Das christliche Leben* (Zurich, 1976), pp. 443-50.

8. In Möttlingen Blumhardt experienced the overwhelming power of Jesus in the case of a young woman who manifested phenomena that the gospel describes as possession: J. C. Blumhardt, *Die Krankheitsgeschichte der Gottliebin Dittus* (repr. Göttingen, 1982; included in *Gesammelte Werke* as "Der Kampf in Möttlingen," 2 vols. [Göttingen, 1979]). When she was healed, the whole congregation confessed their sins; many of the sick were healed. See Zündel, *Blumhardt*, pp. 58-147; *A.S.*, 3:250-51.

We should note that Blumhardt was not one of those Christians who wanted to have Jesus without the Jews. He said that we who believe in Christ are fully part of Israel: "In actual fact, the believers in Christ should not have been called Christians, but, having been grafted upon Abraham's stem, they should have been called Jews or Israelites. If that had been done from the beginning . . . we would have seen totally different ideas in our time."[9] He answered a question about mission work among the Jews as follows:

> Christian believers must change considerably before they can begin to convert Jews. . . . I am convinced that Jews will not be converted in great numbers until they have the opportunity to see the power of Christ reflected in signs and wonders in the lives of Christians. In the meantime I am keen to treat them unreservedly as my brothers and to approach them as brothers, since together with them we believe in the God of Abraham, through whom all nations of the earth will be blessed. That is how I have found acceptance with many Jews.

It is noteworthy that when he put parts of the psalms and the prophets into rhyme, he took great care that there would be nothing that a Jew would not be able to sing.[10]

I was struck by the similarity between Blumhardt's expectation for the church and that of Tabaksblat. But I also saw that something was missing from the grounds on which Blumhardt built his expectation. The early church, which he took as his model, was a church of Jews and Gentiles. As long as the church remains a church without Jews in her midst, she will lack the connection with the root from which she must receive her power to grow — as a branch that is cut off from the olive tree Israel. She will never reach the fullness she has been promised if she fails to return to her

---

9. *Blätter aus Bad Boll* (1873), p. 103. Tabaksblat shared this view of the church. By virtue of the fact that she is grafted into the olive tree, the church is *also Israel,* like the synagogue: "a distorted Israel, but Israel nonetheless; I will not retract one word from what I said . . . blind, both are blind to God's Word, the church as well as the synagogue," were among his last words.

10. *A.S.,* 3:254-55; about the hymns: Zündel, 1887, p. 393. At times Blumhardt also refers to the salvation of the world as coming from Israel: "At last all Israel will come forward; then the compassion, which God has promised Israel, *finds its fulfillment!* Yes, the people will be amazed about the great glory that will yet be revealed, arising from Israel over all the world. . . . And even if a long time elapses, until everything has been accomplished, it will happen that the whole world will experience compassion, through him who came into the world" (*Predigt-Blätter aus Bad Boll* [Bad Boll, 1880], p. 342).

place at the side of Israel. Only then can the Spirit give her what the early church possessed — not temporarily, as a reminder of what God has in mind, but always.

This leads us to another similarity between Tabaksblat and Blumhardt: We are not dealing here with a future that must be awaited, but a task that must be taken up. The way must be prepared for the coming of the Messiah. "We must put out the red carpet for him [the Messiah]," Tabaksblat used to say, "otherwise we might have to wait a long time!"[11] For that reason we must not, at any price, passively accept the present division and powerlessness in the church. The church must become what God purposes her to be: a church in which the presence of Jesus as the great Compassionate One is seen; a church that is fulfilling her mission toward Israel and the world. There will be setbacks and disappointments, but ultimately she cannot fail. For it is his commission, and he is with us always, until the end of the world (Matt. 28:20).

Once we talked about "the fullness of the Gentiles" (Rom. 11:25). That must be taken in a *qualitative* sense, he said — a term I already used earlier. Then he added: "*The church will be as a sparkling gem — Jesus will shine through his church.* When that happens, Israel will become jealous." "And," so he writes in the "Pages from My Life's Story," "when all Israel is saved, Messiah's rule will begin" (p. 25).

Good expectations for the church! No one perceived more clearly than he did how far she had strayed from the way the apostles had shown. Yet unshakable hope for the church's future — and for the future of this world! I had glimpsed something of the hope and good expectation of Paul himself.

11. For the same thought, see Blumhardt, *A.S.*, 2:203-14; also pp. 7-18, 277.

Bibliography

(Literature quoted in an abbreviated form)

Bible Translations and Confessional Documents

Septuagint (LXX): The Greek translation of the Old Testament commonly used in the three centuries before the beginning of the Christian era.

Vulgate: The Latin translation of the Roman Catholic Church (largely the work of the church father Jerome; ca. 347-420).

States-General Bible (Statenvertaling), also called the Dutch Authorized Version, first published in 1637.

AV: Authorized Version, or King James Version, first published in England in 1611.

RSV: Revised Standard Version, published in 1952 (an English revision of the American Revised Version, published in 1901).

NRSV: The New Revised Standard Version, an authorized revision of the Revised Standard Version, published in 1989. This translation has been used throughout this book, except in cases where the AV or RSV uses a preferred wording. These instances have been indicated.

Buber: German translation of the Old Testament by Martin Buber, in collaboration with Franz Rosenzweig (*Die Fünf Bücher der Weisung*, Cologne-Olten, 1968 [repr. of 1854 ed.]; *Bücher der Kündung*, Cologne, 1958.

Luther: *Biblia/das ist/die gantze Heilige Schrift Deutsch*, 1534; facs. ed. Reclams-Universal Bibliothek. Leipzig, 1983.

Schaff: Philip Schaff, *The Creeds of Christendom,* vol. 3. New York, 1931 (for the Heidelberg Catechism, Canons of Dort, and Belgic Confession).

Schlatter: German translation of the New Testament in A. Schlatter, *Erläuterungen zum Neuen Testament.* Stuttgart, 1947-50 (repr.).

Church Fathers and Later Authors

Augustine, *The City of God:* Trans. Henry Bettenson. In *St. Augustine: The City of God.* New York, 1984.

Augustine, *Enchiridion:* Trans. Whitney J. Oakes. In *Basic Writings of Saint Augustine,* vol. 1. New York, 1948.

Barth, *CD: Church Dogmatics,* 13 vols. Edinburgh, 1957.

Bavinck, *Dogmatiek:* H. Bavinck, *Gereformeerde Dogmatiek,* 4 vols., 4th ed. Kampen, 1928-30.

Calvin, *Institutes:* Trans. John T. McNeil, The Library of Christian Classics, vols. 20 and 21: Calvin, *Institutes of the Christian Religion.* Philadelphia, 1975 ed.

Calvin, *Romans:* Trans. Ross MacKenzie. John Calvin, Commentaries: *The Epistle of Paul the Apostle to the Romans and the Thessalonians.* Edinburgh, 1961.

Origen, *De Principiis:* Trans. Fred. Crombie. In *The Writings of Origen,* vol. 1. Edinburgh, 1899. Additional use has been made of the work of H. Görgemanns and H. Karpf (Darmstadt, 1976), which offers the Latin text with a German translation and comments.

Origen, *Ad Romanos:* "Commentaria in epistolam B. Pauli ad Romanos." In Migne, *Patrologia Graeca,* vol. 14, 832-1294. Since 1990 the text and a German translation are being published in the series Fontes Christiani: Commentarii in epistolam ad Romanos, 5 vols. Freiburg.

Commentaries on Romans

Baarlink, *Romeinen 1,2:* H. Baarlink, *Romeinen.* Kampen, 1987-89.

Calvin, *Romans* (see above).

Godet, *Romains 1,2:* F. Godet, *Commentaire sur l'épître aux Romains.* Paris/Geneva/Neuchâtel, 1879, 1880.

Greijdanus, *Romeinen 1,2:* S. Greijdanus, *De Brief van de Apostel Paulus aan de gemeente te Rome.* Amsterdam, 1933.

Jeremias, *Sprachliche Beobachtungen:* J. Jeremias, "Einige vorwiegend sprachlicher Beobachtungen zu Röm. 11,25-36," in W. G. Kümmel et al., *Die Israelfrage nach Röm. 9–11.* Rome, 1977, pp. 193-215.

Lekkerkerker, *Romeinen 1,2*: A. F. N. Lekkerkerker, *De Brief van Paulus aan de Romeinen,* 3rd ed. Nijkerk, 1974-75.

Origen, *Ad Romanos* (see above).

Ridderbos, *Romeinen*: Herman Ridderbos, *Aan de Romeinen.* Kampen, 1959.

Schlatter, *Erläuterungen* (see Bible translations).

Schlatter, *Gerechtigkeit*: A. Schlatter, *Gottes Gerechtigkeit, ein Kommentar zum Römerbrief.* 3rd ed. Stuttgart, 1959.

Stuhlmacher, *Römer*: P. Stuhlmacher, *Der Brief an die Römer.* Göttingen, 1989.

Wilckens, *Römer 1, 2, and 3*: U. Wilckens, *Der Brief an die Römer.* Neukirchen, 1978, 1980, 1982.

Dictionaries

EDNT: Exegetical Dictionary of the New Testament. Eds. H. Balz and G. Schneider. Grand Rapids, 1990-93 (3 vols.).

TDNT: Theological Dictionary of the New Testament. Ed. G. Kittel. Trans. Geoffrey W. Bromiley. Grand Rapids, 1964-76 (10 vols.).

TDOT: Theological Dictionary of the Old Testament. Eds. G. J. Botterweck and H. Ringgren. Grand Rapids, 1979-97 (8 vols. published).

TLOT: Theological Lexicon of the Old Testament. Eds. E. Jenni and C. Westermann. Peabody, MA, 1997 (3 vols.).

Index of Scripture References

45:20-21	199	23:40	212n.14, 215	16:55	50, 51
45:21	199	25:9	212n.14, 213	16:58	53
45:21b-25	198	25:12	212n.14	16:60	205, 208
45:22	154, 204	30:24	214	16:60-61	210
45:22-23	161	31:3	146n.18	16:60-63	50
45:22-24	49	31:3-4	214	16:61	205
45:22-25	203	31:18-19	207	16:63	205, 206
45:23	154, 217, 220	31:20	146n.18	18:23	77
45:23-24	210	31:28	170	22:31	204
45:24	154, 201, 203,	31:31-34	208, 215	23:35	204, 205
	204	31:31-37	146n.18	23:49	204, 205
45:25	83, 145, 154	31:31-40	219	31:18-19	210
49:6	161	31:33	209	31:34	210
53:6	208n.8	31:34	208, 209	31:37	210
55:1	83	31:34-37	145	34:11-12	63
55:8	154, 194	31:35-37	170	36	185
55:12-13	113	31:36	145n.16	36:22	208
56–66	216	31:38-40	213	36:24-32	209
59:20	186n.30	49:13	212n.14	36:25	208
65:2	156	49:33	212n.14	36:25-26	210
65:6	216	50:39	212n.14	36:25-27	206
65:13	216	51:26	212n.14	36:26-27	50, 186, 209
65:15	216	51:39	212n.14	36:27	54
66:24	216, 217	51:57	212n.14	36:31	216
		51:62	212n.14	36:31-32	206
Jeremiah				36:32	208
3:17	161, 210	*Lamentations*		37	185
3:21	207	3:31-32	224	37:1-14	209
3:22	207	3:33	224	37:9	186
3:25	207			37:10	185
4:2	210	*Ezekiel*		37:11	185
4:4	212n.15	5:5-7	204	37:11-14	185
7:20	212n.15	7:3-9	204	37:23	208
12:8	146n.18	9:10	204	37:26	208
12:16	210	11:19-20	209	44:10	204
16:19	161, 210	11:21	204	44:12	204
17:4	212, 214, 216,	14:3-11	210	44:13	205
	219	14:10	204		
17:27	212, 216	16	48-49, 54, 204	*Daniel*	
18:15-16	215	16:38	204	7:18	126
18:16	212n.14	16:42	204	12:2	216, 217
18:40	219	16:43	50, 53, 204		
20:11	207, 212n.14,	16:46-48	49	*Hosea*	
	215	16:52	205	1:9-10	146n.18
21:12	212n.15	16:53	50, 51, 52	9:15	146n.18
23:20	214	16:54	205		